Latter Day Lawyers

Brian Craig

Foreword by Senator Harry Reid

Library of Congress Control Number: 2018911829

Cover image: Pixabay

Kindle Direct Publishing

First Edition
Printed in the United States

Dedication

This book is dedicated to my sixth great grandfather, Thomas Rankin I (1724–1810), and my fifth great grandfather, William Rankin (1759–1833). Thomas Rankin served as a captain in the Revolutionary War and his four sons also fought in the war. Private William Rankin fought in the Battle of Kings Mountain in 1780 and the siege of Yorktown in 1781. My fifth great grandfather, Thomas Craig (1752–1832), also fought in the Revolutionary War for seven years. My son, Marshall Rankin Craig, is named after these great patriots. I express my gratitude for the service of these brave men and other patriots who helped establish the freedoms all Americans enjoy today.

Acknowledgements

A work of this undertaking would not be possible without the contributions of many people. I express my gratitude to the dozens of individuals who granted interviews. I am especially grateful for the willingness of Jay Bybee, Larry Echo Hawk, Thomas Griffith, Roger Hunt, Kent Jordan, Mike Lee, Michael Mossman, Dallin H. Oaks, and Milan Smith, Jr. While members of the Church strive for humility, I am grateful for their cooperation to share insights on their careers. As a lawyer, professor, and writer, I tried to rely on as many original sources as possible, including judicial opinions, government documents, and personal interviews. I also express my appreciation for the other individuals who agreed to be interviewed for this book. Special thanks are given to Allan Brinkerhoff, Shima Barawaran Baughman, Dr. David Dalin, and James W. Parkinson. I also recognize the contributions of John B. West in establishing West Publishing Company to publish and preserve American legal opinions, now available on Westlaw, which served as a valuable research tool.

I express my gratitude to Senator Harry Reid for agreeing to write the foreword and for his insight on the manuscript. I also appreciate the other reviewers, including John Berube, Shaun Jamison, and Eric Richards. I am also grateful for the support of my wife, Valerie, and our children. This project truly has been a labor of learning and love.

Contents

Foreword

By Senator Harry Reid

I practiced law for 18 years. I was a trial lawyer. I tried over 100 cases to juries. It was a rewarding time for me as it gave me lasting memories of America's court system. A system showing the wisdom of our founding fathers in establishing the unique separation of powers doctrine; the legislative, the judicial, and executive branches of government. Professor Brian Craig has written a book that helps fill a void. In the past, there has been little written about the legal contributions of members of the LDS church. I found his book, written with individual chapters on church members and their contributions to the law, fascinating. He writes of trial lawyers, judges, legal scholars, executive branch employees, and legislators. I did my undergraduate work in Utah. It was at that time that a nemesis of nearly everyone and every institution, Federal Judge Wallis Ritter, was presiding as Chief Judge. He was Utah's only federal judge. President Dwight D. Eisenhower, upon the recommendation of Senator Arthur Watkins, an enemy of Judge Ritter, appointed Sherman Christensen to be a Utah Federal Judge to serve with Judge Ritter. A longstanding battle ensued as Judge Ritter did everything to diminish Judge Christensen's authority and power. I enjoyed this chapter above others. I have had the good fortune of knowing some of the individuals Professor Brian Craig writes about. I was Rex and Mike Lee's home teacher. I was the U.S. Senate Leader when Judge Milan Smith, Jr., Judge Jay Bybee, and Judge Thomas Griffith were confirmed. I was fortunate to have worked with Larry Echo Hawk when he was the Assistant Interior Secretary. Having apostle James Faust as a personal friend has been one of the highlights of my life. Judge Levi Udall was the patriarch of Senators Mark and Tom Udall and he helped raise Rex Lee. I enjoyed my work with all three of Judge Udall's protégés. It is unfortunate we have not had LDS women who have chapters in this book. But, times are changing as I write this, and the time will soon come when they will be recognized. I am grateful for Professor Craig's arduous work. It is a timely piece of legal history.

Harry Reid served as a Democratic U.S. Senator from Nevada from 1987 to 2017. He served as Senate Majority Leader from 2007 to 2015.

Introduction

Daniel Webster, the famed politician and orator, once said that justice is "the greatest interest of man on earth. It is the ligament which holds civilized nations together. Wherever her temple stands, and as long as it is duly honored, there is a foundation for social security, general happiness and the improvement and progress of our race."[1]

Even though some mock the legal profession, including many lawyers themselves, the legal field remains a noble profession in a quest to promote justice and fairness. In my first week of law school, the dean discouraged law students from telling "lawyer jokes" which demean the legal profession. While some people engaged in duels in the past as a way of resolving disputes, as illustrated by the death of Alexander Hamilton, the justice system provides for a resolution of disputes through fair, just, and non-violent means.

This collection of short biographies of judges and lawyers—who are also members of The Church of Jesus Christ of Latter-day Saints—profiles individuals who have raised the bar for the legal profession. The persons featured in the book are not perfect, yet they set a standard of excellence and professionalism for all to follow. Inspired by *Profiles in Courage*, John F. Kennedy's Pulitzer-Prize winning book which recounts courageous efforts by U.S. Senators, this book attempts to shed light on ways a select group of lawyers and judges have influenced the constitutional and legal rights of all Americans. While *Jewish Justices of the Supreme Court: From Brandeis to Kagan* by David G. Dalin (Brandeis University Press, 2017) profiles U.S. Supreme Court Justices of the Jewish faith, *Latter Day Lawyers* shows how individuals of another religious sect and minority have impacted American legal history despite an early history of discrimination toward their religion. The chapters recount the lives and legal careers of accomplished people, most of whom remain unknown on the national level, under the backdrop of intriguing and some landmark legal cases.

While some people have referenced the so-called "White Horse Prophecy" that elders who are members of the Church will preserve the U.S. Constitution as it hangs by a thread in the last days, the Church issued a statement that the prophecy is based on accounts that have not been substantiated by historical research and is not embraced as Church doctrine.[2] While the formal name of the Church is The Church of Jesus Christ of Latter-day Saints, some references use the terms "LDS" and "Mormons" before Church President Russell M. Nelson issued a statement in 2018 to emphasize using the formal name of the Church.[3] Other historical references also use the term "Mormon" such as the "Mormon Test Oath" in the Idaho Constitution.

The primary objective is to share a small segment of legal history with readers in following the counsel to "seek . . . out . . . the best books words of wisdom" and to "obtain a knowledge of history, and of countries, and of kingdoms, of laws of God and man."[4] It is my hope that those who fought for American freedom and independence would find satisfaction in the principles of the American legal system today.

Brian Craig

---

[1] C. La Rue Munson, *How Far Shall the Justice and Rights of the Particular Cause Prevail over A Strict Application of Established Rules of Law*, 13 Yale L.J. 124, 125 (1904).
[2] The Church of Jesus Christ of Latter-day Saints, Newsroom, Church Statement on "White Horse Prophecy" and Political Neutrality, Jan. 6, 2010, https://www.mormonnewsroom.org/blog/church-statement-on-white-horse-prophecy-and-political-neutrality [https://perma.cc/7EVN-VTRW].
[3] See Tad Walch, *Christ-centered lives, home-centered church*, Deseret News, Oct. 8, 2018, 2018 WLNR 31097269.
[4] See Doctrine & Covenants 88:118; Doctrine & Covenants 93:53.

⚖

Chapter 1

Jay S. Bybee: Judge with a Passion for Legal Education

The Kabuki Dance of Senate Confirmation

Jay S. Bybee experienced one of the most bizarre confirmations of a federal judge in recent memory. Some legal experts have described the highly-scripted and politicized confirmation process of federal judges as a "Kabuki" dance.[1] A "Kabuki" dance is a traditional Japanese popular drama performed with highly stylized singing and dancing.[2] President George W. Bush originally nominated Bybee in 2002 to the U.S. Court of Appeals for the Ninth Circuit. After the Senate recessed without approving the nomination, President Bush renominated Bybee in 2003. In reflecting on the confirmation process, Bybee said "The whole thing was very strange. I was first nominated in 2002 and I had to be renominated in 2003. At that time, the Senate had just flipped because of Senator [Jim] Jeffers. It was very, very contentious." Bybee recalled, "There were a number of nominees behind me. There was just a lot of infighting. I had the backing of both Senator [Harry] Reid and Senator [John] Ensign from Nevada. Then the groups came out of the woodwork. It was really interesting to see that."[3]

As a law professor and legal scholar, Bybee authored many law review articles published in top journals which became the focus of some criticism during the confirmation process. Bybee said, "The law reviews are looking for provocating and groundbreaking things."[4] In one article appearing in the Yale Law Journal, Bybee examined the tensions between Congress, the judiciary, and the President over presidential use of advisory committees.[5] Bybee concluded that the President has the inherent power to seek the views of outside advisers: "This implied power secures a constitutional enclave within which the President may obtain outside advice free of congressional control. It is constitutional elbow room for the President to seek the advice he believes relevant, and from a source he considers competent to render it."[6]

In another law review article published in the Harvard Journal of Law and Public Policy, Bybee analyzed the Tenth Amendment to the U.S. Constitution with reference to Plato's Allegory of the Cave. In the allegory, Plato describes a cavernous chamber in which men are imprisoned. Although a large fire lights the cave, the prisoners cannot see the light source. Instead, they can only make out figures that dance and parade in front of them illuminated by the fire. Bybee observed, "In some sense we are prisoners of our Constitution. As a law superior to all other laws, the Constitution circumscribes our political institutions and holds us as a people securely within its walls."[7]

Some of Bybee's ground-breaking legal scholarship and analysis in law review articles drew criticism from the Senate. But on the same day as Bybee's confirmation hearing before the Senate Judiciary Committee, U.S. Secretary of State Collin Powell delivered a speech before the United Nations. Many Senators on the Senate Judiciary Committee slipped out to watch Powell testify and failed to ask more probing questions of Bybee. With a 12-6 endorsement from the Senate Judiciary Committee, Bybee's nomination went to the full Senate. With support across the aisle from U.S. Senator Reid, a Democrat from Bybee's home state of Nevada, the full Senate confirmed Bybee's confirmation by a 74-19 vote.

Building a Stellar Legal Resume

Bybee's interest in the law stems from his early childhood. "I wanted to be a lawyer since I was eight years old," said Bybee. Bybee traces his interest in the law to his grandfather who was a lawyer and municipal judge in California. "I always felt a draw to the law because of him. I always felt a kinship," said Bybee.[8] As an undergraduate student at Brigham Young University (BYU), Bybee was recruited by Rex Lee, founding dean of the law school, and BYU President Dallin H. Oaks to attend the new J. Reuben Clark Law School at the university. "Rex was very aggressive recruiting the best and the brightest," recalled Bybee. "Dallin Oaks and Rex Lee were enormous influences in my life."[9]

Bybee boasts an impressive legal resume. After graduating cum laude from the J. Reuben Clark Law School at BYU, Bybee clerked for Judge Donald Russell of the U.S. Court of Appeals for the Fourth Circuit and then worked in private practice for the prominent law firm Sidley & Austin. In 1984, he accepted a position with the U.S. Department of Justice, first joining the Office of Legal Policy, and then working with the appellate staff of the Civil Division. From 1989 to 1991 Bybee served as Associate Counsel to President George H.W. Bush. From 1991 to 1999, Bybee served on the faculty of the Paul M. Hebert Law Center at Louisiana State University and then joined the founding faculty of the William S. Boyd School of Law at UNLV in 1999. President George W. Bush later appointed Bybee as Assistant Attorney General for the Office of Legal Counsel at the U.S. Department of Justice, a position he held from 2001 to 2003.[10]s

Throughout his accomplished legal career as an Assistant U.S. Attorney General, esteemed law professor, legal scholar, and federal appeals court judge, Jay Bybee has found the greatest satisfaction in teaching law students and law clerks. Bybee has left an enduring legacy with many of his former students and law clerks who have gone on to have their own stellar legal careers. The William S. Boyd School of Law at the University of Nevada Las Vegas (UNLV) recognized Bybee as Professor of the Year in 2000, the school's inaugural year, reflecting Bybee's passion for education. Thomas J. Miles, a former law clerk of Bybee, became Dean of the prestigious University of Chicago Law School in 2015.[11] Another former law clerk, Shima Barawaran Baughman, a law professor at the University of Utah, praised Bybee's legal reasoning: "Judge Bybee is a phenomenal writer, legal thinker and mentor. He is one of the greatest disciplined legal thinkers and writers of our time."[12] Bybee continues to teach courses at UNLV, including constitutional law, while serving as a judge on the influential and sometimes controversial U.S. Court of Appeals for the Ninth Circuit.

Facing Criticism on Post 9/11 Security Issues

Soon after his appointment to the bench, Bybee became surrounded in controversy involving his previous work in the Office of the Legal Counsel (OLC). The Assistant Attorney General who heads the OLC, appointed by the President and confirmed by the Senate, assists the Attorney General in his function as legal advisor to the President providing legal advice to the Executive Branch on all constitutional questions and reviewing pending legislation for constitutionality. Formal written opinions by the OLC constitute "controlling legal advice to Executive Branch officials in furtherance of the President's constitutional duties to preserve, protect, and defend the Constitution" and the "Take Care" Clause found in Article II, Section 3 of the U.S. Constitution that provides "[The President] shall take Care that the Laws be faithfully executed . . ."[13] Former Assistant Attorneys General in the OLC include U.S. Supreme Court Justices William H. Rehnquist and Antonin Scalia.[14] In 2002 following the terrorist attacks on September 11, 2001, Bybee signed two memoranda drafted by the OLC on the standards of conduct for interrogations used in investigations of suspected terrorists.[15]

After the public release of the "torture memos" in 2004 as they were described by some critics, U.S. Senator Russ Feingold, a Democrat from Wisconsin, and others called for Bybee's impeachment and removal as a judge on the Ninth Circuit.[16] Some even accused Bybee as a "war criminal" and labeled him the "torture judge."[17] After an investigation, the Office of Professional Responsibility (OPR) in the U.S. Department of Justice concluded that Bybee did not violate any ethical standards and his conduct did not rise to the level of professional misconduct.[18] Congress refused to consider any articles of impeachment against a sitting federal judge. While some Democrats in Congress, including Senator Patrick Leahy, former chairman of the Senate Judiciary Committee, renewed his call for Congress to investigate the Bush administration's interrogation policies, Senator Reid, who served as Senate Majority Leader from 2007 to 2015, backed Bybee. Senator John Cornyn, a Republican from Texas, said the report "should put to rest any notion that Jay Bybee and John Yoo should deserve anything other than the grateful thanks of the nation." Senator Jeff Sessions said attacking the attorneys amounted to "second guessing good people who made tough decisions at difficult times."[19]

Bybee has taken the high road declining to discuss the memoranda. Article III, Section 1 of the U.S. Constitution states "The Judges, both of the supreme and inferior Courts, shall hold their Offices during good Behaviour." The founders of the U.S. Constitution created an independent judiciary with lifetime tenure not subject to the political whims of the day. Baughman defended Bybee's legal position taken in the controversial memoranda: "Judge Bybee is a moral and careful thinker. I believe that under the circumstances that Judge Bybee was in—right after 9/11 with the pressures he was presented with of trying to avoid a second 9/11, that many of us would have made the same decision he did to sign that memo." Baughman added, "It is hard to judge years later without the benefit of that perspective and given that a second 9/11 did not happen."[20]

Prolific Legal Writer

While Bybee's decisions as a federal appeals court judge often take a more conservative approach than his more liberal colleagues on the Ninth Circuit, Bybee has forged a strong working relationship with the other judges who sit on the Ninth Circuit. "I was a little nervous coming to the Ninth Circuit being a liberal bastion with interesting and strong personalities. For a court as interesting as ours, the court of the judiciary, the court is remarkably collegial. . . I enjoy my colleagues and I have enormous respect for them. I think our court has worked very hard on that" said Bybee.[21] Judge Stephen Reinhardt, appointed by President Jimmy Carter and regarded as one of the nation's most liberal judges, served with Bybyee on the Ninth Circuit. Reinhardt and Bybee decided cases together on both three-judge panels and en banc panels while maintaining a professional relationship.

Bybee has continued his legal writing and scholarship while serving on the bench. Bybee co-authored a book on the Ninth and Tenth Amendments to the U.S. Constitution with Thomas B. McAffee and A. Christopher Bryant. In *Powers Reserved for the People and the States: A History of the Ninth and Tenth Amendments*, Bybee sheds light on the history and development of the Ninth and Tenth Amendments and provides insight on the relationship between state and federal governments.[22] In an article on the empirical measures of judicial performance published in the Florida State University Law Review and co-written with Miles after Bybee's appointment to the bench, Bybee and Miles analyzed a proposed "Tournament of Judges" with a series of ideologically neutral measures that identify which appellate judges "merit" elevation to the Supreme Court in an attempt to avoid partisan battles. While Bybee and Miles praised the valiant attempt to measure judges, the proposal, in the opinion of Bybee and Miles, fails to present a convincing case that choosing Supreme Court nominees by tournament should replace selecting them by the Constitution's more political process with appointment by the President with the advice and consent of the Senate.[23]

Bybee even defended his colleagues from personal attacks in a formal opinion and recognized the importance of an independent judiciary. In *Washington v. Trump*, 858 F.3d 1168 (9th Cir. 2017) where the court analyzed the executive order issued by President Donald Trump to ban immigrants and visitors from seven Muslim countries, Bybee wrote, "Even as I dissent from our decision not to vacate the panel's flawed opinion, I have the greatest respect for my colleagues. The personal attacks on the distinguished district judge and our colleagues were out of all bounds of civic and persuasive discourse—particularly when they came from the parties."[24]

Bybee recognizes that while writing a dissenting opinion offers more flexibility than writing the majority opinion for the court, the majority opinion controls. Bybee observed, "You can do a lot more in a dissent than you can in an opinion. If you want to have an impact on things, you have to be writing the majority opinion. A dissent is just not going to get you far."[25]

In *United States v. Alvarez*, 617 F.3d 1198 (9th Cir. 2010) dealing with the constitutionality of the Stolen Valor Act, Bybee wrote an extensive and passionate 24-page dissent. In *Alvarez*, Bybee recognized that the First Amendment freedom of speech protects satirical and theatrical statements claiming receipt of military awards. Bybee referenced a satirical claim made by comedian Stephen Colbert about winning the Congressional Medal of Honor. Bybee also offered two movie examples of Congressional Medal of Honor winners: *Forest Gump* (1994) and *The Karate Kid* (1984). In *Forest Gump*, the title character, portrayed by Tom Hanks, received the prestigious medal. *The Karate Kid* film also represented that Mr. Miyagi, played by actor Pat Morita, received the Congressional Medal of Honor for his heroism in World War II. Bybee observed "But we all understood the context. . . I do not believe it realistic that anyone would think to accuse Colbert or Hanks of violating the Stolen Valor Act in these contexts." Bybee further wrote, "Assuming, as I must, that the Act will be applied with some modicum of common sense, it does not reach satire or imaginative expression. . . Although the Supreme Court has never so held, I am quite confident that satirical or theatrical statements claiming receipt of a military award are protected under the First Amendment."[26] In reflecting on the *Alvarez* case, Bybee lamented "It was a great dissent."[27]

Bybee also recognized the importance of preserving First Amendment rights in another high-profile case involving Sheriff Joseph "Joe" Arpaio. In *Lacey v. Maricopa County*, 693 F.3d 896 (9th Cir. 2012). Bybee and other judges on the Ninth Circuit examined allegations of unlawful conduct by officials in the Maricopa County Sheriff's Office, led by Sheriff Arpaio, and the Maricopa County Attorney's Office, involving the owners of the Phoenix *New Times*, a small, free weekly newspaper in Arizona. The *New Times* published a series of articles critical of

Sheriff Arpaio. Arpaio is known as "America's toughest sheriff," based on the 1996 book written by Arpaio with Len Sherman entitled *America's Toughest Sheriff: How We Can Win The War Against Crime*.

On July 1, 2004, the *New Times* published an article entitled "Sheriff Joe's Real Estate Game," authored by *New Times* reporter John Dougherty, which questioned Arpaio's commercial real estate transactions. A week later, in an article by Dougherty entitled "Stick it to 'Em," the paper again questioned Arpaio's redaction of personal information from public records, pointing out that Arpaio's home address was available from other websites; at the end of the article, the paper published Arpaio's home address.

Arpaio's "Selective Enforcement Unit" then arrested the newspaper owners, Michael Lacey and Jim Larkin, at their homes late at night. Following the late-night arrests, the co-owners of the newspaper, filed a civil action alleging numerous federal and state causes of action, including an action under 42 U.S.C. § 1983 for violation of constitutional rights. On appeal, the U.S. Court of Appeals for the Ninth Circuit held that the newspaper owners adequately alleged several causes of action. The federal appeals court rejected the claims for immunity asserted by Arpaio, the prosecutors, and the other defendants. Bybee wrote the opinion of the court observing: "Prosecutors are absolutely immune from liability for the consequences of their advocacy, however inept or malicious, because it is filtered through a neutral and detached judicial body; they are not necessarily immune for actions taken outside this process, including actions logically—though not necessarily temporally—prior to advocacy. . . It is hard to conceive of a more direct assault on the First Amendment than public officials ordering the immediate arrests of their critics."[28]

The court recognized that the special prosecutor's motions for arrest warrants, contempt findings, and fines show that he meant the *New Times* to fear them as valid. The special prosecutor appointed had also subpoenaed the names of everyone who read the *New Times* online and details about the websites they had browsed before and after reading the *New Times*. The prosecutor did not wait for the warrants or other official approval before authorizing Arpaio's "Selective Enforcement Unit" to arrest Lacey and Larkin at their homes. The court also observed that "[a]rresting someone in retaliation for their exercise of free speech rights is sufficient to chill speech is an understatement."[29]

After the federal appeals court remanded the case to the district court, the Maricopa County Board of Supervisors unanimously approved a $3.75 million legal settlement in 2013 with the co-owners of the *New Times* newspaper whose false arrests in 2007 were orchestrated by Sheriff Arpaio.[30] In August 2017, President Donald Trump pardoned Arpaio for his criminal-contempt conviction stemming from a different case amid much controversy.[31]

Bybee does not hold back and he has become quite forthright in his formal written opinions. Writing opinions is one of the essential attributes of judges.[32] In a complex decision involving sentencing in criminal cases with divisible and indivisible statutes, *United States v. Martinez-Lopez*, Bybee wrote "concurring in part and dissenting in part, *but frustrated with the whole endeavor*."[33] Bybee agreed with the outcome of the decision but lamented about the process with his candid assessment. He added, "[W]e have struggled to understand the contours of the Supreme Court's framework. Indeed, over the past decade, perhaps no other area of the law has demanded more of our resources."[34] Normally judges write "concurring in part and "dissenting in part" but adding the phrase "but frustrated with the whole endeavor" reflects Bybee's true sentiments. The *Texas Lawyer* magazine selected Bybee for its 2017 "Judicial Honesty" Award for this opinion commenting, "Wow—tell us how you really feel, Judge Bybee. What's next, 'Bybee Circuit Judge, concurring because the Supreme Court won't look at this one anyway?'"[35]

In a case involving a petition for habeas corpus relief, *Smith v. Baldwin*, Bybee sat on a three-judge panel with Judge Reinhardt and voiced another strongly worded opinion.[36] While burglarizing a home, either the defendant or his criminal companion, bludgeoned an 87-year-old man to death with a three-foot long crowbar. The jury found Roger Paul Smith guilty of felony murder and Smith sought habeas corpus relief in federal court. In a split 2-1 decision, the three-judge panel granted habeas corpus relief. In his vehement 24-page dissent, Bybee wrote:

> My view of the majority's analysis of the evidence can perhaps best be described by paraphrasing author Mary McCarthy: I disagree with nearly every word the majority has written, including "and" and "the." My profound disagreement is not limited to the facts, but runs throughout the majority opinion. . . There isn't a jury in the country that wouldn't convict Smith today on a charge of felony murder. . . I vigorously disagree with the majority. But most egregiously, even if we indulge in all of the majority's legal innovations, the majority cannot escape the facts of this case. Smith is guilty of felony murder. . . [N]o amount of prying and tugging—not even with a crowbar and a rope—can get it open.[37]

When the Oregon Attorney General's Office asked for "en benc" reconsideration by the Ninth Circuit in *Smith v. Baldwin*, the panel sided with Judge Bybee's reasoning and reversed the earlier decision. The en banc panel, by a 13-2 decision, held that Smith, the petitioner, failed to demonstrate his "actual innocence" as required by the U.S. Supreme Court when a person seeks habeas corpus relief for felony murder.[38]

Serving Others and Giving Back

Besides his devotion to public service as a judge, law school professor, and government lawyer, as a lifelong member of the Church, Bybee has spent considerable time serving and helping others. He served a mission for the Church in Santiago, Chile from 1973 to 1975 and has also served as a counselor to bishops and served in stake young men presidencies. Baughman, a former law clerk, recalled, "Judge Bybee always cared about individuals and put people first every time. Regardless of how busy Judge Bybee was, he would take as long as necessary to talk to people who visited or called or for any clerks who wanted to chat."[39] Bybee said that his most rewarding church calling has been teaching seminary to high school students. "I really enjoyed working with the kids," he said. While church members do not normally ask for specific callings, Bybee admitted that the only church calling that he actively campaigned for was primary pianist where he played the piano during church services for children. "One thing that I firmly believe in teaching youth is that they are far more capable of understanding the gospel. . . They are capable of being far more mature."[40]

"[P]ersonal attacks [on judges] treat the court as though it were merely a political forum in which bargaining, compromise, and even intimidation are acceptable principles. The courts of law must be more than that, or we are not governed by law at all." Judge Jay Bybee, in his dissenting opinion in *Washington v. Trump* over the travel ban executive order issued by President Donald Trump.[41]

---

[1] Arrie W. Davis, *The Richness of Experience, Empathy, and the Role of A Judge: The Senate Confirmation Hearings for Judge Sonia Sotomayor*, 40 U. Balt. L.F. 1, 38 (2009).
[2] Merriam-Webster's Collegiate Dictionary 680 (11th ed. 2004).
[3] Phone interview with Jay S. Bybee, Judge, U.S. Court of Appeals for the Ninth Circuit, Jul. 20, 2017 (hereinafter "Bybee (2017)").
[4] *Id.*
[5] Jay S. Bybee, *Advising the President: Separation of Powers and the Federal Advisory Committee Act*, 104 Yale L.J. 51, 53–54 (1994).
[6] *Id.* at 128.
[7] Jay S. Bybee, *The Tenth Amendment Among the Shadows: On Reading the Constitution in Plato's Cave*, 23 Harv. J.L. & Pub. Pol'y 551 (2000).
[8] Bybee (2017).
[9] *Id.*
[10] Hearing before the Committee on the Judiciary, S Hrg No. 108-13, 103th Cong, 2d Sess, 2 (2004).

[11] Hon. Jay S. Bybee & Thomas J. Miles, *Judging the Tournament*, 32 Fla. St. U. L. Rev. 1055 (2005).

[12] Shima Baradaran Baughman, Professor, Utah of Utah College of Law, email to the author, Aug. 21, 2017 (hereinafter "Baughman (2017)").

[13] Avidan Y. Cover, *Supervisory Responsibility for the Office of Legal Counsel*, 25 Geo. J. Legal Ethics 269, 273 (2012).

[14] Dawn E. Johnsen, *Faithfully Executing the Laws: Internal Legal Constraints on Executive Power*, 54 UCLA L. Rev. 1559, 1611 (2007).

[15] Memorandum from Jay S. Bybee, Assistant Att'y Gen., Dep't of Justice, Office of Legal Counsel, to White House Counsel Alberto S. Gonzales, Re: Standards of Conduct for Interrogations under 18 U.S.C. §§ 2340-2340A (August 1, 2002).

[16] John Nichols, *Feingold is Right on Torture Judge*, Wisconsin State Journal, April 26, 209, B3, 2009 WLNR 7962717.

[17] Erwin Chemerinsky, *Civil Liberties and the War Terror: Seven Years After 9/11: History Repeating: Due Process, Torture and Privacy During the War on Terror*, 62 SMU L. Rev. 3, 12 (2009).

[18] Steve Tetreault, *"Torture Memo" Author Backed*, Las Vegas Review-Journal, Feb. 27, 2010, 4B, 2010 WLNR 4248796.

[19] *Id.*

[20] Baughman (2017).

[21] Bybee (2017).

[22] McAffee, Bybee, and Bryant, *Powers Reserved for the People and the States: A History of the Ninth and Tenth Amendments (Reference Guides to the United States Constitution)* (Praeger, 2006).

[23] Hon. Jay S. Bybee & Thomas J. Miles, *Judging the Tournament*, 32 Fla. St. U. L. Rev. 1055, 1076 (2005).

[24] 858 F.3d at 1885.

[25] Bybee (2017).

[26] 617 F.3d at 241.

[27] Bybee (2017).

[28] 693 F3d at 917.

[29] *Id.*

[30] *New Times' Journalists Were Arrested in Dead of Night*, Arizona Republic, Dec. 21, 2013, A1, 2013 WLNR 33054676.

[31] Yvonne Wingett Sanchez and Michael Kiefer, Pardon. Politics. Power. For Arpaio, *Pardon Is a Symbol of Loyalty Rewarded*, Arizona Republic, Aug. 27, 2017, A21, 2017 WLNR 26369888.

[32] David R. Stras & Shaun M. Pettigrew, *The Rising Caseload in the Fourth Circuit: A Statistical and Institutional Analysis*, 61 S.C. L. Rev. 421, 441 (2010).

[33] 864 F.3d 1034, 1058 (9th Cir. 2017) (emphasis added).

[34] 864 F.3d at 1058 (citing *United States v. Aguila-Montes de Oca*, 655 F.3d 915, 917 (9th Cir. 2011)).

[35] John G. Browning, *And the Envelope Please*, Texas Lawyer, Nov. 1, 2017, https://www.law.com/texaslawyer/sites/texaslawyer/2017/11/01/1117magooobrowning/ [https://perma.cc/7JQJ-3U6K].

[36] *Smith v. Baldwin*, 466 F.3d 805 (9th Cir. 2006), reh'g en banc granted, 482 F.3d 1156 (9th Cir. 2007); rev'd by 510 F.3d 1127 (9th Cir. 2007).

[37] 466 F.3d at 829, 853.

[38] 510 F.3d at 1139.

[39] Baughman (2017).

[40] Bybee (2017).

[41] 858 F.3d 1168, 1885 (9th Cir. 2017).

Chapter 2

A. Sherman Christensen: Dreamer of the American Inns of Court

Making the American Inns of Court a Reality

A. Sherman Christensen dreamed that one day the American legal system could create a standard for legal excellence akin to the monumental Great Halls of the Inns of Court in England. The venerable English Inns of Court began in 1292 when King Edward I directed his chief justice to satisfy a growing need for skilled advocates at the Royal Court in Westminster. The English Inns of Court grew in number and importance during the Middle Ages. They emphasized the value of learning the craft of lawyering from those individuals already established in the profession. Their collegial environment fostered common goals and nurtured professional ideals and ethics.[1]

U.S. Supreme Court Chief Justice Warren Burger traveled to England in 1977 as part of the Anglo-American Exchange to learn more about the English legal system. Burger was particularly impressed with the collegial approach of the English Inns of Court and with the way in which the Inns passed on to new lawyers the decorum, civility and professional standards necessary for a properly functioning bar. Burger thought that the American legal system could adopt many of the positive values of the English Inns, such as integrity, civility, and collegiality, integral concepts of the English Inns.[2]

After visiting England, the Chief Justice appointed U.S. District Judge A. Sherman Christensen as chairman of the ad hoc committee on the American Inns of Court of the Judicial

Conference of the United States to spearhead a project of creating Inns of Court in America patterned after the English Inns of Court.[3] Christensen, Burger, and Rex E. Lee founded the first American Inn of Court in 1980 in affiliation with the J. Reuben Clark School of Law at Brigham Young University in Provo, Utah with J. Clifford Wallace as the keynote speaker.[4] Although the number of Inns increased slowly at first, the organization grew rapidly with the creation of the American Inns of Court Foundation in 1985.[5]

Christensen envisioned small, intimate gatherings for the American Inns of Court. In encouraging the establishment of locals Inns of Court, Christensen wrote in 1980 during the infancy of the movement, "We remain convinced that a series of small and intimate organizations designed for these purposes could make a unique contribution by helping to provide, as it were, an insightful, professional soul for trial practice permeated by the vision we thought could be caught from common law traditions and English Inn relationships." Christensen advocated, "We could find no better general model for structuring these ideas than the English Inn itself."[6]

Howard T. Markey, chairman of the board of the American Inns of Court Foundation, in a report entitled "The Cathedral of the American Inns of Court," wrote:

> In his essay, "Some Suggestions for Effective Case Presentation," Justice [Robert] Jackson tells a parable of three stonemasons. A questioner asks each of the stonemasons what they are doing. The first replied, without looking up, "earning my living." And the second answers, "I am shaping this stone to pattern." But the third stone mason pauses and responds, "I am building a Cathedral." Since its creation, the American Inns of Court has been about a vision of legal excellence. This is our Cathedral. When we visit our counterparts in England and stand in the monumental Great Halls of the Inns of Court, we are humbled by the vision of those who, 800 years ago, gave birth to the Anglo-American practice of law and first set forth the ideals we aspire to.[7]

15

Christensen founded the American Inns of Court which now comprise more than 400 local chapters in forty-eight states and the District of Columbia. The American Inns of Court involve more than 130,000 active and alumni members who include judges, lawyers, law professors, and law students.[8] Christensen played an instrumental role in the American Inns of Court movement which established a standard for excellence, civility, professionalism, and ethics in the legal profession.

Serving Alongside a Tyrant

Christensen pursued a career in the law following the path set by his father. "My father was my model," said Christensen. "I vividly remember going to his courtroom, which was in an old building in Manti, Utah. You had to go up a rickety flight of stairs to the second floor. There was a big pot bellied stove that the sheriff kept stoked with coal," he recalled.[9] Born in Manti, Utah in 1905, Christensen attended the National University School of Law in Washington, D.C. National University School of Law later merged with the George Washington Law School in 1954.[10] After law school, Christensen returned to Utah and joined his father's law firm and his brothers later joined him in the practice of law. In his early career before becoming a judge, Christensen became a successful and well-respected trial lawyer. Sherman also served in the Navy for four years during World War II commanding the auxiliary Naval Air Stations along the West Coast and was also a Navy pilot.[11]

After his nomination by President Dwight D. Eisenhower and confirmation by the Senate in 1954, Christensen became the first federal judge in Utah who was a member The Church of Jesus Christ of Latter-day Saints. When Christensen went to the White House to be interviewed by President Eisenhower, the President entered the room, shook his hand and said, "I want to meet the only judicial candidate thus far in my Presidency who the FBI has given a perfect score in its background check."[12] In a biography of Christensen published by the Tenth Circuit Historical Society, Allan T. Brinkerhoff, who worked as a law clerk for Judge Christensen, recognized that this statement by Eisenhower is consistent with the integrity and straight forward manner in which Judge Christensen had practiced law and otherwise conducted his life.[13]

But the honeymoon of praise did not last long for Judge Christensen. While most federal judges generally have mutual respect, Christensen experienced hostility with fellow U.S. District Judge Willis W. Ritter. U.S. Supreme Court Justice Sandra Day O'Connor described Ritter's conduct as "obnoxious, capricious, or even tyrannical at times." One of the most controversial jurists ever to sit on the federal bench, Ritter once ordered the arrest of 26 postal workers because the creaking of an elevator they were riding disturbed proceedings in his courtroom. Neither rain nor sleet nor snow can stop the mail, but on that fateful day a disgruntled federal judge did just that. O'Connor observed that this is just one of various stories where it may be fair to conclude that Judge Ritter may have abused his authority as a judge, but he did not commit a high crime or misdemeanor warranting impeachment.[14]

"They didn't have a very close relationship. It wasn't Judge Christensen's fault. Judge Ritter was an egotist and didn't think they needed a new judge. He came in with four strikes against him. [Judge Ritter] thought it was a Republican conspiracy to dilute his almighty power," said Brinkerhoff. "Judge Ritter was the tyrant here in Utah. He didn't like Sherman the day he got there."[15]

Judge Christensen's style contrasted with the style of Judge Ritter. "[Judge Christensen] was very formal and very respectful to you. He had a very formal personality. On the bench, he was formal to the attorneys who appeared before him. He was very friendly, not real chummy," recalled Brinkerhoff. "He was extremely precise and fair and well prepared and sober and all of the things that Judge Ritter wasn't. Everybody was very laudatory and very respectful. He was highly respected even more so because of the antics of Judge Ritter. Because of the juxtaposition, everybody thought Judge Christensen was great. Even if he ruled against you, people always thought he was fair."[16]

Judge Christensen displayed fairness and compassion from the bench. When a deaf and blind immigrant, Aslaug Vaieland, appeared before Judge Christensen to take the oath to become a United States citizen, the compassionate judge first offered to waive the repeating of the oath. But Vaieland, with tears in her eyes, told the judge she wanted to repeat the oath. Vaieland, who lost her hearing at the age of six through scarlet fever and experienced similar disabilities as Helen Keller with deafness and blindness, repeated the oath in a loud clear voice with the assistance of an interpreter using sign language and touching Vaieland's hand. Christensen said he purposely kept another case outside his courtroom, concerning a man who faced deportation, so the man would not have to witness the moving ceremony of new citizens taking the citizenship oath.[17]

As federal judge, Christensen decided many important cases, including anti-trust cases with complex and often protracted issues. While he had no formal academic background in economics, his early Washington D.C. experience in the Bureau of Foreign and Domestic Commerce as assistant business specialist while attending law school stimulated an interest and at least some perception in this field. He became very adept in handling antitrust and other complicated commercial cases. Those practitioners who often appeared before Judge Christensen during his years on the bench overwhelmingly characterized his preparation, judicial temperament, hard work, and demeanor in the most laudatory terms.[18]

In an anti-trust case involving computer-giant IBM in 1973, Judge Christensen ruled against IBM, the first time IBM had ever lost a major anti-trust case.[19] Christensen initially awarded $352.5 million to Telex, which at the time was one of the highest awards in anti-trust law history. Christensen found that IBM violated Section 2 of the Sherman Act when confronted with the unresolved issue of what pricing actions a lawfully acquired monopoly may take. IBM appealed the case, and in a rarity, the U.S. Court of Appeals for the Tenth Circuit reversed the trial court decision rendered by Christensen.[20]

Christensen also decided important cases involving constitutional questions. In *Potter v. Murray City*, 585 F. Supp.

1126 (D. Utah 1984), Christensen decided a case interpreting the free exercise of religion. In *Potter*, a terminated Utah police officer filed a civil rights action alleging the termination of his employment because of his practice of plural marriage violated his right to free exercise of his religion. The police officer argued that the bigamy law was forced upon the state through the requirement that Utah's constitution prohibit polygamy.

Christensen ruled that the government did not violate the officer's right to free exercise of religion. In the opinion, Christensen held that Constitution's protection of religious freedom from the First Amendment, applicable to state and local governments through the Fourteenth Amendment's Due Process Clause, states that local governments should be able to effectively exercise police powers to benefit their citizens is implicit throughout the Constitution and is explicit in the Tenth Amendment providing that "the powers not delegated to the United States by the Constitution, nor prohibited by it to the states, are reserved to the states respectively or to the people."[21] As was the usual case with cases decided by Judge Christensen, the U.S. Court of Appeals for the Tenth Circuit agreed with Christensen's analysis and affirmed the decision.

Because of the conflicts with Ritter, Christensen elected to take "senior" status as soon as he became eligible. Judge Christensen acknowledged that the years of conflicts with Ritter "finally led to my taking Senior Judge Status in 1971 before ordinarily I would have considered it."[22] A form of semi-retirement, federal judges have the option of electing senior status after meeting certain age and service requirements with a reduced caseload.[23]

Finding Satisfaction in "Retirement"

While Christensen experienced challenges and frustration because of Judge Ritter's antics, Christensen enjoyed the time he spent on the Temporary Emergency Court of Appeals and as a visiting judge sitting by designation after he attained senior judge status. Chief Justice Burger appointed Christensen to the Temporary Emergency Court of Appeals, where he eventually served longer than any of the other 27 judges with the court.[24] During the oil embargo of the early 1970s, Congress passed the Economic Stabilization Act Amendments of 1971 and created the Temporary Emergency Court of Appeals.[25] The court's jurisdiction exclusive initially focused on appeals arising from implementation of the wage and price control program embodied in the Economic Stabilization Act of 1970.[26] The Temporary Emergency Court of Appeals acted more like a regular circuit court of appeals in that it reviewed decisions of the federal district courts instead of a specialized agency. Congress added other specialized statutes, typically in the energy area, to its exclusive jurisdiction after the initial price control act expired.[27] Congress abolished the Temporary Emergency Court of Appeals in 1992 and transferred cases to the U.S. Court of Appeals for the Federal Circuit.[28]

Along with his service on the Temporary Emergency Court of Appeals during the energy crisis, Chief Justice Burger also appointed Christensen to sit as a visiting judge by designation. Under the federal statute, the Chief Justice may designate and assign temporarily a district judge of one circuit for service in another circuit, either in a district court or court of appeals.[29] Christensen travelled the country deciding cases in various federal appellate courts, including cases in the Second, Third, Seventh, and Ninth Circuits. Christensen served on the panel in 118 different court of appeals cases from 1972 to 1992.[30] On one occasion, Judge Christensen invited Brinkerhoff, his law clerk, to California. Brinkerhoff and Christensen included their wives on the trip and they stayed at the luxurious Biltmore Hotel in Los Angeles. Recently married, Brinkerhoff attended half-day hearings at the court and then spent the rest of the time enjoying a honeymoon in California with his bride. Christensen's beloved wife, Lois, told Brinkerhoff, "Yours was one of the best honeymoons I have been on."[31]

Christensen also traveled to Chicago sitting by designation on the Seventh Circuit and sat on the panel with John Paul Stevens—the year before Stevens became a U.S. Supreme Court Justice. In *Epperson v. United States*, 490 F.2d 98 (7th Cir. 1973), Christensen wrote the opinion of the court holding that the closing argument of the lawyer for the government which mentioned the taxpayer was a rich man and should not be allowed to avoid paying his "fair share" of taxes, while in "bad taste if not reprehensible," did not result in prejudicial error and the taxpayer should not receive a new trial. Judge Christensen would not have had such as happy career if he had not decided as many cases by designation."[32]

Deciding the Fate of General George Washington

The venerable and self-styled "country lawyer" presided over many cases during his 36-year career as a federal judge, but the one trial that Christensen enjoyed the most involved the mock trial of none other than General George Washington.[33] In a mock trial held in the oak-paneled panoply and high stained-glass of the Great Hall of Lincoln's Inn in London, Christensen served as one of three judges deciding the fate of Washington with British barristers trying to prove Washington was a traitor to the crown. It was the connection between two Inns of Court that led to the mock trial. Lord Goff of Chieveley, a "law lord" of the English House of Lords, a position equivalent to a U.S. Supreme Court justice, issued a friendly challenge to the American Inns of Court Foundation meeting in Washington. Goff said George Washington was a traitor and should have been tried for high treason. Supreme Court Justice Warren Burger was first asked to serve as a judge, but Burger asked his good friend Christensen to serve in his place.

The trial was set in 1779, after the Declaration of Independence, under the imaginary premise that General George Washington had been indicted for treason and returned to London to face and defend the charge before a British court. Treason was defined on the basis of the Statute of Treasons of 1351, for "levying war against the king." The late seventeenth century penalty for treason was severe. A convicted person was drawn (dragged to the gallows), usually with a blanket or sled to avoid abrasion, then hanged and his body quartered, with its parts to be at the disposition of the king. The expression "drawn and quartered" derives from this cruel punishment.

Christensen served as the lone American judge on the three-judge panel. Lord Bridge of Harwich, a senior British Law Lord, and Sir Patrick Neill, a British appellate judge and one of England's leading historians, also decided the fate of the American general. Prosecuting Washington under the Treason Act of 1351 was Sydney Kentridge, the human rights lawyer who defended Steven Biko in South Africa. The American attorneys, led by Michael Coffield and Jim Figliulo of the Chicago Inn of Court, took up the challenge to defend the American general.

Thomas Jefferson, Benjamin Franklin, and Washington, portrayed by members of the Philadelphia-based Royal Pickwickians, a troupe that combines acting with historical research, testified for the defense in attire appropriate for the eighteenth century. Acting for the crown, Kentridge only cited the undisputed historical truth, that the accused, Washington, had organized and led the revolutionaries. In 1775, he had taken over as commander-in-chief of the colonial forces with the sole aim of overturning the crown's authority. Washington had three defenses: the right of a people to rise up against oppression and a right of self-determination, the right of self-defense and provocation, and a breach of the social compact between the king and his people. Coffield argued for the defense, saying, "We are establishing the case that our client owed no allegiance to the crown after the British levied punitive taxation and denied the colonies democratic representation."

In a blending of two great, complementary systems of justice, the three-judge panel unanimously found that Washington would avoid the gallows. The judges found that the way Britain governed the colonies had forced the Americans to react. The colonists "only as a last resort were driven to the Declaration of Independence," Bridge said. The judges agreed that Washington and all Americans were entitled to revolt against repression. "The conduct of the Crown was in violation of the right of self-determination," Christensen recalled.

"It was exciting to see the interface of the two systems of justice," remarked Christensen. "The American lawyers who were perhaps less polished and more direct, dressed in their contemporary American business suits, and the British, calm, articulate and more disciplined in their colonial dress. The trial was a very moving one. I tried to practice judicial impartiality." Christensen found the advocacy highly effective on both sides, and he was especially stirred by the words of Thomas Jefferson. During the trial, Christensen confessed "predisposition" in view of his "sojourn in the Colonies" and his "distant acquaintance with some of the witnesses," but vowed with the other judges "to decide the case without fear or favor." Judge Christensen said: "My contribution may have been in recognizing the synergistic relationship of the three defenses, and distinguishing between individual unregulated self-determination—which was not what the Revolution was about—and the self-determination of a people fighting against insufferable oppression and discrimination. I asked Lord North what single unalienable right, if any, were recognized by the crown, and he said, 'The right to protection by our law.' That was the heart of the case. If it were the only right protected it should have been enough to effect Washington's release." Christensen concluded that "it was British law that oppressed the Americans as much as British actions did. To give the Colonies the right only to the laws that were oppressing them would be like sending lettuce home with a rabbit." Christensen described the mock trial, which later aired on television in Great Britain and the United States, as the "experience of a lifetime."[34]

Receiving Recognition for a Lifetime of Service

Christensen received many honors and awards for his distinguished lifetime service in the legal profession. The American Bar Association (ABA) presented him in 1990 with its highest honor, the ABA Medal, recognizing Judge Christensen's "conspicuous service to the cause of American jurisprudence."[35] Past recipients of the ABA Medal, first awarded in 1929, include U.S. Supreme Court Justices Oliver Wendel Holmes, Felix Frankfurter, and Thurgood Marshall.[36] The Utah State Bar recognized Christensen for the Judge of the Year Award in 1977 and the Federal Bar Association awarded Christensen the Distinguished Jurist Award in 1989.[37] Despite these and many other accolades, perhaps Christensen's greatest recognition lies in the view of those who knew him best and described him as a "wonderful human being" and a "consummate gentleman."[38]

The A. Sherman Christensen Award is awarded annually by the American Inns of Court Celebration of Excellence held at the Supreme Court of the United States. The award is bestowed upon a member of an American Inn of Court who, at the local, state, or national level has provided distinguished, exceptional and significant leadership to the American Inns of Court movement.[39] Christensen's dream was fulfilled with the American Inns of Court and the prestigious service award that now bears his name recognizes the person who best exemplifies the qualities of leadership and commitment displayed by Judge A. Sherman Christensen. While Judge Ritter left his mark as a tyrant, Judge Christensen left a legacy with a commitment to leadership, service, ethics, and professionalism during his 91 years of life.

"The right to worship according to the dictates of one's own conscience and reason and to be free from molestation or restraint in his person, liberty, or estate in such worship, is a natural, fundamental and inalienable right, available to every individual, subject only to a proper exercise of the police power when action is coupled with belief. Freedom to believe or not to believe is absolute. Freedom to act, however, is not absolute but limited or qualified by the power of the state within reasonable limits to protect society pursuant to a compelling state interest." A. Sherman Christensen, on the freedom of religion.[40]

---

[1] American Inns of Court, History of the American Inn of Court, http://inns.innsofcourt.org/for-members/inns/the-barney-

masterson-american-inn-of-court/history-of-the-american-inn-of-court.aspx [https://perma.cc/F522-85YC].

[2] *Id.*

[3] Justice Hugh Maddox, *An Old Tradition with A New Mission the American Inns of Court*, 54 Ala. Law. 381 (1993).

[4] *Id.*

[5] American Inns of Court, *supra* note 1.

[6] A. Sherman Christensen, *The Concept and Organization of an American Inn of Court: Putting A Little More "English" on American Legal Education*, 93 F.R.D9. 807, 813 (1981).

[7] Maddox, 54 Ala. Law. at 383.

[8] United Stats Courts for the Ninth Circuit, Public Information Office, Judge J. Clifford Wallace to Receive the 2016 American Inns of Court A. Sherman Christensen Award, News Release, Sept. 19, 2016, http://cdn.ca9.uscourts.gov/datastore/ce9/2016/09/19/Wallace_Sherman_Award.pdf [https://perma.cc/Y9AK-2C68].

[9] Allan T. Brinkerhoff, Judge A. Sherman Christensen, Tenth Circuit Historical Society, Biographies of Judges of the Tenth Judicial Circuit, p. 3, https://tenthcircuit-historicalso.squarespace.com/s/Christensen_bio.pdf [https://perma.cc/6H68-QWLY] (hereinafter "Brinkerhoff, Tenth Circuit Historical Society").

[10] Robert M. Jarvis, *A Brief History of Law School Names*, 56 J. Legal Educ. 388, 410, note 59 (2006).

[11] Brinkerhoff, Tenth Circuit Historical Society.

[12] *Id.*

[13] *Id.*

[14] Sandra Day O'Connor, *Judicial Independence and Civics Education,* Utah B.J. September/October 2009, 10, 12.

[15] Phone interview with Allan Brinkerhoff, Utah lawyer and former law clerk to Judge A. Sherman Christensen, Sept. 27, 2017 (hereinafter "Brinkerhoff (2017)").

[16] *Id.*

[17] Citizenship-Her Greatest Day, *Salt Lake Tribune*, Apr. 9, 1964, 13.

[18] Brinkerhoff, Tenth Circuit Historical Society.

[19] *Telex v. IBM: Monopoly Pricing Under Section 2 of the Sherman Act*, 84 Yale L.J. 558, 583 (1975).

[20] *Telex Corp. v. International Business Machines Corp.*, 367 F.Supp. 258 (N.D. Okla. 1973), rev'd 510 F.2d 894 (10th Cir. 1975).

[21] *Potter v. Murray City*, 585 F. Supp. 1126, 1137 (D. Utah 1984), aff'd as modified, 760 F.2d 1065 (10th Cir. 1985).

[22] Patricia F. Cowley & Parker M. Nielson, *Thunder Over Zion* (Salt Lake City: University of Utah Press, 2007), 214.

[23] 28 U.S.C. § 371; David R. Stras & Ryan W. Scott, *Are Senior Judges Unconstitutional?*, 92 Cornell L. Rev. 453, 461 (2007).

[24] *Death: Judge A. Sherman Christensen*, Deseret News, Aug. 16, 1996, https://www.deseretnews.com/article/507735/DEATH--JUDGE-A-SHERMAN-CHRISTENSEN.html [https://perma.cc/MJ6S-FBVE].

[25] Pub. L. No. 92-210, 85 Stat. 743 (1971).

[26] Pub. L. No. 91-379, 84 Stat. 799 (1970).

[27] Theodore W. Ruger, *The Judicial Appointment Power of the Chief Justice*, 7 U. Pa. J. Const. L. 341, 363–64 (2004); See generally James R. Elkins, *The Temporary Emergency Court of Appeals: A Study in the Abdication of Judicial Responsibility*, 1978 Duke L. J. 113 (1978).

[28] Federal Courts Administration Act of 1992 Pub. L. No. 102-572, 106 Stat. 4506.

[29] 28 U.S.C. § 292.

[30] Search conducted on Westlaw in Federal Courts of Appeals Cases for "PA(christensen) & utah /s designation" (without quotation marks), September 28, 2017.

[31] Brinkerhoff (2017).

[32] *Id.*

[33] Dennis Lythgoe, Utah Judge Stirred by his Part in Mock British Trial of George Washington, *Deseret News*, Oct. 29, 1990, https://www.deseretnews.com/article/129454/UTAH-JUDGE-STIRRED-BY-HIS-PART-IN-MOCK-BRITISH-TRIAL-OF-GEORGE--WASHINGTON.html [https://perma.cc/KY6A-VGYX].

[34] Associated Press, Mock Trial: George Washington Found Not Guilty, *St. Louis Post-Dispatch*, Oct. 21, 1990, 12A, 1990 WLNR 479789.

[35] Jim McCarthy, ABA Honors Thurgood Marshall Retired Justice Will Receive ABA Medal at Annual Meeting, 78 ABA Journal 104 (1992); American Bar Association, Guidelines for Awarding the ABA Model, https://www.americanbar.org/content/dam/aba/administrative/boa rd_of_governors/aba_medal_guidelines_past_recipients_2015.auth checkdam.pdf [https://perma.cc/6A68-LFQ7].

[36] *Id.*

[37] *Death: Judge A. Sherman Christensen, supra* note 24.

[38] Rachel Sterver, *Federal Appeals Court Judge J. Clifford Wallace Seeks Inspiration, Chances to Serve*, Church News, The Church of Jesus Christ of Latter-day Saints, Jan. 10, 2017, https://www.lds.org/church/news/federal-appeals-court-judge-j-clifford-wallace-seeks-inspiration-chances-to-serve?lang=eng [https://perma.cc/37XC-KHXN].

[39] United States Courts for the Ninth Circuit, Public Information Office.

[40] *Potter*, 585 F. Supp. at 1137.

$$\underline{\overline{\top}}$$

Chapter 3

J. Reuben Clark, Jr.: International Lawyer, Statesman, and Diplomat

Drafting the Landmark Memorandum on American Foreign Policy

Before his 28 years in Church leadership as a member of the First Presidency, J. Reuben Clark, Jr. was an accomplished international lawyer, statesman, and diplomat described by Church President Heber J. Grant as "the greatest International lawyer in the U.S."[1] Philander Knox, the former U.S. Secretary of State, U.S. Senator, and U.S. Attorney General, considered Clark "the most helpful man in international law in the United States."[2] Clark's crowning achievement in international law was his 238-page paper entitled "Memorandum on the Monroe Doctrine" later known as the Clark Memorandum.[3]

Written in December 1928 and later published by the administration of President Herbert Hoover in 1930, the Clark Memorandum "is one of the most powerful and influential documents against imperial, colonial, or interventionist policies ever drafted by an American in high office" and considered a "master treatise."[4] The memorandum, written while Clark acted as Undersecretary Secretary of State during the administration of President Calvin Coolidge, provides a restatement and history of United States policy in Latin America based on the Monroe Doctrine. The Monroe Doctrine, first announced by President James Monroe in 1823, is the principle that the United States will allow no intervention or domination in the Western Hemisphere by any non-American country, including European nations.[5]

Clark drafted the memorandum in response to Secretary of State Frank B. Kellogg's inquiry who asked to "give me everything that had ever been said on the Monroe Doctrine by presidents, secretaries of state and other officials." The memorandum, later reprinted in countless textbooks and in Department of State manuals, states in part, "These various expressions and statements . . . detract not a little from the scope popularly attached to the Monroe Doctrine, and they relieve that Doctrine of many of the criticisms which have been aimed against it."[6] Clark concluded that the "Big Stick" policy utilized by President Theodore Roosevelt was not a proper interpretation of the doctrine because a "Big Stick" was not necessary to assure the national security interests of the United States.[7] Clark wrote, "[I]t is not believed that this [the Roosevelt] corollary is justified by the terms of the Monroe Doctrine, however much it may be justified by the application of the doctrine of self-preservation."[8] In other words, the Clark Memorandum repudiated the "Roosevelt Corollary" that "in case of financial or other difficulties in weak Latin American countries, the United States should attempt an adjustment thereof lest European Governments should intervene, and intervening should occupy territory."[9]

In effect, the Clark Memorandum removed Teddy Roosevelt's militarism and colonialism from the Monroe Doctrine and from American foreign policy.[10] In embarking on a "Good Neighbor" policy, President Hoover gave his support to the views expressed by Clark.[11] Both the American public and foreign governments accepted the Clark Memorandum as an official interpretation of the Monroe Doctrine. The memorandum has since become one of the landmark documents of American foreign relations.[12] Many documents have since cited the Clark Memorandum. For example, in a memorandum addressed to Attorney General Robert Kennedy on August 30, 1962, the Office of the Legal Counsel cited the Clark Memorandum in part as the basis for the United States to take action against the Soviet Union for establishing missile bases in Cuba that led to the Cuban Missile Crisis.[13]

Embarking on a Journey to Study the Law

Joshua Reuben Clark was born on September 1, 1871, in the small farming town of Grantsville, a settlement located 35 miles southwest of Salt Lake City in Tooele County, Utah. Even as a child, Clark showed a love for learning. His father once related that young Reuben would "rather miss his meals than to miss a day from school."[14] After four years at the University of Utah, Clark completed all the requirements for both his high school diploma and his bachelor of science degree. He graduated first in his class—in addition to having served as student-body president, managing editor of the student newspaper, and secretary to university president James E. Talmage. On September 14, 1898, J. Reuben Clark married Luacine Annetta Savage in the Salt Lake Temple, with Talmage officiating at the ceremony. For the next four years, Clark held various positions around the state as a teacher and administrator on both high school and college levels.[15]

While working as an educator and school administrator, Clark attempted to study the law on his own, but he decided he needed a formal legal education. At the time, no law school existed in Utah as the University of Utah School of Law would not have its first graduating class until 1913.[16] In 1903, the Clarks, including two small children, moved to New York City, where Clark entered law school at the prestigious Columbia University. Joseph Nelson provided an interest-free loan to Clark that enabled him to attend Columbia and finance his education.[17] Before departing for the East Coast with his wife and two daughters, Clark received counsel and official sanction to lead his family in to "Babylon" from Church President Joseph F. Smith, who set him apart on a type of mission "to be an exemplary Latter day Saint among the gentiles of the world."[18]

Clark excelled as a student at Columbia. His work was of such a high quality that in the beginning of the second year, he was elected one of three second-year students to the editorial board of the Columbia Law Review. During the summer of 1905, Dr. James Brown Scott, one of his professors, asked Clark to compile and annotate materials for a case book.

Clark's work impressed Dr. Scott so much that the following summer, Scott asked Clark to compile and annotate the major portion of two volumes of cases on equity jurisdiction. Scott then received appointment as Solicitor of the State Department. With Scott's recommendation, Clark was appointed Assistant Solicitor of the State Department by Elihu Root, Secretary of the State under President Theodore Roosevelt. By the end of his second year, Clark was admitted to the New York Bar and he received an LL.B. degree in 1906. Thus began Clark's journey into the field of international law. Shortly thereafter, Clark became an assistant professor of law at George Washington University, where he taught until 1908.[19]

Becoming an Acclaimed International Lawyer

In July 1910, under the administration of President William Howard Taft, Clark received an appointment to serve as Solicitor of the U.S. Department of State, the chief law officer for the Department of State. As part of his responsibilities as Solicitor, Clark represented the United States government in a dispute with Chile. In 1879, war broke out between Chile and Bolivia. Peru also became involved in the conflict and the port of Arica passed into the possession of Chile by the Treaty of Peace in 1904. The Government of the United States took up the matter, and in 1890, a claims commission was appointed to resolve the controversy between Chile and the United States. In the *Alsop* case, Clark handled the diplomatic negotiations with Chile which led to arbitration before King George V, the king of Great Britain. Clark prepared the entire case of the United States in the controversy covering 350 pages of arguments. King George V, acting as arbitrator, awarded nearly $1 million in favor of the United States, which was one of the largest international arbitration awards ever made at the time.[20] After the reduction of certain expenses, the sum of $863,493 remained in the Federal Treasury for distribution among the beneficiaries by the Secretary of State.[21]

Clark drafted the legal opinion for Secretary of State Philander C. Knox that the distribution of the award was a matter, not of international, but of municipal law. A decision by the Orphans' Court of Pennsylvania in Philadelphia County, determining distribution of the estate of Ann McCall, recognized Clark's hand in deciding the distribution of claims.[22]

Clark also worked on the extradition case involving Russian national Jan Pouren who sought asylum in the United States.[23] Jan Janoff Pouren fled to the United States from the Baltic region of Russia after participating in the disorders accompanying the 1905 Revolution. In January 1908, the Russian government applied to U.S. Secretary of State Elihu Root for Pouren's return, claiming that he was a common criminal whose offenses came under the extradition clauses of the United States-Russian treaty of 1887. Fortunately for Pouren, a great many Americans disputed this claim and worked actively to convince Washington officials that he was a political refugee and was therefore not subject to extradition. By the time extradition proceedings were finally resolved in Pouren's favor, thousands of Americans had rallied to his defense and thousands more had come to regard the autocratic regime of Czar Nicholas II with pronounced hostility.[24] In the aftermath of the Pouren case, Clark gave a speech on the definition of a political offense in international extraditions.[25]

Secretary of State Knox praised Clark's abilities as a lawyer: "I am doing him but justice in saying that for natural ability, integrity, loyalty, and industry, I have not in a long professional and public service met his superior and rarely his equal."[26]

During the Taft Administration, Clark wrote his "Memorandum on the Right to Protect Citizens in Foreign Countries by Landing Forces," which was later billed as the "classic authority on the subject." As Solicitor, he was appointed to the International Relief Board of the American Red Cross and was made chairman of the Committee on Civil Warfare where he drafted procedures to handle insurrection, civil war, and revolution. He was appointed chairman of the American Preparatory Committee to represent the United States at the Third Hague Conference. He was also a member of the Board of Directors of the American Peace Society, and was appointed as counsel for the United States before the Tribunal of Arbitration between the United States and Britain.[27]

After Woodrow Wilson's election and the Democratic Party control of the executive branch, Clark left the State Department in 1913 and entered private law practice for the first time in his life. Clark formed a law partnership with Preston D. Richards under the firm name Clark and Richards in the nation's capital. Richards previously worked with Clark with the U.S. Department of State. Clark's clients included the Japanese Embassy, Philander C. Knox, the Cuban Legation, the Guatemalan Ministry, the Equitable Life Assurance Society, and J. P Morgan & Company. The firm later opened offices in New York City and Salt Lake City.[28] Clark focused on transactional legal work rather than litigation. As such, his name does not appear in any published decisions as a litigator.[29] In 1916, Clark scored a major victory bringing in a new client. He became counsel to the newly organized American International Corporation (AIC), one of the early American-based multinational conglomerates, with a capitalization of $50 million.[30]

Answering the Call of Duty During World War I

During World War I, Clark temporarily left his growing private law practice and joined other Americans in answering the call of service to support the war effort. Today, it is not unusual to find judge advocates who entered the Corps from civilian life, as directly commissioned officers. At the time, however, it was a radical idea to invite civilian attorneys, who had no military experience, to don uniforms and join the Judge Advocate General's Department.[31] In February 1917, Clark received a direct commission as a major in the Army Judge Advocate General's Officer Reserve Corps as one of the first civilian attorneys given direct commissions in the corps. Clark joined Felix Frankfurter, a Jewish Harvard Law School professor who later became a U.S. Supreme Court Justice, and other lawyers at the top of the American legal profession in the early 20th Century in receiving direct commissions as Army lawyers.[32] Clark received an assignment to work as a special assistant to the U.S. Attorney General where he prepared "Emergency Legislation and War Powers of the President."[33] He later assisted Judge Advocate General Enoch Crowder with the implementation of the Selective Service Act. After the war, Clark received recognition with the Distinguished Service Medal for his "zeal, great industry, and eminent legal attainments." Clark's citation reads, in part: "[F]rom June 1917 until September 1918 . . . he rendered conspicuous services in the compilation and publication of an extremely valuable and comprehensive edition of the laws and analogous legislation pertaining to the war powers of our Government since its beginning. From September 1918 to December 1918, as executive officer of the Provost Marshal General's Office, he again rendered services of an inestimable value in connection with the preparation and execution of complete regulations governing the classification and later the demobilization of several million registrants."[34]

Answering the Call to Service Yet Again

Following the war, Clark continued his private law practice focusing on international law but Clark's practice struggled. Clark returned to Utah 1920 and assumed active partnership with Richards while still traveling back East to represent some clients. Later, Clark took a position as personal legal advisor to U.S. Ambassador to Mexico Dwight Morrow, who had been impressed with Clark's work in the State Department.[35] As a private practitioner, his achievement fell considerable short of his aspirations. Although the Utah practice was respected, he never stayed with it long enough to reach commanding heights as a practical lawyer.[36]

Clark then answered the call again to public service. Clark accepted the position as Under-Secretary of State in 1928 to serve in the administration of Calvin Coolidge.[37] During this time, Clark wrote his celebrated memorandum on the Monroe Doctrine. As Under-Secretary, Clark experienced a level of personal accomplishment and recognition. In the Secretary's absence, Clark assumed the role as acting Secretary of State, and like his former days at the State Department, made critical decisions regarding international emergencies and recommended courses of action to the president.[38]

When Morrow resigned as ambassador to serve in the U.S. Senate, President Herbert Hoover appointed Clark to fill the void. Clark became Ambassador Extraordinary and Plenipotentiary of the United States to Mexico on October 3, 1930, a key post in U.S. foreign relations that earned him instant prestige. In a profile of his great-grandfather, Stephen S. Davis recognized that the ambassadorship to Mexico for Clark "was a fulfillment of his highest aspirations and dreams."[39] In his farewell address to the president and people of Mexico, Clark poignantly expressed his love for them: "To no one could come a greater honor than the assurance you give me of the sympathy and affection of the Mexican people. To possess a place in the hearts of a people is the most priceless heritage that can come to any man, however high may be his degree and however lowly may be his station."[40]

While Clark experienced professional success, Clark's legendary work habits took their toll on his family relationships. After moving back to Utah in 1920, Clark still spent considerable time commuting to the East. A photograph of his wife, Luacine, and the children, taken about 1920 bears the revealing caption, "No mere happenstance that daddy was missing from the picture."[41] Driven by an unquenchable determination to make his mark in law and public service, he worked days, evenings, and weekends, often including Sundays.[42] In one of the full-length biographies written of Clark, Frank W. Fox wrote: "[T]he Clark home life was none too idyllic. Luacine had been less than enthusiastic about the law school adventure in the first place. But she was the faithful Mormon wife, and she had gone to New York without a whimper. Now she found herself confronting all the old difficulties of Heber City [Utah] and three or four new ones besides." Fox added, "Her husband was scarcely ever home and even then scarcely ever available. Luacine kept a calendar and drew X's across it as the weeks passed by. She was like a prisoner awaiting parole."[43] Biographer D. Michael Quinn noted that Clark's daughter Marianne fondly reminisced that even though her father worked or studied every night until late, his children were always a welcome interruption. "I always remember him working. You just took it for granted. But we could always go up and visit him."[44]

Overcoming a Crisis of Faith and Becoming a Spiritual Giant

Before his call to the First Presidency in 1933, Quinn noted that Clark experienced a crisis of faith, decades of church inactivity, and a near-descent into atheism.[45] For much of his public life, Clark was a doctrinal skeptic.[46] While teaching a Sunday School class in Utah, Clark experienced a renewed sense of faith. In a letter addressed to his brother, Frank, he wrote, "I believe our whole scripture. Much of it I am not able to understand, but I take it on faith, because I am sure it is a living faith."[47]

When the call came from Church President Hebert J. Grant to serve as a counselor in the First Presidency, Clark originally drafted a diplomatic response neither accepting nor rejecting the assignment. But after spiritual contemplation, Clark, at age 62, drafted a second response to the First Presidency accepting the call: "I have never aspired to Church office. . . but when, as now, a call comes from my superior officers, charged with the responsibility of presiding over the Church and acting under the inspiration of the Lord, then I, responsive to my training and my faith, must answer to the call, not only as a clear duty but as a great privilege." Clark added, "It is for the Lord to say how and where I shall serve. I trust Him to help me meet the responsibility of my task. I know, at least in part, my own shortcomings and unworthiness. I appreciate the honor the call brings to me."[48]

Clark served a total of 28 years in the First Presidency of the Church, longer than any other man who has not been

President of the Church. After serving with President Grant, Clark also served as a counselor to presidents George Albert Smith and David O. McKay. Even after his death, Clark remains one of the most prolifically quoted, revered, and beloved counselors to have ever served in the First Presidency.[49]

While Clark had his flaws, next to Rex E. Lee, J. Reuben Clark is considered one of the most impactful Church members and lawyers at the national level. When the Board of Trustees at Brigham Young University decided to establish a law school at the church's flagship institution, leaders named the law school after the great statesman. President Marion G. Romney, then Second Counselor in the Church First Presidency, gave the dedicatory address and prayer of the new J. Reuben Clark Law Building at Brigham Young University on September 5, 1975 with U.S. Supreme Court Chief Justice Warren E. Burger and Associate Justice Lewis F. Powell, Jr. in attendance.[50] Romney declared: "I . . . desired to have perpetuated on this campus the memory and influence of President J. Reuben Clark, Jr.—a great lawyer, patriot, statesman, and church leader. It's my hope that all faculty and student body members will familiarize themselves with and emulate his virtues and accomplishments."[51]

The J. Reuben Clark Law School at Brigham Young University that now bears his name has produced decades of lawyers who have left an impact on society and the law. The J. Reuben Clark Law Society, the international law society comprising hundreds of local chapters and thousands of members around the world, also bears his name. In addition, the J. Reuben Clark Law Society uses the name "Clark Memorandum" from his famous work on the Monroe Doctrine for its semi-annual publication, first published in 1978.[52]

J. Reuben Clark died in 1961 at age 90 devoting much of his life in service to his county and his faith. Church President Thomas S. Monson said it best in praise of Clark: "the biographies, plaudits and honors relating to the life of resident J. Reuben Clark do not begin to capture his warmth of personality, his depth of compassion and his keen sense of humor."[53]

"So far as Latin America is concerned, the [Monroe] Doctrine is now, and always has been, not an instrument of violence and oppression, but an unbought, freely bestowed, and wholly effective guaranty of their freedom, independence, and territorial integrity against the imperialistic designs of Europe." J. Reuben Clark, Jr. in his Memorandum on the Monroe Doctrine.[54]

[1] D. Michael Quinn, *Elder Statesman: A Biography of J. Reuben Clark* (Salt Lake City, UT: Signature Books, 2002), 38 (citing Letter from Lute Clark to J. Reuben Clark, Jr., August 15, 1918, fd 1, box 332, JRCP; C, 438).

[2] Jonathan Zasloff, *Law and the Shaping of American Foreign Policy: The Twenty Years' Crisis*, 77 S. Cal. L. Rev. 583, 642 (2004).

[3] Memorandum on the Monroe Doctrine, December 17, 1928 (Washington: Government Printing Office, 1930); U.S. Dep't of State, Memorandum on the Monroe Doctrine, S. Doc. No. 114, 71st Cong., 2d Sess. xxii-iv (1930) (hereinafter "Clark Memorandum (1930)").

[4] J. Reuben Clark Law Society, Clark Memorandum, Vol. 1, Issue 1, p. 4 (1978) (hereinafter "J. Reuben Clark Law Society (1978)").

[5] Monroe Doctrine, Black's Law Dictionary (10th ed. 2014).

[6] Clark Memorandum (1930).

[7] Philip B. Taylor, Jr., *Law and Politics in Inter-American Diplomacy. by C. Neale Ronning. New York: John Wiley & Sons, Inc. 1963. 167 Pages. $5.95*, 16 Stan. L. Rev. 774, 779 (1964).

[8] Clark Memorandum (1930).

[9] *Id.*

[10] Edwin B. Firmage, *Mx: Democracy, Religion, and the Rule of Law-My Journey*, 2004 Utah L. Rev. 13, 35 (2004).

[11] Thomas A. Bailey, *A Diplomatic History of the American People* (Appleton-Century-Crofts, 1955), 681.

[12] J. Reuben Clark Law Society (1978).

¹³ U.S. Department of Justice, Supplemental Opinions of the Office of Legal Counsel in Volume 1, Memorandum Opinion for the Attorney General, Authority Under International Law to Take Action If the Soviet Union Establishes Missile Bases in Cuba, Aug. 30, 1962, https://www.justice.gov/file/20791/download [https://perma.cc/AD5E-Y6N5].

¹⁴ D. Michael Quinn, *J. Reuben Clark: The Church Years* (Provo, Utah: Brigham Young University Press, 1983), 7 (citing Journal of Joshua R. Clark).

¹⁵ J. Reuben Clark Law Society (1978).

¹⁶ The University of Utah S.J. Quinney College of Law, College of Law History, https://www.law.utah.edu/alumni/college-of-law-history/ [https://perma.cc/GBE5-K8CY].

¹⁷ Quinn, (2002), 13.

¹⁸ *Id.*

¹⁹ George D. Parkinson, *How a Utah Boy Won his Way*, The Improvement Era, Volume 17, No. 1, November 1913, 559.

²⁰ *Id.*

²¹ *In re McCall's Estate*, 28 Pa. D. 433, 1919 WL 3356, at *1–2 (Pa. Orph. 1919).

²² *Id.*

²³ J. Reuben Clark, Jr., *Nature and Definition of Political Offense in International Extradition,* Proceedings, Am. Soc. of Int. Law, 95, 120 (1909).

²⁴ Frederick C. Giffin, *The Pouren Extradition Case*, Social Science, Vol. 56, No. 2 (Spring 1981), pp. 88-93.

²⁵ Clark (1909).

²⁶ Parkinson (1913).

²⁷ J. Reuben Clark Law Society (1978), at 3.

²⁸ *Id.*

²⁹ A search on Westlaw in combined federal and state cases for "at("reuben clark") & da(bef 1933)") retrieves no results (search conducted Nov. 25, 2017).

³⁰ Robert E. Riggs, *J. Reuben Clark: The Public Years. By Frank W. Fox,* 1981 BYU L. Rev. 226, 234 (1981) (book review).

[31] Fred L. Borch, *Civilian Lawyers Join the Department: The Story of the First Civilian Attorneys Given Direct Commissions in the Corps*, Army Lawyer, May 2013, 1

[32] *Id.*

[33] J. Reuben Clark Law Society (1978), 4.

[34] *Id.*

[35] Frank W. Fox, *J. Reuben Clark: The Public Years* (Provo, Utah: Brigham Young University Press and Deseret Book Company, 1980), 444.

[36] Riggs, 1981 BYU L. Rev. at 239.

[37] J. Reuben Clark Law Society (1978), 4.

[38] Fox (1980), 505.

[39] Stephen S. Davis, *J. Reuben Clark, Jr.: Statesman and Counselor*, in Michael K. Windor, ed., *Counselor to the Prophets* (Salt Lake City, Utah: Eborn Books, 2001), 354.

[40] *Id.*

[41] Fox (1980), 383.

[42] Riggs, 1981 BYU L. Rev. at 241.

[43] Fox (1980), 36–37.

[44] Quinn (2002), 19.

[45] *Id.* at viii.

[46] Riggs, 1981 BYU L. Rev. at 243.

[47] Fox (1980), 446.

[48] Quinn (2002), 44.

[49] Davis (2001), 347–348.

[50] Brigham Young University, Howard W. Hunter Law Library, The BYU Law School Building: A Short History, http://huntersquery.byulaw.info/wordpress/wp-content/uploads/2011/04/The-Law-School-Building.A-Short-History.March-2011.pdf [https://perma.cc/2GCN-Q3QG].

[51] Marion G. Romney, Why the J. Reuben Clark Law School? Dedicatory Address and Prayer of the J. Reuben Clark Law Building (September 5, 1975) (2009). Vol. 2: Service & Integrity. 29. https://digitalcommons.law.byu.edu/life_law_vol2/29 [https://perma.cc/477Q-33Y5].

[52] Scott Wolfley, *Welcome to the Clark Memo, J. Reuben Clark Law Society*, Clark Memorandum, Vol. 1, Issue 1 (1978).

[53] Davis (2001), 306 (citing Thomas S. Monson, letter to Janice Stewart).
[54] Clark Memorandum (1930).

Chapter 4

Larry Echo Hawk: Champion for Native American Rights and a Symbol of Bravery

Epitomizing Bravery as Idaho Attorney General

Larry Echo Hawk's last name, given to his great-grandfather, has special meaning. The hawk is a symbol of bravery among the Pawnee people. Because the elder's brave deeds were spoken of from one side of the village to the other, the elders of the tribe gave the name "Echo Hawk."[1] Indeed, Larry Echo Hawk's lifelong service epitomizes that symbol of bravery in the name bestowed upon his great-grandfather.

Larry Echo Hawk, a member of the Pawnee Tribe, became the first American Indian in U.S. history to win a statewide constitutional office, such as Governor or Attorney General, when he won the race for Idaho Attorney General in 1990.[2] "That kind of gave me a little extra incentive," said Echo Hawk. "That was very significant to have that opportunity."[3]

But that opportunity did not come without its challenges. When Echo Hawk was elected as Attorney General, Idaho voters passed a state constitutional amendment for a state lottery, but the language opened the door for Las Vegas style gaming operations that went beyond the state lottery. At the urging of Echo Hawk, the Idaho Legislature convened a special session to amend the loophole in the constitutional language. "The tribes, of course, in Idaho saw a payday. This was their opportunity to get full scale gaming operations in Idaho," said Echo Hawk. Legislative leaders asked Echo Hawk to present the proposed amendment on the floor of the House and the Senate despite opposition from his own community. "I knew that the major opposition was the tribes. I had been their champion for years. But I had a job to do. . . Up in the gallery were the tribal elected leaders. It was first time I had ever been on the opposite side of them. It was a tough thing to do what my constitutional oath of office required of me in very difficult circumstances."[4]

As Idaho Attorney General, Larry Echo Hawk faced many challenges but fulfilled his constitutional oath of office to defend the U.S. Constitution and the Idaho Constitution. In 1994, he oversaw Idaho's first scheduled execution in 37 years of Keith Wells. Hanging was the method used for most of Idaho's history. Idaho's last execution prior to scheduled execution of Wells took place on October 18, 1957, when Raymond Allen Snowden, a 35-year-old laborer, was hanged for the murder and mutilation of a woman he met at a bar.[5] With the first scheduled execution in the state in nearly four decades, both opponents and proponents of the death penalty lined up outside the prison to voice their positions. The Idaho Maximum Security Institution (IMSI) in Boise opened just five years earlier in 1989 to confine Idaho's most disruptive male offenders and house the death penalty chamber where Wells faced capital punishment by lethal injection. Wells was sentenced to death after being found guilty by a jury for killing John B. Justad, a bar patron, and Brandi Kay Rains, the bartender, at the Rose Pub Bar in Boise, Idaho on December 20, 1990 with a baseball ball. Wells had taken approximately $400 from the cash register at the bar along with Justad's wallet.[6] Wells stated that "it was time for them to die." Wells, who was on parole for armed robbery at the time of the killings, chose not to appeal the death sentence, although the American Civil Liberties Union (ACLU) appealed the case on his behalf.

With the execution scheduled for midnight, Echo Hawk made the difficult decision to postpone the execution of Keith Wells on the cold winter night of January 6, 1994 for 40 minutes awaiting a possible stay by the U.S. Supreme Court.[7] At the time, Idaho judges, rather than juries, made the factual findings necessary to impose the death penalty. The U.S.

Supreme Court later ruled in *Ring v. Arizona*, 536 U.S. 584 (2002) that the Sixth Amendment of the U.S. Constitution requires the jury, rather than the judge, to make all factual findings necessary to impose the death penalty.[8] This decision *in Ring v. Arizona* invalidated the death penalty statutes in Arizona, Idaho, Colorado, Montana and Nebraska, as these states allowed the trial judge to determine whether aggravating circumstances exist.[9] Echo Hawk was on the phone with a clerk for the U.S. Supreme Court to see if the nation's high court would grant review. Ultimately, the U.S. Supreme Court denied a last-minute appeal and Wells died by lethal injection. Echo Hawk said, "When you are in office, you have to made decisions like that. When you get to the big league, there are big league decisions. Lawyers have to be prepared to do the right thing in the right circumstances."[10] After the execution of Wells, Idaho did not execute an inmate for another 17 years until triple murderer Paul Ezra Rhoades died by lethal injection in 2011.[11]

Passionately Defending the Rights of Tribal People

Prior to becoming Attorney General, Echo Hawk worked in many ways to help Native Americans become more economically self-sufficient and overcome the false stereotype of lazy Indians.[12] As Chief General Legal Counsel for the Shoshone-Bannock Tribes of the Fort Hall Indian Reservation in Idaho from 1977 to 1986, the first time in history a Native American served as chief tribal counsel, he helped secure grazing rights of the Tribes on National Forest lands within the Caribou National Forest in Idaho. When Echo Hawk first became the tribal counsel, one of the first things he did was read the original Fort Bridger Treaty of 1868 between the United States and the Eastern Band of Shoshone and Bannock Tribes and the Agreement of February 5, 1898 between the United States and the Shoshone-Bannock Tribes both ratified by Congress.

The Fort Bridger Treaty of 1868 and Agreement of 1898 reserved priority grazing rights in ceded lands which were a part of the Caribou National Forest to the Tribes. Article IV of the 1898 Agreement provides for the reservation of grazing rights: "So long as any of the lands ceded . . . remain part of the public domain, [the Tribes] shall have the right . . . to pasture their livestock on said public lands."[13]

After reading the language in the original treaty, Echo Hawk asked the tribal leaders how many heads of cattle they owned. The tribal leaders responded that the Tribes did not have any cattle because the U.S. government prohibited them from using public land for grazing. The Tribes then petitioned the U.S. government for grazing rights, but the government refused because the land had already been leased to white cattle ranchers. After failing to reach any protection from the U.S. Forest Service, Echo Hawk filed an action in court on behalf of the Tribes. The U.S. District Court ruled that the Tribes had continuing grazing rights in the ceded lands but that their rights encompassed only a "fair proportion" of grazing capacity on the ceded lands still in federal ownership. Both the Tribes and the white cattle ranchers appealed the decision to the U.S. Court of the Appeals for the Ninth Circuit.

The federal appeals court held in *Swim v. Bergland* that the Fort Bridger Treaty of 1868 and Agreement of 1898 reserved priority grazing rights in ceded lands which were a part of the Caribou National Forest to the Tribes.[14] The court held that the rights of the Indians superseded the grazing rights of non-Indian ranchers who had grazed their cattle on the lands in question for many years. The Ninth Circuit affirmed that the U.S. Forest Service could cancel the permits as needed to implement the Tribes' reserved grazing rights. The appeals court also reversed the limitation of those rights to a "fair proportion" of available grazing capacity by the district court ruling.[15]

"The United States had ignored the treaty," said Echo Hawk. "The non-Indian ranchers and farmers were not happy. I had a client that had a treaty right that the United States knew about. [The United States government] failed to recognize and had taken actions inconsistent with their role as the trustee for the tribe."[16]

One of Echo Hawk's greatest legal accomplishments came not through contentious litigation, but rather through negotiation and compromise with the Snake River Basin Adjudication settlement. The Snake River Basin Adjudication commenced in 1987 to quantify all claims to water rights in the Snake River in Idaho. With over 150,000 water rights claims and factual issues addressing two hundred years of historical, anthropological, ecological, and sociological analysis of life in Idaho, all of the interested parties reached a settlement avoiding years of lawsuits. The cost of the final settlement had an estimated value exceeding $200 million.[17] Ultimately, the stakeholders—including the tribal nations, the Idaho state government, and the federal government—were able to reconcile their philosophical and cultural differences to reach a pragmatic solution.[18] "Rather than go through expensive and contentious litigation, it made more sense to negotiate," Echo Hawk observed. "It turned out to be the correct policy position because it did not go on for years in litigation. It was a quicker process that yielded a result that had mutual benefits."[19]

Narrowly Losing the Gubernatorial Bid in Idaho

After serving as a state legislator and later as Attorney General of Idaho, Echo Hawk campaigned in 1994 to serve as the Governor of Idaho to replace four-time Governor Cecil Andrus who previously announced his retirement. But Echo Hawk had three strikes against him: (1) he was a Democrat; (2) he was an Indian; and (3) he was a member of the Church.[20] Besides being a Democrat in a Republican dominated state, Echo Hawk was also in the minority as an Indian and as a member of The Church of Jesus Christ of Latter-day Saints.

Despite a large percentage of Church members living in the state, Idaho has a long history of discrimination toward members of the Church. The so called "Mormon Test Oath" in the Idaho Constitution required voters to take an oath before voting, swearing that they were not bigamists or polygamists. The Test Oath, as a legal device, could be far more widely and immediately implemented than the prohibitions enacted by Congress. The Mormon Test Oath led directly to Idaho statehood in 1890. From 1872 until 1885, the Territorial Legislature was controlled by a coalition of Democrats and Mormons. By the summer of 1889, no Mormon could vote and the Legislature came under control of the Republicans, supported by the Independent Anti-Mormon Party. In *Territory v. Evans*, 2 Idaho 627, 23 P. 232 (1890), the Supreme Court of the Territory of Idaho excluded church members from serving as jurors holding "[W]e think the legislature meant to exclude from jury service those belonging to the so–called 'Mormon Church.' "[21] In *Davis v. Beason*, 133 U.S. 333 (1890), the U.S. Supreme Court upheld the constitutionality of the Mormon Test Oath in the Idaho Constitution. The "Mormon Test Oath" formally remained in the Idaho Constitution until 1982.[22]

While Echo Hawk led early in the polls, he narrowly lost the race to Republican Phil Batt, an onion farmer and former lieutenant governor. The 1994 "Republican Revolution" election took place on November 8, 1994, in the middle of President Bill Clinton's first term. As a result of the historic 54-seat swing in membership from Democrats to Republicans, the Republican Party gained a majority of seats in the U.S. House of Representatives for the first time since 1952. Voters across the nation overwhelmingly supported Newt Gingrich's Contract with America which led to strong Republican gains across the board. With a strong outpouring of Republican support across the nation, including Idaho, Echo Hawk, a Democrat, failed in his bid to serve as governor of the Gem State.

Overcoming Adversity

After narrowly losing the gubernatorial race, Echo Hawk faced dejection and disappointment. But then he learned an important life lesson: when one door closes, another door opens. The very next day after he lost the race, H. Reese Hansen, then dean of BYU's law school and a former classmate of Echo Hawk during their days at the University of Utah law school, called Echo Hawk on the phone and offered him a position to serve on the faculty of Brigham Young University's J. Reuben Clark Law School.[23]

Larry Echo Hawk previously attended the University of Utah Law School in a special program to train Indian lawyers. His older brother, John Echo Hawk, another prominent Indian lawyer, became the first graduate of the program. John Echo Hawk, Executive Director of the Native American Rights Fund, persuaded his younger brother, Larry, to attend law school to use their legal training to improve the lives of their people. Larry Echo Hawk, who initially thought about being a high school football coach, first thought about pursuing a career in the law and public service while at BYU. As a student, Echo Hawk heard Church President Spencer W. Kimball speak several times. Kimball was well known as the apostle who had a great love for Indian people. He gave a speech titled "This Is My Vision" in which he related a dream about the Indian people. Kimball said, "I saw you as lawyers. I saw you looking after your people. I saw you as heads of cities and of states and in elected office."[24] Echo Hawk recounted, "To me it was like a challenge from a prophet of God. I carried an excerpt from that talk in my scriptures. At a certain point in my life, I reread the passage where he said we could become leaders of cities and states, and even though I had never envisioned running for elective office, I knew that I could and should do it."[25]

Larry Echo Hawk accepted the position at BYU and became one of the nation's leading authorities on Indian law. As a law professor, he taught courses in Indian Law and focused his research agenda on legal issues affecting Native Americans writing many leading articles. In one article published in the Idaho Law Review, Echo Hawk analyzed balancing state and tribal power to tax in Indian country. Echo Hawk quoted John Marshall that the "power to tax [is] the power to destroy." Echo Hawk concluded, "This power must be exercised with great care when states deal with Indian tribes on a government-to-government basis. Neither state nor tribal governments should unilaterally impose taxes without carefully studying whether proposed new taxes are reasonably necessary to provide essential governmental services to the affected community."[26] Echo Hawk loved his "dream job" as a law professor.

Leaving His Dream Job to Serve Others

Echo Hawk served as a faculty member for 15 years until he received another call to public service. "I was sitting in my office in early January of 2009 and the phone rang. It was the [Barack Obama] presidential transition team," he said. After first replying that he was not interested in a job, the caller on the other end of the phone pled, "Would you give the courtesy to the next President of the United States to come for one day for a short interview?" Echo Hawk reluctantly agreed to an interview but cautioned, "You need to know I am not leaving." Echo Hawk loved his position as a law professor and he had also been serving as a stake president for the Church in a young single adult stake. In addition, BYU President Cecil O. Samuelson appointed Echo Hawk to serve as the NCAA Faculty Athletics Representative for the university. As a student-athlete who attended BYU on a football scholarship as an undergraduate student, Echo Hawk started at safety for the Cougars and earned Academic All-Western Athletic Conference during his senior year in 1969 recording 25 solo tackles, 29 assisted tackles, and nine pass deflections.[27] The faculty athletics representative plays an important role providing oversight of the academic integrity of the athletics program and serving as an advocate for student-athlete well-being. The National Collegiate Athletic Association (NCAA) requires each of its member institutions to appoint a faculty athletics representative who must be on the faculty or administrative staff and may not hold a position in the athletics department.[28]

After an interview in the nation's capital, the transition team extended an offer to Echo Hawk to serve as Assistant Secretary of the Interior over the Bureau of Indian Affairs. After re-reading *Bury My Heart at Wounded Knee* by Dee Brown, which recounts the atrocities of the federal government on Native Americans, combined with deep spiritual contemplation, prayer, and temple attendance with his wife,

49

Echo Hawk accepted the call to serve his country and his people. "I went from having one teaching assistant to having 10,000 employees. When you talk about having an impact on tribal communities, that was very significant to have those opportunities," said Echo Hawk. "It turned out to be the most satisfying professional thing I ever did to take on that responsibility. I just couldn't believe what we were able to accomplish in those difficult times."[29]

Those who worked closely with Echo Hawk during his stint as head of the Bureau of Indian Affairs commended his service. U.S. Secretary of the Interior Ken Salazar said, "With Larry Echo Hawk's leadership, we have opened a new chapter in our nation-to-nation relationships with American Indian and Alaska Native tribal governments, accelerated the restoration of tribal homelands, improved safety in tribal communities, resolved century-old water disputes, invested in education and reached many more milestones that are helping Indian nations pursue the future of their choosing."[30] During his tenure, Echo Hawk worked across the federal government, including the U.S. Department of Justice, to help build safer communities and implement the Tribal Law and Order Act that President Obama signed into law in 2010. Echo Hawk also strengthened law enforcement and launched an intense community policing pilot program on four reservations experiencing high crime rates.[31] U.S. Senator Daniel K. Akaka, a Democrat from Hawaii and Chairman of the Senate Committee on Indian Affairs, echoed Salazar's sentiments touting the accomplishments of Echo Hawk: "Larry Echo Hawk has been a great friend to the American Indian, Alaska Native, and Native Hawaiian communities. Whether advocating for the protection of tribal sovereignty, trust responsibility, or the right to self-sufficiency, Larry has spent his tenure working for what is pono—right and just." Akaka added that Echo Hawk "strengthened the government-to-government relationship between tribes and the federal government. His leadership and vision will be greatly missed."[32]

Echo Hawk received many awards and accolades for his lifelong commitment to public service. Echo Hawk received the distinguished Alumnus Awards from both Brigham Young

University (1992) and the University of Utah (2003). Echo Hawk also was honored in 1995 as the first BYU graduate ever to receive the National Collegiate Athletic Association's prestigious Silver Anniversary Award. The Silver Anniversary Award annually recognizes distinguished individuals on the 25th anniversary of the conclusion of their college athletics careers who have distinguished themselves in their careers and personal lives. Former winners of the NCAA Silvery Anniversary Award include Bo Jackson, Sally Ride, Troy Aikman, Bill Walton, and Steve Largent. He also received the J. Reuben Clark Law Society's Distinguished Service Award in 2013. "I think that you really can't describe Larry Echo Hawk with only words," Hansen recognized. "I think you have to meet him, shake his hand, look into his eye, hear him talk (and) the tone of his voice and the sincerity of what he says—and you'll know it's all true. He is absolutely authentic."[33]

After serving for three years in Washington, D.C. as head of the Bureau of Indian Affairs, Echo Hawk accepted a higher call to serve as a General Authority for the Church. He previously held church callings as a bishop, stake president, and gospel doctrine instructor. General Authorities are men called to serve at the highest levels of leadership in The Church of Jesus Christ of Latter-day Saints. After faithfully serving as a General Authority and reaching age 70, the age when General Authorities are normally released, Echo Hawk was given an honorable release and given emeritus status. While his connections in Washington, D.C. would allow him to rake in big money as a lobbyist, he hopes to return to serving the poor and disadvantaged upon his release as a General Authority. "I feel like I want to go back where I started and go into native communities and help people, particularly individuals," he said. "I want to go back to my legal services days and take on the disadvantaged and those that don't have much hope and give them a chance in the system."[34]

"It was very meaningful for me to realize . . . that great dream of Martin Luther King that regardless of your race, your religion, your ethnic heritage, your economic station in life, this can be a

land of opportunity for all people. What a blessing it has been to have these opportunities that my forefathers would never have thought possible." Larry Echo Hawk, on being asked to the speak during the commemoration at the Idaho State Capitol in Boise when Idaho became one of the last states to recognize the Martin Luther King, Jr. statewide holiday.[35]

[1] Sarah Harris, *Elder Echo Hawk Connects Pawnee Indian Ancestors with Mormon Pioneers*, Church News, The Church of Jesus Christ of Latter-day Saints, Jun. 29, 2017, https://www.lds.org/church/news/elder-echo-hawk-connects-pawnee-indian-ancestors-with-mormon-pioneers?lang=eng [https://perma.cc/8PXU-45KW].
[2] Sandra Lee Nowack, *So That You Will Hear Us: A Native American Leaders' Forum*, 18 Am. Indian L. Rev. 551, 575 (1993).
[3] Interview with Larry Echo Hawk, former Assistant Secretary of the Interior for Indian Affairs, in discussion with the author, Apr. 26, 2017, in Salt Lake City, Utah (hereinafter "Echo Hawk (2017)").
[4] *Id.*
[5] Associated Press, *Murderer Is First Person Executed in Idaho Since 1957*, Philadelphia Inquirer, Jan. 7, 1994, B07, 1994 WLNR 2085642.
[6] *State v. Wells*, 864 P.2d 1123, 1124 (Idaho 1993).
[7] *Glenn Seeks Probe of Non-Radiation Tests*, Baltimore Sun, 1994 WLNR 865755, Jan. 7, 1994, 6A.
[8] Danielle J. Hunsaker, *The Right to A Jury "Has Never Been Efficient; but It Has Always Been Free": Idaho Capital Juries After Ring v. Arizona*, 39 Idaho L. Rev. 649, 650 (2003).
[9] *Id.*
[10] Echo Hawk (2017).
[11] Betsy Z. Russell, *Triple Killer Rhoades Executed in Idaho*, The Spokesman-Review (Spokane, Wash.), Nov, 18, 2011, 2011 WLNR 24147316.
[12] See John H. Moore, *The Myth of the Lazy Indian: Native American Contributions to the U.S. Economy*, 2 Nature, Soc'y, & Thought 2, 198–201 (1989).
[13] *Swim v. Bergland*, 696 F.2d 712, 716 (9th Cir. 1983) (citing 371 Stat. 674).

[14] *Id.* at 712.

[15] *Id.* at 720.

[16] Echo Hawk (2017).

[17] Francis E. McGovern, *Mediation of the Snake River Basin Adjudication*, 42 Idaho L. Rev. 547, 549 (2006).

[18] *Id.* at 562.

[19] Echo Hawk (2017).

[20] Hugh Dellios, *Native American Beating Odds in Idaho*, Chicago Tribune, Oct. 4, 1994, http://www.chicagotribune.com/news/ct-xpm-1994-10-04-9410050052-story.html [https://perma.cc/6JQV-UBB8].

[21] 23 P. at 233.

[22] Dennis C. Colson, *Idaho's Founders and Their Mormon Test Oath*, 50 Advocate 11, 12 (2007).

[23] Echo Hawk (2017).

[24] Dell Van Orden, *Emotional Farewell in Mexico*, Church News, The Church of Jesus Christ of Latter-day Saints, Feb. 19, 1977, p. 3.

[25] Larry Echo Hawk, *"Why I'm a Mormon": Larry Echo Hawk*, Deseret News, Feb. 7, 2012, 2012 WLNR 2640739 (excerpt from *Why I'm a Mormon*, edited by Joseph A. Cannon (Salt Lake City, UT: Ensign Peak, 2012).

[26] Larry Echo Hawk, *Balancing State and Tribal Power to Tax in Indian Country*, 40 Idaho L. Rev. 623, 655 (2004) (quoting *McCullough v. Maryland*, 17 U.S. (4 Wheat.) 316, 327 (1819)).

[27] BYU Athletics, Larry Echo Hawk, Player Profile, http://byucougars.com/athlete/m-football/larry-echohawk [https://perma.cc/9M5E-ATKQ].

[28] National Collegiate Athletics Association, Roles, Responsibilities and Perspectives of NCAA Faculty Athletics Representatives, Feb. 2013 Report, 10.

[29] *Id.*

[30] United States Department of the Interior, Assistant Secretary of Indian Affairs Larry Echo Hawk to Conclude Successful Tenure at Interior, Press Release, Apr. 9, 2012, https://www.doi.gov/news/pressreleases/Assistant-Secretary-of-Indian-Affairs-Larry-Echo-Hawk-to-Conclude-Successful-Tenure-at-Interior [https://perma.cc/LY22-EFJC].

[31] *Id.*

[32] United States Senate Committee on Indian Affairs, Statement by Senator Akaka on the Resignation of Larry Echo Hawk, Press Release, Apr. 26, 2012, https://www.indian.senate.gov/news/press-release/statement-senator-akaka-resignation-larry-echo-hawk [https://perma.cc/2NKG-U6QR].

[33] Jahmshid Ghazi Aska, *Elder Echo Hawk Reflects on Law Career*, Deseret News, March 15, 2013, 2013 WLNR 6484120.

[34] Echo Hawk (2017).

[35] *Id.*

Chapter 5

James E. Faust: Prolific Appellate Advocate and Civil Rights Lawyer

Appearing Before the Utah Supreme Court

Many lawyers would consider arguing a case before the state supreme court a major highlight of their career. James E. Faust had the opportunity to argue a total of 17 cases before the Utah Supreme Court between 1954 and 1972, likely more than any other lawyer in private practice during the same period.[1]

After more than two decades of experience in his legal career as a lawyer in Salt Lake City, Utah, Faust represented Warren's Holladay Pharmacy to challenge the constitutionality of a Sunday closing law passed by the Utah Legislature in 1970. The case reached the Utah Supreme Court in 1971. In *Skaggs Drug Centers, Inc. v. Ashley*, 26 Utah 2d 38, 484 P.2d 723 (1971), the court considered the constitutionality of the Sunday closing law passed in the state with a large percentage of members of the Church. Faust, and the other lawyers who represented a variety of retail stores in the consolidated action, argued that the law failed to meet the constitutional requirement of the Due Process Clause protected under the Fourteenth Amendment. The law generally prohibited Sunday sales, with various exemptions including ones for the sale of goods or rendering of services necessary to the maintenance of health, safety, or life, essential or incidental to customarily continuous operations such as transportation facilities, essential to travel, or normally associated with or incidental to the operation of recreational, educational, or entertainment facilities.

The validity of Sunday observance laws has been assailed for violation of the Due Process Clause because of alleged vagueness and uncertainty in the language used. Sunday legislation must, to avoid its invalidation on the ground of vagueness or uncertainty, constitute a reasonable guide for conduct, permitting an individual of ordinary intelligence to determine in advance what acts are prohibited and what are permitted.[2] Although the Utah Legislature had good intentions in enacting the Sunday closing law to encourage people to observe a day of rest, the Utah Supreme Court invalidated the Sunday closing law in *Skaggs Drug Centers* and held that "any statute whose terms are so vague that a person of ordinary intelligence could only guess at its meaning and differ as to its application fails to meet the standard of due process."[3]

While Faust successfully challenged the compelled Sunday closing law in *Skaggs Drug Centers*, Faust also preached the importance in choosing sabbath day observance from the pulpit. He taught that keeping the Sabbath day holy is much more than just physical rest. It involves spiritual renewal and worship. Faust observed, "Over a lifetime of observation, it is clear to me that the farmer who observes the Sabbath day seems to get more done on his farm than he would if he worked seven days. . . The doctor, the lawyer, the dentist, the scientist will accomplish more by trying to rest on the Sabbath than if he tries to utilize every day of the week for his professional work."[4]

Practicing "Door Law" in Salt Lake City

Even though the name James E. Faust is well known among faithful members of the Church as a long-time member of the First Presidency, many people, including Church members, do not know the full extent of Faust's legal career prior to his service in church leadership. Before his call to serve as a member of the Quorum of the Twelve Apostles, Faust had a distinguished career as a lawyer in Salt Lake City representing clients in a variety of practice areas, including estate planning, family law, criminal law, and medical malpractice.[5] Faust also made significant contributions to the legal community establishing the Utah Bar Foundation and advancing civil rights as a member of the ABA Lawyer's Committee for Civil Rights under the Law.

Born in Delta, Utah in 1920, James Esdras Faust attended school in the Granite School District and grew up in the south side of the Salt Lake Valley. He was one of five sons of George A. and Amy Finlinson Faust. George Faust worked as an attorney and district court judge in the Salt Lake Valley. At home and on the farms of his grandparents in central Utah, James enjoyed the love and support of a Christ-centered family and honed the virtues of honesty, hard work, and service as a youth. "No man ever had a better father than did I," he said. Of his mother he recalled, "She was a deeply spiritual, saintly woman who fully exemplified Christlike living."[6] Faust enrolled at the University of Utah in 1937, where he participated as a member of the track team and ran the quarter-mile and mile relay. His college career was interrupted first to serve as a missionary in Brazil and later by World War II, during which he served in the U.S. Army Air Force and was honorably discharged as a first lieutenant. In 1945, he returned the University of Utah and graduated in 1948 with a B.A. and a Juris Doctor degree.[7]

Faust recalled his experience and valuable lessons learned from attending law school at the University of Utah: "The dean of the law school that I attended constantly impressed upon us that his primary mission was not to teach us the law, for the law would change; rather, his primary mission was to teach us to think straight, based upon sound principles."[8]

After graduating from law school, Faust worked as a solo attorney in Salt Lake City, a common situation before the heyday of the mega-firms that became popular in the 1980s. Historically, legal practice was almost exclusively the domain of solo-practitioners.[9] In the late 1950s only 38 law firms in the United States had more than 50 lawyers-and more than half of these were in New York City. Larger law firms emerged in the 1980s. By 1985, over 500 firms had 51 or more lawyers, and firms with more than 100 lawyers grew from less than a dozen in 1960 to 251 in 1986.[10]

Many lawyers, especially those first starting out, practice "door law," taking virtually any client and matter that walks through the door.[11] Faust was no exception. He recalled:

> When I began to practice law in 1948 I couldn't afford to be selective about my clients. We took care of just about anybody who came in the door. I came out of law school and went into the chambers of a small Catholic office which was founded by George J. Gibson. Mr. Gibson was very reputable and highly regarded. He represented the Salt Lake Tribune and the Kearns family interests. He had some domestic help who were African-American. In those days some of the prestigious law offices would not accept poor African-American clients. But we took care of their legal problems even after he died. They did not want charity and agreed to pay their legal bills at the rate of $10 a month. They were very faithful in keeping their commitment. I confess that I received more satisfaction taking care of the legal needs of this family than I did for more affluent clients of less integrity.[12]

Faust argued his first case before the Utah Supreme Court in a will contest proceeding in 1954, six years after graduating from law school. Faust represented one of the parties challenging the will and estate of Florence P. Howard, a resident of Salt Lake City. Even though the Utah Supreme Court decided against his client's interests, Faust gained valuable experience arguing before the Utah Supreme Court that would help him later in his career as he advocated on behalf of his clients.[13]

In a speech given to the Utah Bar Association in 1996, Faust recalled one divorce case from his early legal career. He said, "In those days divorces were not as common as they are now. My associate, John D. Rice, agreed to represent an unfortunate woman who had a drinking sickness. We spent countless hours trying to get some justice for this woman. We did not even keep track of the time. We were paid a pittance. However, my senior associate, Jack Rice, was never more heroic in my eyes than when he stood before the Supreme Court of Utah and said, 'Mrs. Jones is a drunk. She has been abandoned by her church, her husband, and her family, and everybody except her lawyers.' "[14]

Faust also worked on criminal cases. Faust recalled, "I found myself in my first pro bono case before Judge Tillman D. Johnson, the venerable federal judge, who was at the time over ninety years of age. I was appointed to defend a young man who had taken a stolen motorcycle across state lines. At the time of the arraignment when the case was called up, my client and I approached the bench. Judge Johnson asked, 'Which one of you is the accused?' "[15] Faust learned humility early in his professional career.

Serving in the Utah Legislature

Faust served as an elected representative in the Utah House of Representatives and remained active in politics for many years. Faust was just 28 years old and fresh out of law school when he first ran for public office. Faust, a Democrat, represented Utah's eighth district, which included Salt Lake County, from 1949 to 1951.[16] During the one-term Faust served in the 28th Utah State Legislature, Utah passed several important pieces of legislation. With the increased popularity of automobiles after World War II, the legislature for the Beehive State enacted the Motor Vehicle Business Regulation Act.[17] The Utah Legislature also confirmed the Upper Colorado River Basin Compact in 1949. Representatives for the Upper Colorado River Basin States, Arizona, Colorado, New Mexico, Utah and Wyoming, adopted the Upper Colorado River Basin Compact at Santa Fe, New Mexico, on October 11, 1948.[18] Utah, and the other arid states in the basin, depend on the waters of the Colorado River to make the region productive and inhabitable.[19]

Faust supported the two-party system and encouraged Church members to run for political office. He admonished, "It is in the interest of the Church to have a two-party system. . . Both locally and nationally, the interest of the Church and its members are served when we have two good men or women running on each ticket, and then no matter who is elected, we win."[20] Oscar McConkie Jr., a Democrat leader from Utah, recognized that "President Faust was one of the prominent political figures of this state."[21]

Faust returned to the Utah State Legislature 46 years after serving as an elected representative—this time offering the prayer convening the new legislative session. Faust, then Second Counselor in the First Presidency of The Church of Jesus Christ of Latter-Day Saints, expressed gratitude and asked for spiritual guidance for the legislature in the prayer:

> Our Holy Father in Heaven, On this historic day, we pause in thanksgiving for the blessings which have been bestowed upon this great state. . . We also pray that thy spirit will attend each member of this body to give them wisdom, understanding, and humility. We celebrate this year the sesquicentennial of the arrival of the pioneers in this valley who began the beginnings of the marvelous blessings which we collectively enjoy. And, we also stand at the beginning of a new century, which is historic. This legislature will put in place many things which are needful and beneficial for this state, carrying over for many years into the next century. Give to this body vision and leadership, and may they work together in harmony, disagree but not being disagreeable, finding it easy to cross from one side of the aisle to the other. We're grateful for the families of our citizen legislators and pray thy blessing to be upon them, that they will have the discipline to support and sustain our legislators in their important roles. Now we pray for all the blessings for which we're needful, express the gratitude of our hearts for the many cultures,

many peoples which have contributed so greatly to this state. We invoke a blessing upon all of them, every race, religion, creed. I pronounce these blessings humbly in the name of thy son, the Lord Jesus Christ, Amen.[22]

Faust's prayer at the Utah Legislature reflects his respect for the important role of legislators and the need for guidance from the Almighty.

Establishing the Utah Bar Foundation

Faust provided leadership to the Utah State Bar and helped promote legal services to those in need. He was elected as President of the Utah State Bar on May 31, 1962 and served as President from 1962 until 1963.[23] In December 1963, Faust, along with Calvin Behle, Earl D. Tanner, Julius Romney, and Charles Welch Jr., had an idea to form a charity that would promote legal education and increase the knowledge and awareness of legal services and needs in the community. This new organization would assist in providing funds for legal services to the disadvantaged, improvement to the administration of justice, and service worthwhile law-related education and public purposes. That idea became a reality with the founding of the Utah Bar Foundation. Since the establishment of the Utah Bar Foundation under the direction of Faust, the organization has provided ongoing financial support for organizations such as the Utah Law Related Education, the Legal Aid Society of Salt Lake, Utah Legal Services, the Southern Utah Community Legal Center, the Salt Lake Community Legal Center, the Disability Law Center, the refugee resettlement/immigration programs at both Catholic Community Services and Holy Cross Ministries, the Rocky Mountain Innocence Project, DNA People's Legal Services, Divorce Education Classes for Children, and Utah Dispute Resolution.[24] The Utah State Bar recognized Faust with the Distinguished Lawyer Emeritus Award in 1995 for his faithful service, including the establishment of the Utah Bar Foundation.[25]

Leading the Charge to Protect Civil Rights

As a lawyer, Faust used his legal skills and experience to help advance the civil rights of all Americans. On June 11, 1963, President John F. Kennedy told the country on national television that justice demanded legislation to ensure the civil rights of all Americans. The next day, a Ku Klux Klan member murdered civil rights leader Medgar Evers. On June 21, President Kennedy summoned 250 prominent lawyers from the American Bar Association (ABA) to the White House and urged them to provide legal assistance to advance civil rights. The Lawyers Committee for Civil Rights Under Law was founded as a result of that meeting.[26] President Kennedy appointed Faust to the Lawyers' Committee for Civil Rights Under Law and the ABA Board of Governors created the Special Committee on Civil Rights and Racial Unrest. The ABA Board of Governors directed the Committee "to study the grave problems with respect to observance of law and legal processes which have arisen throughout the country on civil rights issues and to make recommendations which will encourage respect by all concerned for, and observance of, the rule of law." Faust, one of the 17 committee members selected by the ABA Board of Governors, also worked with Rush H. Limbaugh, Sr., grandfather of Rush Limbaugh III, the popular conservative talk radio show host, on the committee.[27]

The Committee sent scores of talented lawyers, such as Faust, into courts throughout the country to ensure the protection of civil rights. Arlan M. Adams, Circuit Judge for the U.S. Court of Appeals for the Third Circuit, noted that the Committee succeeded in stirring the bar from its apathy by issuing a clarion call to informed responsibility in this all-important area, at a most crucial time.[28] McConkie also recalled, "Bobby Kennedy asked President Faust to serve on this important committee, and he did. A very important work, and President Faust did that for several years."[29] Judge Adams recognized that the Lawyers' Committee remains a vigorous force today in the continuing campaign to make equal justice a reality, providing the vehicle through which bright and able lawyers from eminent law firms contribute their talents to public service work.[30]

Faust used his legal skills to help those who often only had limited means. His son, Marcus, said, "I recall with fondness piling into the family car just before Christmas to deliver to father's clients both presents and goodwill. Most of those we visited were poor or disadvantaged, people who had turned to my father, their attorney, to resolve some personal crisis." Marcus Faust added, "I witnessed the trust, respect, admiration, and love these people had for their lawyer and I saw something noble in using one's knowledge of the law to help people through difficulties in their lives. For me, the work my father did as an attorney helping people solve their legal problems was another form of administering Christlike service."[31]

Faust also served on the advisory board for the ABA Journal from 1966 to 1969.[32] The ABA Journal is the flagship magazine for the nation's largest volunteer bar association. The ABA, founded in 1878 and one of the world's largest voluntary professional organizations, is committed to improving the legal profession, eliminating bias and enhancing diversity, and advancing the rule of law throughout the United States and around the world.[33] During the time Faust served on advisory board, the ABA Journal published several notable articles, including "Dangers to the Rule of Law" by U.S. Supreme Court Justice Abe Fortas and "Improving the Criminal Justice Act" by Dallin H. Oaks.[34] Faust would later serve with Oaks in the Quorum of the Twelve Apostles for the Church for 23 years, from 1984, when Oaks was first called, until Faust's death in 2007.

Faust found joy in the practice of law to help people solve problems. "There were many satisfactions in my professional life," he said. "I tell my three boys, all of whom are lawyers, that if I had to do it over, I'd do it just the same way." According to his son Marcus, "[H]e instilled in his boys the idea that people are more important than things—and that we needed to remember that in our own practices."[35]

Applying Legal Experience to Church Leadership

When the call came to serve as an Assistant to the Quorum of the Twelve Apostles in 1972, Faust did not hesitate and made immediate plans to close his law practice and devote full time to church service.[36] He was later called to the Quorum of the Twelve Apostles in 1976, a lifetime calling, and also served as a member of the First Presidency of the Church with President Gordon B. Hinckley and Thomas S. Monson from 1995 until his death in 2007.[37]

In church leadership, Faust continued his advocacy on important yet controversial issues. As a litigator, Faust advocated the interests of his clients. As an ecclesiastical leader, Faust advocated the interests of the Church and his religious convictions. Faust spoke out on salient topics, including abortion and same-sex marriage. In 1975, two years after the landmark U.S. Supreme Court decision in *Roe v. Wade,* 410 U.S. 113 (1973), Faust, then an Assistant to the Quorum of the Twelve Apostles, lamented that "we have come to a time when the taking of an unborn human life for nonmedical reasons has become tolerated, made legal, and accepted in many countries of the world. But making it legal to destroy newly conceived life will never make it right. It is consummately wrong."[38]

Faust was a member of the First Presidency with President Gordon B. Hinckley and Thomas S. Monson when the Church issued The Family: A Proclamation to the World in 1995. The "Proclamation" states in part that "We, the First Presidency and the Council of the Twelve Apostles of The Church of Jesus Christ of Latter-day Saints, solemnly proclaim that marriage between a man and a woman is ordained of God and that the family is central to the Creator's plan for the eternal destiny of His children." The proclamation continues, "The family is ordained of God. Marriage between man and woman is essential to His eternal plan." The Proclamation ends with the following admonition: "We warn that the disintegration of the family will bring upon individuals, communities, and nations the calamities foretold by ancient and modern prophets. We call upon responsible citizens and officers of government everywhere to promote those measures designed to maintain and strengthen the family as the fundamental unit of society."[39]

Faust's received many accolades for his professional and church service. Along with the Distinguished Lawyer Emeritus Award from the Utah Bar Association, Faust received an Honorary Doctors Degree of Christian Service from Brigham Young University in 1997. He was honored as a Distinguished Alumni at the University of Utah in 1999, and was awarded the Honorary Order of the Coif at Brigham Young University in 2000. In 2003, he received the Marion G. Romney Distinguished Service Award by Brigham Young University Law School, and he was awarded an Honorary Doctors of Law degree by the University of Utah. In 1998, Faust received a Brazilian national citizenship award — an honor given to only a select few leaders—and was awarded honorary citizenship of the city of São Paulo.[40]

The James E. Faust Law Library at the University of Utah S.J. Quinney Law School building, dedicated in 2015, now bears his name. Law students and other library patrons for generations to come will now study and conduct legal research in the library named after the distinguished lawyer and church leader.[41]

As one of the top leaders of the Church, Faust gained the admiration of many people, but also the ire of critics. In *Treff v. Hinckley*, 2001 UT 50, 26 P.3d 212 (2001), a prison inmate filed a civil case against church leaders, including Faust, and others, based on claims of alienation of affections and violation of parental rights. Robert Treff was incarcerated after shooting and killing his wife. His two children were placed in the custody of his wife's sister and later baptized as members of The Church of Jesus Christ of Latter-day Saints. Treff filed suit several years later, alleging causes of action for violation of his parental rights and alienation of affections. The inmate also claimed that the trial judge improperly refused to recuse himself for religious bias. On appeal, the Utah Supreme Court affirmed the dismissal of the lawsuit by the district court and held that the inmate's demands lack merit. The Utah Supreme

Court did not even address the merits of the claim about recusal of the judge.[42]

Along with his inspirational messages, Faust also sought opportunities to speak to lawyers and law students. Faust encouraged lawyers to "[l]ook upon [their] learning and license to practice law as a way to do great things for little people and little things for everyone."[43] Faust also advised law students, "Do not expect your professor . . . to concentrate his lessons out of the scriptures, although occasionally he may wish to do so. His obligation is to teach you the secular rules of civil and criminal law and matters that relate to them, such as procedures." Faust also related, "Your obligation is to learn the rules of law and related matters. The whisperings of the Holy Spirit will no doubt help you, but you must learn the rules of law, using [Winston] Churchill's phrase, by 'blood, sweat, and tears.' . . . Just having a good heart does not get the job done."[44]

While faithful Latter-Day Saints will remember Faust for his inspirational messages and leadership, Faust also left behind a model of service and excellence for all members of the legal community to follow. Kristin Gerdy, a Utah lawyer, remarked, "His example is one that attorneys of all faiths would be wise to emulate."[45]

"Our legal system with all of its imperfections has stood the test of time and preserved the rule of law. There is certainly very much to commend our system to so many other countries of the world where some of us travel or have lived. . . [T]he law should continue to be more of a profession than a business. Perhaps we ought to be a little more concerned about doing our job and a little bit less concerned about what's in it for us." James E. Faust, on the legal system.[46]

---

[1] See *In re Howard's Estate*, 2 Utah 2d 112, 269 P.2d 1049 (1954); *Weber Basin Water Conservancy Dist. v. Moore*, 2 Utah 2d 254, 272 P.2d 176 (1954); *In re Howard's Estate*, 3 Utah 2d 76, 278 P.2d 622 (1955); *Weber Basin Water Conservancy Dist. v. Gailey*, 5 Utah 2d 385, 303 P.2d 271 (1956); *Huggins v. Hicken*, 6 Utah 2d

233, 310 P.2d 523 (1957); *Weber Basin Water Conservancy Dist. v. Gailey*, 8 Utah 2d 55, 328 P.2d 175 (1958); *Application of Conde*, 10 Utah 2d 25, 347 P.2d 859 (1959); *Shields v. Dry Creek Irr. Co.*, 12 Utah 2d 98, 363 P.2d 82 (1961); *Morrison v. Horne*, 12 Utah 2d 131, 363 P.2d 1113 (1961); *Hinckley v. Swaner*, 13 Utah 2d 93, 368 P.2d 709 (1962); *Amundson v. Mutual Benefit Health & Acc. Ass'n*, 13 Utah 2d 407, 375 P.2d 463 (1962); *Acme Crane Rental Co. v. Ideal Cement Co.*, 14 Utah 2d 300 383, P.2d 487 (1963); *Green Ditch Water Co. v. Salt Lake City*, 15 Utah 2d 224, 390 P.2d 586 (1964); *Clack-Nomah Flying Club v. Sterling Aircraft, Inc.*, 17 Utah 2d 245, 408 P.2d 904 (1965); *Greguhn v. Mutual of Omaha Ins. Co.*, 23 Utah 2d 214, 461 P.2d 285 (1969); *Skaggs Drug Centers, Inc. v. Ashley*, 26 Utah 2d 38, 484 P.2d 723 (1971); *Hardy v. Hendrickson*, 27 Utah 251, 495 P.2d 28 (1972). A search on Westlaw in Utah Supreme Court cases for "DA(aft 1953 & bef 1973)" retrieves 2,774 cases. A review of these cases shows Faust argued more cases than any other lawyer in private practice during this time period (search conducted Oct. 19, 2017). Utah Attorney General Vernon B. Romney had the most cases appearing in 251 cases from 1964 to 1972.

[2] 73 Am. Jur. 2d Sundays and Holidays § 23.

[3] *Skaggs Drug Centers, Inc. v. Ashley*, 26 Utah 2d 38, 42, 484 P.2d 723, 726 (1971).

[4] James E. Faust, *The Lord's Day, Ensign*, November 1991, 35.

[5] *Hardy v. Hendrickson*, 27 Utah 251, 495 P.2d 28 (1972) (estate administration); *Huggins v. Hicken*, 6 Utah 2d 233, 310 P.2d 523 (1957) (medical malpractice); *Application of Conde*, 10 Utah 2d 25, 347 P.2d 859 (1959) (family law).

[6] *President James E. Faust, Beloved Shepherd*, Ensign, October 2007, 3.

[7] The Utah State Bar Presents Lifetime Achievement Awards at 75th Anniversary Celebration Dinner, Utah B.J. 75th Anniversary Edition 2006, 40, 41.

[8] James E. Faust, *The Doctrine and Covenants and Modern Revelation*, in Sperry Symposium Classics: The Doctrine and Covenants, ed. Craig K. Manscill (Provo, UT: Religious Studies Center, Brigham Young University, 2004), 1–9.

[9] Darya V. Pollak, *"I'm Calling My Lawyer . . . in India!": Ethical Issues in International Legal Outsourcing*, 11 UCLA J. Int'l L. & Foreign Aff. 99, 159 (2006).

[10] Marc S. Galanter, *Why the Big Get Bigger: The Promotion-to-Partner Tournament and the Growth of Large Law Firms*, 76 Va. L. Rev. 747, 749 (1990).

[11] Bradley H. Hodge, *Starting A Business Practice*, 1 Transactions: Tenn. J. Bus. L. 26, 29 (1999).

[12] President James E. Faust, *Thoughts on the Justice System and Lawyers*, Utah B.J. November 1996, 12.

[13] *In re Howard's Estate*, 2 Utah 2d 112, 269 P.2d 1049 (1954).

[14] *President James E. Faust, Beloved Shepard, supra* note 6.

[15] *Id.*

[16] BYU Religious Studies Center, James E. Faust, Author Profile, https://rsc.byu.edu/authors/faust-james-e [https://perma.cc/B9BE-RME3].

[17] Motor Vehicle Business Regulation Act, Utah Laws 1949, c. 67, § 7; codified in Utah Code § 41-3-601, et. seq.

[18] Utah Laws 1949, c. 19, § 1; codified in Utah Code § 73-13-9.

[19] See *Arizona v. California*, 373 U.S. 546 (1963).

[20] James E. Bell, *In the Strength of the Lord: The Life and Teachings of James E. Faust* [Salt Lake, UT: Deseret, 1999], 86.

[21] Bob Bernick Jr. and Geoffrey Fattah, *Officials Mourn President Faust's Passing, Deseret News*, Aug. 10, 2007, 2007 WLNR 25852867.

[22] Senate Journal, 1997 General Session of the Fifty-Second Legislature, State of Utah, Jan. 20, 1997, http://le.utah.gov/~1997/journal/s0001.txt [https://perma.cc/LPG4-V5NT].

[23] The Utah State Bar Presents Lifetime Achievement Awards at 75th Anniversary Celebration Dinner, 2006 Utah B.J. at 41.

[24] The Honorable Augustus Chin & Kim Paulding, *The Utah Bar Foundation Celebrates 50 Years of Service*, Utah B.J. November/December 2013, 36.

[25] The Utah State Bar Presents Lifetime Achievement Awards at 75th Anniversary Celebration Dinner, 2006 Utah B.J. at 41.

[26] Charles J. Merten, *Mississippi, 1966*, 64 Or. St. B. Bull. 25 (2003).

[27] Board Authorizes Special Committee on Civil Rights and Racial Unrest, 49 ABA Journal 743 (1963).

[28] Arlin M. Adams, *Bernard G. Segal*, 129 U. Pa. L. Rev. 1023, 1027 (1981).

[29] Bob Bernick Jr. and Geoffrey Fattah, "Officials Mourn President Faust's Passing," *Deseret News*, August 10, 2007, 2007 WLNR 25852867.

[30] Arlin M. Adams, *Bernard G. Segal*, 129 U. Pa. L. Rev. 1023, 1027 (1981).

[31] Marcus G. Faust, *Lawyer, Lobbyist, and Latter-Day Saint*, 27 Tex. Tech L. Rev. 1117, 1117–18 (1996).

[32] See Advisory Board of the Journal, 52 ABA Journal 994 (1966); 55 ABA Journal 104 (1969).

[33] American Bar Association, About the American Bar Association, https://www.americanbar.org/about_the_aba.html [https://perma.cc/L4Q3-AFPV].

[34] Abe Fortas, *Dangers to the Rule of Law*, 54 ABA Journal 957 (1968); Dallin H. Oaks, *Improving the Criminal Justice Act*, 55 ABA Journal 217 (1969).

[35] Elder William Grant Bangerter, *Elder James E. Faust: Sharing His Love for the Lord*, Ensign, October 1986, 6.

[36] Eleanor Knowles, *Elder James E. Faust Assistant to the Council of the Twelve*, Ensign, January 1973, 14.

[37] The Utah State Bar Presents Lifetime Achievement Awards at 75th Anniversary Celebration Dinner, 2006 Utah B.J. at 41.

[38] Elder James E. Faust, *The Sanctity of Life*, Ensign, May 1975, 27.

[39] The Family: A Proclamation to the World, The Church of Jesus Christ of the Latter-day Saints, Ensign, May 2017.

[40] The Utah State Bar Presents Lifetime Achievement Awards at 75th Anniversary Celebration Dinner, 2006 Utah B.J. at 41.

[41] Bob Nelson, *University of Utah Breaks Ground on the New S. J. Quinney College of Law Building*, KUER, Jun. 4, 2013, http://kuer.org/post/university-utah-breaks-ground-new-s-j-quinney-college-law-building#stream/0 [https://perma.cc/6QAE-26CD].

[42] 26 P.3d at 212.

[43] Kristin B. Gerdy, *Clients, Empathy, and Compassion: Introducing First-Year Students to the "Heart" of Lawyering*, 87 Neb. L. Rev. 1, 27–28 (2008).
[44] James E. Faust, *The Study and Practice of the Laws of Men in Light of the Laws of God*, Clark Memorandum, 16, 18–19 (Fall 1988).
[45] Gerdy, 87 Neb. L Rev. at 28.
[46] Faust, Utah B.J. November 1996, 12.

Chapter 6

Thomas B. Griffith: Beltway Judge for the Nation's Second Most Influential Court

Forging Political Connections Early in Life

There is a saying in politics and networking that it's all about who you know—and who they know.[1] A little bit of luck and fortunate timing certainly do not hurt either. Growing up in the suburbs of the metropolitan Washington, D.C. area in Virginia, Thomas B. Griffith forged political connections and interests early in life. Those early political ties and interests helped Griffith later become chief legal counsel for the U.S. Senate and then a judge on the nation's second most influential court with the U.S. Court of Appeals for the District of Columbia Circuit.

When he was just 15 years old, Griffith started working as an aide for Congressman Mo Udall, a Democrat who represented Arizona, in the U.S. House of Representatives. A former professional basketball player with the Denver Nuggets, Udall was one of the few members of the U.S. House of Representatives with a national profile. Udall is best known for finishing second to Jimmy Carter in the Democrat nomination in the 1976 presidential election.[2] Griffith, who didn't even have a driver's license at the time, carpooled with Udall from his home in Virginia to the Capitol each day for two summers learning from the long-serving and quick-witted Congressman. "I had the good fortune of living in his neighborhood. He just happened to live near me. Those were glorious days for a 15-year-old kid. He was just so kind to me

71

and took a special interest that I didn't deserve," recalled Griffith. "He had just high standards of public service. Not everyone was as principled as he was. He was a great public servant and a good man."[3]

Griffith also credits the role of Fred Field in advancing his legal career and political connections. In the 1990s, Field was the so-called "dean of Republican lawyers" in Washington, D.C. Field served as deputy counsel to John Dean in the Nixon Administration and was one of the few lawyers in the administration with his reputation in tact after the Watergate scandal. President Ronald Reagan later asked Field to serve as his chief counsel. Griffith recalled his early experience working with Field, "He had an illustrious career. I was an associate and later a partner at Wiley [D.C. law firm Wiley Rein & Fielding; later Wiley Rein LLP]. I worked for Fred. He was always just helpful to me along the way." Griffith added, "He played a large role in helping me become the Senate Legal Counsel. That was a really important fork in the road for me. Fred was very helpful in that regard. I didn't have a lot of political experience. I am confident his recommendation went a long way. He was a remarkable figure."[4]

Becoming a Compromise Judicial Selection

As Senate Legal Counsel, Griffith oversaw the trial of President Bill Clinton in the Senate after the U.S. House of Representatives passed articles of impeachment. Griffith helped moderate and establish the trial procedures used by the Senate. In providing legal advice to the Senate during the contentious and politically-charged trial of a sitting president, only the second time in history, Griffith handled the proceedings with diligence and gained respect and admiration from both Democrat and Republican Senators along with the rest of the Washington legal community.[5]

When a vacancy arose on the D.C. Circuit, widely perceived as the second most powerful and influential court in the United States, trailing only the U.S. Supreme Court, President George W. Bush first nominated Miguel Estrada in 2001. But Senate

Democrats used the filibuster to block the nomination. The filibuster in the Senate imposes an effective supermajority requirement of 60 votes, rather than a simple majority, to pass legislation and confirm nominations.[6] Bush then nominated Griffith to the influential "feeder-court" or "stepping-stone" court to the U.S. Supreme Court that has produced many U.S. Supreme Court Justices, including Justices Antonin Scalia, Clarence Thomas, Ruther Bader Ginsburg, and John Roberts.[7]

Griffith survived a somewhat contentious confirmation process despite his impressive qualifications to serve on the court and endorsement from many influential people inside Washington. After graduating summa cum laude from Brigham Young University and earning his law degree from the University of Virginia, Griffith worked in private practice in North Carolina and later became a partner with the distinguished firm of Wiley, Rein & Fielding in Washington, D.C. After serving as Senate Legal Counsel, Griffith became the counsel for Brigham Young University (BYU). Some Democrats, including Senator Patrick Leahy, harped on Griffith for his failure to pay his dues to the D.C. bar and not being admitted to practice law in the State of Utah while acting as university general counsel. Griffith accepted responsibility for the oversight in not paying dues. At BYU, Griffith oversaw one of the nation's largest private universities that has an international presence with students from all over the world. The executive director of the Utah Bar wrote a letter to the Senate Judiciary Committee, also signed by the five former presidents of the Utah State Bar Association, that Griffith's conduct as general counsel at BYU did not constitute the "unauthorized practice of law."[8]

Reflecting on his confirmation before the Senate, Griffith observed "I can't be too critical of the process. I got caught in a political crossfire that had little to do with me. I was pretty calm about it. I was given assurances by senior Senate Democrats that I was going to be confirmed." Griffith added, "Obviously, Senator Leahy took after me. In those moments, they are not fun but I was really gratified by the number of people who came to my defense. Chief among them were a number of Washington lawyers who were Democrats. . . I respect Senator Leahy."[9]

Abner Mikva, former chief judge of the D.C. Circuit appointed by President Jimmy Carter and later White House Counsel for President Clinton, led the charge in support of Griffith. Other Washington insiders, including Democrats, also voiced support for Griffith. Seth Waxman, who served as U.S. Solicitor General for President Bill Clinton, said "[l]itigants would be in good hands with a person of Tom Griffith's character as their judge."[10] President and Senator Hillary Clinton's personal counsel David Kendall had this to say: "The Federal bench needs judges like Tom, an excellent lawyer who is supported across the political spectrum." Kendall said Griffith "has the intellect and judgment to be an excellent judge."[11] Griffith reflected, "Anytime you are criticized in public, it is not a fun thing. The fact that I had so many people that I admire and respect come to my defense was very gratifying."[12]

On the confirmation process for federal court judges, Griffith opined, "These are important decisions and nominees ought to be highly criticized. That is what happens when people vote. It is rough and tumble. I wouldn't relish doing that again. It comes with the territory. The scrutiny is fine. What I do object to is when [nominee's] records are mischaracterized for political points. That's bothersome. These are human beings who have families, friends, and reputations. These are real people you are talking about."[13]

Griffith recognizes that he would not have secured his position as a judge on the influential court but for the controversial filibuster rule in the Senate. "I am on the D.C. Circuit because for four years, I was chief legal officer of the U.S. Senate and I managed to make friends on both sides of the aisle. That is why I was nominated by President Bush." Griffith recognized that he became a compromise selection after the tumultuous filibuster by Senate Democrats with Estrada's nomination. Griffith added, "I was told that one reason why I was nominated is because President Bush knew I would be confirmed and wouldn't be filibustered because I had friends on both sides of the aisle."[14]

Sitting on the Nation's Second Most Influential Court

The D.C. Circuit regularly handles high-profile and complex cases involving questions of broad significance such as health benefit exchanges under the Patient Protection and Affordable Care Act (ACA).[15] As a judge on the D.C. Circuit, Griffith has many opportunities to engage with cutting-edge issues in constitutional and administrative law with national scope, including constitutional rights for suspect terrorists, gun rights, campaign finance law, and national air-quality standards.[16] In many cases, the relatively even-handed and ideologically unpredictable Griffith plays a vital role as a key swing vote drawing similarity to Justice Anthony Kennedy on the U.S. Supreme Court. In fact, the *New Republic* magazine recognized Griffith in 2011 as one of Washington's Most Powerful, Least Famous People.[17]

Griffith has decided many challenging and emotionally charged cases as a jurist. One of the most difficult cases personally for Griffith was the Abigail Alliance case. The legal question in *Abigail Alliance for Better Access to Developmental Drugs v. von Eschenbach*, 495 F.3d 695 (D.C. Cir. 2007) was whether the U.S. Constitution provides the right of terminally ill patients access to experimental medications. Abigail Burroughs was just 19 years old when she was diagnosed with neck cancer. Abigail was an honor student and high school athlete who devoted much of her time to charity work making beds at homeless shelters and creating a free tutoring program. Soon after her diagnosis, Abigail's family learned of a new experimental drug in Erbitrux. Abigail's oncologist at Johns Hopkins Hospital believed that Abigail would be a good candidate for the drug, but Abigail was denied access to participate in the clinical trials because the nature of the trials was limited both by size and type of patients. After months of trying to access the drug, Abigail lost her fight with cancer dying at age 21. Soon after his daughter's death, Frank Burroughs, Abigail's father, established the Abigail Alliance for Better Access to Developmental Drugs to petition the Food and

Drug Administration (FDA) and Congress to change the rules on patient access to experimental medications.[18]

A three-judge panel of the D.C. Circuit originally ruled in favor of the Abigail Alliance and found that the Constitution protects the right of terminally ill patients to access to experimental drugs. The FDA requested that the full panel of the Court of Appeals reconsider the case. The American Society of Clinical Oncology (ASCO) also filed an amicus brief supporting the FDA's position. The U.S. Court of Appeals for the District of Columbia reheard the case "en banc" with all ten of the judges on the D.C. Circuit present and participating. In a slit 8-2 decision, the court reversed the earlier decision and held the U.S. Constitution does not provide terminally ill patients a right of access to experimental drugs that have passed limited safety trials but have not been proven safe and effective. In writing the opinion of the court, Griffith recognized that the U.S. Constitution has no fundamental right "deeply rooted in this Nation's history and tradition" of access to experimental drugs for the terminally ill.[19] The court also held that patients have no right to "a potentially toxic drug with no proven therapeutic benefit."[20] The D.C. Circuit noted that "arguments about morality, quality of life, and acceptable levels of medical risk are certainly ones that can be aired in the democratic branches, without injecting the courts into unknown questions of science and medicine."[21]

After the decision by the D.C. Circuit, Frank Burroughs, vowed to pursue an appeal to the U.S. Supreme Court, but the U.S. Supreme Court declined to consider the case.[22] In 2012, five years after the court decision, the FDA approved the use of Erbitrux (cetuximab), in combination with radiation therapy, for the treatment of certain types of cancer.[23] The Abigail Alliance and other right-to-try advocates with the support of the Goldwater Institute continued to lobby Congress and state legislatures to change the rules on patient access to experimental drugs with moderate success at the state level.[24] Ten years after the decision, Griffith reflected "It was a highly charged emotional case with young children dying of cancer. . . That is a hard case emotionally that is still talked about and criticized."[25]

Griffith decided another important case involving a constitutional question under the Fourth Amendment protection against unreasonable searches. In *United States v. Maynard*, 615 F.3d 544, 564 (D.C. Cir. 2010), the D.C. Circuit held that "prolonged GPS monitoring defeats an expectation of privacy that our society recognizes as reasonable." In the case, law enforcement agents installed a GPS tracking device on the undercarriage of the suspect's vehicle while it was parked in a public parking lot. Over the next 28 days, the government used the device to track the vehicle's movements. The signals relayed more than 2,000 pages of data. The U.S. Supreme Court later affirmed the case in *United States v. Jones*, 565 U.S. 400 (2012) holding that the use of longer term GPS monitoring in investigations of most offenses impinges on expectations of privacy. Society's expectation has been that law enforcement agents and others would not and simply could not secretly monitor and catalogue every single movement of an individual's car for a very long period.[26] In reflecting on the GPS monitoring case and the Fourth Amendment, Griffith observed, "We are entering a new era where technology is in place with remarkable powers to take their investigations. Obviously, it raises questions about individual privacy and the Fourth Amendment to protect against unreasonable searches."[27]

Along with the interpreting the right against unreasonable searches under the Fourth Amendment, Griffith has decided key cases construing the right to bear arms under the Second Amendment. In *Parker v. District of Columbia*, 478 F.3d 370 (D.C. Cir. 2007), Griffith joined Judge Laurence Silberman's majority opinion holding that the Second Amendment protects an individual's right to bear arms and that this right is not limited to members of the military or organized militias. In *Wrenn v. District of Columbia*, 864 F.3d 650 (D.C. Cir. 2017), gun owners who were denied concealed-carry licenses filed a suit challenging District of Columbia's "good reason" law limiting the issuance of concealed-carry licenses to those with a special need for self-defense. The D.C. Circuit held that "the individual right to carry common firearms beyond the home for self-defense—even in densely populated areas, even for those lacking special self-defense needs—falls within the core of the Second Amendment's protections."[28]

Besides deciding cases interpreting the U.S. Constitution, the D.C. Circuit often faces complex and meaningful questions interpreting legislation enacted by Congress. In a case involving the Voting Rights Act of 1965, Griffith was part of a 2-1 majority that upheld the Voting Rights Act of 1965 that allowed the U.S. Department of Justice to regulate elections.[29] While the U.S. Supreme Court reversed the case on appeal, Griffith said "I think the Voting Rights Act of 1965 is one of the most important pieces of legislation. It was meaningful to me to uphold that statute even though the Supreme Court thought Congress was not a cohort."[30]

Griffith expresses great admiration for his colleagues on the D.C. Circuit. While many government leaders in the nation's capital routinely bicker over partisan matters, the judges on the D.C. Circuit have great admiration for one another despite the often politically-charged nature of the court docket and their strong personalities. "One of the happy things to report is how well the judges get along. It really is collegial. I don't know how to compare it with other [circuits] but my experience has been remarkable." Judge Griffith added, "These are some of the finest people I have ever met—not just lawyers, but people. Being able to work with them day in and day out is the highest professional honor. I really stand in awe of my colleagues. They are brilliant and collegial. We work really hard to avoid dissents."[31]

Griffith serves alongside Judge Merrick Garland, nominated by President Barack Obama to the U.S. Supreme Court after the death of Justice Antonin Scalia. Senate Republicans blocked Garland's nomination waiting for the outcome of the 2016 presidential election. After the election, President Donald Trump nominated the more conservative Neil Gorsuch.[32] On his relationship with Garland, Griffith said, "I have known Judge Garland very well now. I am at a loss for words because I think so highly of him at so many levels. He is a brilliant and fabulous writer."[33]

A week after Griffith's confirmation by the Senate, Judge Harry Edward, the Senior Circuit Judge and Chief Judge

Emeritus on the D.C. Circuit, sent a package to Griffith with a series of articles on the importance of collegiality. "There was a time when the circuit was sorely divided. This was back in the [1970s]. I just couldn't imagine that. That is no way to run a court. They worked real hard to change the culture," said Griffith. "I got the message from the get go. That fit my personality just fine. Although our political views differ, first and foremost, we are patriots and Americans."[34] Griffith espouses the admonition given by Abraham Lincoln given in his first inaugural address: "We are not enemies, but friends. We must not be enemies. Though passion may have strained it must not break our bonds of affection. The mystic chords of memory, stretching from every battlefield and patriot grave to every living heart and hearthstone all over this broad land, will yet swell the chorus of the Union, when again touched, as surely they will be, by the better angels of our nature."[35]

Relishing the Opportunity to Teach Others

While on the D.C. Circuit, Griffith relishes the opportunity to teach law students and other groups around the country about the law. He has taught law school courses at BYU, Stanford University, and Harvard University as an adjunct professor. "I think in my current position, it gives me an opportunity to travel around the nation. Those teaching moments that come . . . particularly among law students and young lawyers, are very gratifying in teaching the law and what it can represent and can accomplish."[36]

Griffith admits that he has not faced any overt prejudice because of his faith. "I have gotten the impression that I have always been treated better than I deserve—particularly being a lawyer of my generation," said Griffith. "When people find out, they immediately think better of me . . . in large part due to the reputation of Rex Lee."[37]

One challenge that Griffith faced early in his career—a challenge that many young lawyers also experience—was finding a proper balance between his family, church, and professional responsibilities. "When I was an associate and bucking to be partner, I was called to be a bishop, with six children, and a major commute. I went to the partner for whom I did the most work and explained here is what happened and here is what is required of me." Griffith explained to the managing partner, "There will be times when I won't be able to work because of a funeral or counseling. I used this opportunity to explain what it means to be a bishop in the Mormon Church. I said I am going to be the best attorney that I can possibly be but I have this obligation." In the Church, a bishop is the ecclesiastical leader of a congregation or ward, and has comprehensive pastoral and administrative responsibility at that level.[38] Bishops serve without any monetary compensation and devote considerable time each week to watch over and care for the members of their congregation. After explaining his role as a bishop for the newly formed congregation, the firm supported Griffith in his new position as a lay clergy. Griffith recalled, "My law firm was just fabulous about it."[39] As is the case with many lawyers with religious convictions, Griffith tried his best to balance his time with the tug and pull of different responsibilities and competing demands.

A few months after Griffith started working as senior counsel at BYU, church leaders called Griffith to serve as stake president over a stake of young single students. "That was a Camelot like experience," he said. "I am still living off the fumes from that experience. That experience was so unique and so distinctive. It was really just an unbelievable experience."[40]

After moving back to the Washington, D.C. area to serve on the D.C. Circuit, Griffith has taught seminary to the youth in the Church and finds great satisfaction from teaching young people about the gospel. Griffith, who converted to the church as a teenager, previously served as a missionary in South Africa and Zimbabwe.[41] Before attending law school, Griffith worked in the Church Educational System, where he directed seminary and institute programs in the Baltimore, Maryland, area.[42] In teaching seminary, Griffith reflected, "That really resonates with me. I love that."[43] Along with formal church callings, Griffith makes efforts to connect with the communities by speaking to young lawyers and law students who are members of the Church. "I particularly enjoy my interactions with LDS law students. I try to always make time with the LDS students in a small group setting. There, we are able to talk about the law and how to balance our commitment to build the kingdom with our professional obligations."[44]

In a speech delivered to students, Griffith offered his thoughts on constitutional interpretation:

> Some speak of a "living Constitution" whose meaning changes with our times. Using the phrase "living Constitution" suggests, however, that the Constitution that has actually been ratified is not quite alive, or is, in the words of the renowned constitutional scholar Miracle Max, "mostly dead." Proponents of the living Constitution call upon unelected, life-tenured, and politically unaccountable federal judges—like me—to keep the Constitution up to date. According to this view, federal judges should be the arbiters of the nation's evolving standards, which we should read into the Constitution. Of course, that is far easier than submitting to the cumbersome and difficult amendment process set forth in the ratified Constitution. But as is often the case with the easy way out, this approach is fundamentally flawed. . . . [C]itizenship is serious business that requires effort.[45]

"[W]e conclude that the Second Amendment protects an individual right to keep and bear arms. That right existed prior to the formation of the new government under the Constitution and was premised on the private use of arms for activities such as hunting and self-defense." Thomas Griffith, on the Second Amendment, joining the majority opinion in *Parker v. District of Columbia*, 478 F.3d 370, 395 (D.C. Cir. 2007).

---

[1] Ted Knutson, *It's All About Who You Know — and Who They Know*, Washington Post, Jan. 25, 2009, 2009 WLNR 27046158.

[2] David Hess, *Mo Udall, Quick-Witted Congressman, Forced to Retire*, Baltimore Sun, 3A, Apr. 20, 1991, 1991 WLNR 734502.

[3] Phone interview with Thomas B. Griffith, Judge, U.S. Court of Appeals for the District of Columbia Circuit, Sept. 1, 2017 (hereinafter "Griffith (2017)".

[4] *Id.*

[5] Thomas R. Lee, *The Clinton Impeachment and the Constitution: Introduction to the Federalist Society Panel*, 1999 B.Y.U. L. Rev. 1079, 1080 (1999).

[6] Catherine Fisk & Erwin Chemerinsky, *The Filibuster*, 49 Stan. L. Rev. 181, 182 (1997).

[7] John M. Golden, *The Federal Circuit and the D.C. Circuit: Comparative Trials of Two Semi-Specialized Courts*, 78 Geo. Wash. L. Rev. 553, 574 (2010).

[8] Hearing before the Committee on the Judiciary, S Hrg No. 109-853, 109th Cong, 1st Sess (2005).

[9] Griffith, *supra* note 3.

[10] Hearing before the Committee on the Judiciary, S Hrg No. 109-853, 109th Cong, 1st Sess (2005).

[11] *Id.*

[12] Griffith (2017).

[13] *Id.*

[14] *Id.*

[15] See *Halbig v. Burwell*, 758 F.3d 390 (D.C. Cir. 2014), reh'g en banc granted, judgment vacated, No. 14-5018, 2014 WL 4627181 (D.C. Cir. Sept. 4, 2014).

[16] John M. Golden, *The Federal Circuit and the D.C. Circuit: Comparative Trials of Two Semi-Specialized Courts*, 78 Geo. Wash. L. Rev. 553, 556 (2010); Richard H. Fallon, Jr., *Greatness in A Lower Federal Court Judge: The Case of J. Skelly Wright*, 61 Loy. L. Rev. 29, 36–37 (2015).

[17] *Washington's Most Powerful, Least Famous People*, New Republic, October 11, 2011, https://newrepublic.com/article/96131/washingtons-most-powerful-least-famous-people.

[18] Priya Brandes, *Regulation of Drugs: A Death Sentence for the Terminally Ill?*, 46 U.S.F. L. Rev. 1149, 1156–57 (2012); Sue Kovach, "The Abigail Alliance: Motivated by Tragic

Circumstances, Families Battle an Uncaring Bureaucracy," *Life Extension*, Abigail Alliance, Special Edition 2007, 26, http://www.abigail-alliance.org/LEMSEP07pAbigailLR.pdf [https://perma.cc/C5CY-NHFV].

[19] 495 F.3d at 695.

[20] *Id.* at 713.

[21] *Id.*

[22] cert. denied, 552 U.S. 1159 (2008).

[23] National Cancer Institute at the National Institutes of Health, FDA Approval for Cetuximab, https://www.cancer.gov/about-cancer/treatment/drugs/fda-cetuximab [https://perma.cc/4QDN-FQ6M].

[24] Tamara J. Patterson, *The Cost of Hope at the End of Life: An Analysis of State Right-to-Try Statutes*, 105 Ky. L.J. 685, 689 (2017).

[25] Griffith, *supra* note 3.

[26] *United States v. Jones*, 565 U.S. 400, 430, 132 S. Ct. 945, 964 (2012).

[27] Griffith (2017).

[28] 864 F.3d at 661.

[29] *Shelby Cty., Ala. v. Holder*, 679 F.3d 848 (D.C. Cir. 2012), rev'd, 133 S. Ct. 2612 (2013).

[30] Griffith (2017).

[31] *Id.*

[32] See Michael J. Gerhardt, *Justice Scalia's Legacies*, 15 First Amend. L. Rev. 221, 221–22 (2017).

[33] Griffith (2017).

[34] *Id.*

[35] Inauguration of President Abraham Lincoln at U.S. Capitol, March 4, 1861, The Library of Congress.

[36] Griffith (2017).

[37] *Id.*

[38] Don M. Pearson, *Encyclopedia of Mormonism* (New York, NY: Macmillan, 1992), 117.

[39] Griffith (2017).

[40] *Id.*

41 Edward L. Carter, *The Rule of Law*, BYU Magazine, Fall 2015, https://magazine.byu.edu/article/the-rule-of-law-2/ [https://perma.cc/N969-EWMN].
42 Brigham Young University, BYU Speeches, Speaker Profile, Thomas B. Griffith, https://speeches.byu.edu/speakers/thomas-b-griffith/ [https://perma.cc/3PW9-BHAC].
43 Griffith (2017).
44 *Id.*
45 Thomas B. Griffith, The Hard Work of Understanding the Constitution, speech given at Brigham Young University, Sept. 18, 2012, https://speeches.byu.edu/talks/thomas-b-griffith_the-hard-work-of-understanding-the-constitution/ [https://perma.cc/G32N-3FAY] (citing William Goldman, *The Princess Bride,* directed by Rob Reiner, Act III Communications (1987), a film particularly popular among members of the Church).

Chapter 7
Carl S. Hawkins: Beloved Law Professor

Making the Difficult Decision to Leave Michigan

When founding Brigham Young University Law School Dean Rex E. Lee and University President Dallin H. Oaks made personal visits to recruit potential faculty members for the new law school set to open in 1973, all were waiting to see the decision of one man: Carl Hawkins. Dean Lee felt he needed a core of academics for credibility of the new school and to obtain accreditation with the American Bar Association and the Association of American Law Schools.[1] Hawkins, a former law clerk to U.S. Supreme Court Chief Justice Fred M. Vinson and an accomplished Washington, D.C. lawyer, was a tenured law school professor at the prestigious University of Michigan. Hawkins was also a lay leader of the Ann Arbor congregations of The Church of Jesus Christ of Latter-day Saints, co-author of a well-known torts casebook, and respected for both his competence and his personal integrity throughout U.S. legal education. Initially, Hawkins said he wasn't about to leave all of that and take a chance on BYU. Hawkins could not imagine a more satisfactory professional position than being a tenured law professor at Michigan.[2]

An unusually rational and orderly thinker, Hawkins made a list of the reasons for staying and for leaving the University of Michigan. He talked with friends and family. But as the practical deadline drew near, he decided to fast and pray. He reviewed his list of factors for and against going to BYU. Hawkins later wrote in his personal history, as told by his colleague Bruce Hafen, "As I reviewed the list, I drifted into a state that I cannot adequately describe, involving something more than cognitive processes or rational evaluation. Each consideration was attended by a composite of feelings that could not be expressed in words but still communicated something more true and more sure than rational thought." Hawkins continued, "Every consideration that I had listed in favor of going to BYU was validated by a calm, overwhelming sense of assurance. Each consideration I had listed for not going to BYU was diminished to the point where it no longer mattered. . . . I fell asleep, content that I had finally made the right decision."[3]

Hafen recalled that he was sitting in President Oaks's office with Academic Vice President Robert Thomas and Dean Lee discussing law school matters. President Oaks's secretary called to say that Hawkins was on the line. Oaks took the call and talked softly with Hawkins. When Oaks hung up, he looked out the window of his office at Mt. Timpanogos. With tears in his eyes, Oaks said, "I guess the Lord really wants this law school . . . to be a good one. Carl is coming!"[4]

Hafen recounted that they whooped and hollered as if Lancelot were coming to Camelot. Hafen said that years later, Hawkins told him that the decision to leave Michigan and come to BYU was primarily the result of his most personal prayers.[5] The decision by Hawkins, after much prayer and deliberation, to leave his position as a tenured law school professor at one of the nation's preeminent law schools to join the faculty at the new and unproven law school reflects the commitment of Hawkins to his faith. His desire to serve the church was a major factor in his decision to take the new position.[6] Dean Willard Pedrick of the Arizona State University College of Law, told Lee during the initial faculty search that the presence of Hawkins on the faculty gave the new law school "instant credibility."[7]

After Hawkins committed to join the faculty, other faculty members followed. At the time, there were relatively few law professors in the country who were members of the Church. Dale Whitman, a member of the original faculty, recalled, "There's no doubt that this information [of Hawkins] made my decision to join the enterprise much easier, and I'm sure that the same is true of most of my colleagues on the original faculty."[8] Other original faculty members that joined Hawkins and Whitman included Ed Kimball, Keith Rooker, Gerry Williams, Woody Deem, Dave Lloyd, and Hafen under the leadership of Dean Lee. All of the world-class members of the original faculty graduated at or near the top of their respective law classes and were members of the Order of the Coif, a prestigious honors society for legal scholars.[9]

Clerking for the Chief Justice on the Nation's Highest Court

Before becoming a prominent law professor, Hawkins clerked for Chief Justice Vinson where he worked on groundbreaking decisions by the U.S. Supreme Court. Clerking for the U.S. Supreme Court Chief Justice is one of the most sought-after positions for recent law school graduates and a position that requires stellar academic credentials.[10] Hawkins earned his undergraduate degree in political science from Brigham Young University and an LL.B. with honors from Northwestern University Law School where he was elected to the Order of the Coif and served as editor-in-chief of the Illinois Law Review, now the Northwestern University Law Review. He also received the Wigmore Award for reflecting outstanding credit in law school and completed postgraduate work in 1951 as the Harry A. Bigelow Teaching Fellow at the University of Chicago Law School, working in the legal drafting program.[11]

Hawkins clerked for Chief Justice Vinson during the 1952–1953 Term which was the last term of the Chief Justice before he died of a sudden heart attack in September 1953.[12] Hawkins arrived at the U.S. Supreme Court soon after the court's decision in *Youngstown Sheet & Tube Co. v. Sawyer*, 343 U.S. 579 (1952) where the Court held in a split 6-3 decision that President Harry Truman exceeded his authority to seize the nation's steel mills during the Korean War without approval by Congress. Vinson wrote the dissenting opinion in the

Youngstown case arguing that President Truman acted within his authority.[13]

Chief Justice Vinson laid the groundwork for racial desegregation decided in *Brown v. Board of Education*, 347 U.S. 483 (1954). On racial segregation, Vinson recognized the failure of the "separate but equal" doctrine to provide truly equal facilities for all races, and the Court's decision in *Sweatt v. Painter*, 339 U.S. 629 (1950) served as a precursor to *Brown v. Board of Education*. Although Hawkins worked as a law clerk when the Supreme Court granted certiorari in 1953 to review *Brown v. Board of Education*, his one-year clerkship concluded before the U.S. Supreme Court decided the landmark case in 1954.[14]

During the time Hawkins served as a law clerk to the Chief Justice, the U.S. Supreme Court decided several important cases. In *Fowler v. Rhode Island*, 345 U.S. 67 (1953), the U.S. Supreme Court unanimously held that an ordinance aimed to penalize a minister of Jehovah's Witnesses for preaching at a peaceful religious meeting in a public park violated the First Amendment freedom of religion. The Court held that "it is no business of courts to say that what is a religious practice or activity for one group is not religion under the protection of the First Amendment."[15] In *Poulos v. New Hampshire*, 345 U.S. 395 (1953), Chief Justice Vinson joined the majority in another case involving the First Amendment. In *Paulous*, the Court held in a split 7-2 decision that a New Hampshire city ordinance requiring an individual or group to obtain a permit to hold a meeting in a public park did not violate the First Amendment.

The most important case that Hawkins worked on during his time clerking for Chief Justice Vinson was the landmark state secrets privilege case *United States v. Reynolds*, 345 U.S. 1 (1953). Vinson wrote the majority opinion in the 1953 case where the U.S. Supreme Court formally recognized the state secrets doctrine for the first time. In a case involving the crash of a B-29 bomber, the Air Force successfully blocked the widows' efforts to obtain the accident report on the ground that its release would threaten national security. Without the report, the survivors could not establish a prima facie case of negligence.[16] Chief Justice Vinson wrote that recourse to state secrets was not to be "lightly invoked," but where formally asserted by the head of a department with control over the matter, and where a "reasonable danger" to national security existed, information could be withheld.[17] Hawkins played an important role in the *Reynolds* decision and even wrote an earlier draft of the opinion written by Vinson.[18] The *United States v. Reynolds* case involving the state secrets privilege decided in 1953 should not be confused with the U.S. Supreme Court case *Reynolds v. United States*, 98 U.S. 145 (1878) decided in 1878 where the Court ruled that a law banning polygamy was constitutional and did not infringe the First Amendment right to free exercise of religion.

The state secrets privilege enables the government to prevent disclosure of sensitive state secrets in the course of litigation. Some describe the state secrets privilege as the "most powerful secrecy privilege available to the president" and the executive branch.[19] The privilege has been invoked by every administration since the U.S. Supreme Court first recognized the privilege in *United States v. Reynolds*.[20]

Successful Private Practice

After clerking for Chief Justice Vinson, Hawkins worked as a successful lawyer in Washington, D.C. where he became instrumental in the firm's representation of several Indian tribes in claims against the United States government. From 1953 to 1957, he was a partner for the law firm Wilkinson, Cragun, Barker & Hawkins, in Washington, D.C., and engaged in general practice before courts and administrative agencies.[21] Hawkins worked with Ernest L. Wilkinson. The greatest legal accomplishment of Wilkinson, who later became President of Brigham Young University, came when he represented the Confederated Bands of Ute Indians in claims against the United States Government which resulted in a $32 million settlement.[22]

In private practice, Hawkins obtained a judgment of nearly $3 million against the United States government representing the Uintah and White River Bands of Ute Indians involving approximately one million acres. In *Uintah & White River Bands of Ute Indians v United States*, 152 F. Supp. 953 (Ct. Cl. 1957), the U.S. Court of Claims awarded compensation in a case arising under the Ute Jurisdictional Act of 1938. The Indians claimed compensation for land of the former Uintah Indian Reservation in Utah, taken by the United States government for the Uintah National Forest.

The biggest case Hawkins tried involved the Crow Tribe where he successfully defended a $10 million judgment awarded by the Indian Claims Commission involving 30 million acres of land. In *Crow Tribe of Indians v. United States*, 284 F.2d 361 (Ct. Cl. 1960), the U.S. Court of Claims affirmed a decision to award compensation to the Crow Tribe for additional compensation for land, presently located in south central Montana and north central Wyoming, which the Crow Indian Tribe ceded to the United States by the treaty signed in 1868. The Indian Claims Commission decided that the tribe was entitled to recover additional compensation. On appeal, the U.S. Court of Claims held that even though the language of the Treaty of Fort Laramie was not technical language of recognition of title, participation of the United States in the treaty, was, under the circumstances surrounding the treaty and in light of the treaty's overriding purpose to secure free passage for emigrants across tribes, a recognition by the United States of the tribes' titles to areas for which they were to be held responsible.

Becoming a Leading Legal Scholar

Hawkins decided to leave private practice in 1957 and joined the faculty at the University of Michigan Law School in Ann Arbor to pursue a career in academia. As a professor at the University of Michigan, Hawkins was a popular and dedicated teacher. He helped shaped the laws in Michigan by drafting many bills introduced in the Michigan State Legislature. Hawkins also served as executive secretary of the Michigan Law Revision Commission, responsible for upgrading state laws, chairman of the Civil Procedure Committee of the Michigan State Bar, and reporter of the Michigan Supreme Court Committee on Standard Jury Instructions. He co-authored a six-volume work explaining the rule of procedure for Michigan courts and also co-authored two popular torts casebooks.[23] Michigan courts often looked to commentary provided by Professor Hawkins when interpreting statutes. In *Catsman v. City of Flint*, 18 Mich. App. 641, 647, 171 N.W.2d 684, 686 (1969), the Michigan Court of Appeals referenced the "helpful 'Practice Commentary' concerning the contempt power by Carl S. Hawkins, following section 1701 of the Revised Judicature Act, in which Professor Hawkins expresses his opinion that 'It is useless to generalize about the civil or criminal nature of contempt proceedings'. M.C.L.A. s 600.1701."[24] At the University of Michigan, Hawkins also wrote the much-cited 1959 law review article appearing in the *Vanderbilt Law Review* entitled "Professional Negligence Liability of Public Accountants."[25]

Hawkins then left Michigan to join the new law school in Provo, Utah—the same city where he was born and attended high school.[26] Most people make critical decisions at some point during their lives that, in turn, affect the lives of many other people. The decision by Hawkins to leave Michigan impacted the lives of countless others.

Professor Hawkins excelled in all three roles for a law professor as 1) a scholar; 2) a teacher and mentor; and 3) a colleague and member of the faculty.[27] While some law school professors become leading scholars in their field, they do not always relate well to their students. On the other hand, some of the best teachers do not always conduct the most ground-breaking scholarly research. And some law professors do not relate well with their colleagues. Carl Hawkins demonstrated strength in all three areas. Hafen added, "He was probably the most complete colleague of anyone who has been on the faculty. His teaching, scholarship, and professional service set the high-water mark. He simply wanted to be a good law teacher."[28]

As a scholar in the field of tort law, Hawkins conducted ground-breaking and influential research. The Iowa Supreme Court, Kansas Supreme Court, Michigan Supreme Court,

Montana Supreme Court, New Jersey Supreme Court, North Dakota Supreme Court, and Utah Supreme Court all cited scholarly research conducted by Hawkins as persuasive secondary authority.[29] In *Vega by Muniz v. Piedilato*, 154 N.J. 496, 521, 713 A.2d 442, 455 (1998), the New Jersey Supreme Court recognized that a jury should be no less adept at applying the duty of reasonable care in a premises liability suit than in an ordinary negligence case. The New Jersey Supreme Court cited a law article written by Hawkins published in the Utah Law Review nearly two decades earlier concluding ordinary negligence principles have constrained jury discretion in premises liability cases in jurisdictions that abolished the classification system.[30]

Besides his stellar research relied upon by courts as persuasive secondary authority and his leading casebooks on tort law, Professor Hawkins left a lasting impact on the lives of his students as a beloved teacher and mentor at both the University of Michigan and BYU. Albert Einstein said, "I never teach my pupils, I only provide the conditions in which they can learn."[31] Professor Hawkins exhibited attributes of a master teacher to help his students better understand the law. Throughout his career, he served as an advisor and mentor to many colleagues and students.[32] Often found wearing a tweed sport coat, Hawkins was considered warm and approachable.[33]

Tim Zinnecker, a former student, shared the following experiences upon the passing of Carl Hawkins, "One time he gave a lecture to us on a torts-related legal writing project. On my instigation, several of us on the back row held up signs that spelled P-R-O-X-I-M-A-T-E C-A-U-S-E (we were indeed a rowdy group!). I started feeling guilty about my behavior and later that day told him I was to blame for the commotion and any disrespect he felt. He just laughed and laughed (whew!)." Zinnecker added, "I had the pleasure and the privilege of receiving a top-notch legal education from some of the finest minds and kindest hearts in the legal academy." Zinnecker said that Carl Hawkins was one such person and expressed his respect for Hawkins: "I'll be forever grateful that he left his tenured position at Michigan to join the ranks of some other brave souls to create the J. Reuben Clark Law School."[34]

Another former student, Monte Stewart, who later worked as a law clerk for Chief Justice Warren E. Burger on the U.S. Supreme Court, characterized the teaching style of Hawkins. Stewart used the terms "calm mastery," "plain humility," and "influence for good" to describe Hawkins. Stewart recalled:

> One day in the Federal Courts class, he put a question to a student. In the response, the ratio of bold bluff over utter lack of preparation was too great for even Professor Hawkins to endure calmly. It wasn't that he raised his voice; he didn't. And it wasn't that he vented scorn or sarcasm; he didn't do that either. But there was definitely an edge to his voice that conveyed a message beyond the few words he spoke; that message was a mixture of rebuke for not treating seriously what merits seriousness and of no tolerance for such a performance. On reflection, that message's power (and it was powerful) surely derived in large measure from his otherwise constant calm in the classroom setting.[35]

As a colleague, Hawkins was considered an indispensable player. He was regarded as the natural "older brother" of the faculty.[36] Reese Hansen said, "When Carl spoke, people listened." His stature among the faculty was unequaled.[37] J. Clifton Fleming, Jr. recalled that when he initially joined the faculty at the BYU Law School, Hawkins gave him a ride to work and shared invaluable insights while commuting. Fleming only had one car at the time, which was used by his growing family, so Hawkins drove Fleming to the law school building located on the east side of campus each morning until Hawkins gave him an old family car that had become surplus as his own children left home. Hawkins told Fleming, "It's impossible to make exams too easy; students will always find ways to distribute themselves along a spectrum; so don't kill yourself in pursuit of creating the perfect exam" and "No matter how much you prepare, you will have days when you're lousy in the classroom so don't let it get you down."[38] Fleming added that most importantly, Hawkins was a man who had applied a splendidly rigorous mind to the important questions of life and faith and had come out of that process with a balance of secular accomplishment and religious devotion that provided him with an invaluable example.[39]

Hawkins assumed the leadership role of Dean of the BYU Law School on two separate occasions while Dean Lee took a leave from the law school to serve as Assistant Attorney General in the U.S. Department of Justice in 1975 and again as U.S. Solicitor General in 1981. Even though Hawkins did not particularly want the position as dean and preferred to focus on teaching and scholarship, Hawkins assumed the mantle and guided the law school through important accreditation by the American Bar Association and approval for membership in the Association of American Law Schools.[40]

A Lifetime of Service

Besides his service to the University of Michigan and Brigham Young University as a law professor, Hawkins dedicated his time serving his country and the legal community. Hawkins served as a radio operator in the Army Air Corps, stationed in the Pacific theater of operations, in World War II. He also was a commissioner and vice chair of Utah's Alcoholic Beverage Control Commission and chair of the Attorney General's Utah Administrative Law Advisory Committee, which drafted a comprehensive Administrative Procedure Act in 1987. At the national level, he was a charter member of the National Conference of Bar Examiners' Multi-State Essay Examination Drafting Committee and served on the Association of American Law Schools' Accreditation Committee. President Jimmy Carter also appointed Hawkins to serve on Judge Nominating Commission of the U.S. Court of Appeals for the 10th Circuit.[41]

Hawkins, a faithful member of the Church, served in a variety of callings throughout his life, including bishop of the Ann Arbor (Michigan) Ward, counselor to President George Romney of the Detroit Michigan Stake, and president of the

Detroit and Dearborn, Michigan, stakes. He also served in leadership positions in BYU student stakes and was a member of the Church's evaluation correlation committee for more than eight years. His favorite calling was instructor of the high priests' group. Later in life, Hawkins served as a stake coordinator for the name extraction program and submitted thousands of names through the volunteer Family Search Indexing Program. He also contributed to the Encyclopedia of Mormonism.[42]

Carl Hawkins left an enduring legacy as a scholar, teacher, mentor, and colleague. The impact of Hawkins will last for generations to come. In a tribute to his friend and colleague, Hafen, who later served as Dean of the BYU Law School and as a General Authority for the Church, said the life of Carl Hawkins puts into action the eloquent words of the prophet Micah: "He hath shewed thee, O man, what is good; and what doth the Lord require of thee, but to do justly, and to love mercy, and to walk humbly with thy God." (Micah 6:8).[43]

"[S]ome people seem to have implicit faith in the untested premise that good legal education requires students and faculty with widely diverse religious backgrounds and beliefs. . . It is because we have untested beliefs as to the necessary conditions for good legal education that we need to allow room for diversity among law schools, so that diverse approaches can be tested through experience." Carl S. Hawkins, on the accreditation of church-related law schools.[44]

---

[1] *Obituary: Hawkins, Carl*, Deseret News, May 1, 2010, https://www.deseretnews.com/article/700028853/Obituary-HAWKINS-CARL.html [https://perma.cc/XX5C-JGJP] (hereinafter "Obituary: Hawkins, Carl"); Elder Bruce C. Hafen, *Carl Hawkins Tribute*, 2010 B.Y.U. L. Rev. 803, 803–04 (2010); Ed Kimball, *Carl Hawkins*, 2010 B.Y.U. L. Rev. 809 (2010).
[2] *Id.*

[3] Bruce C. Hafen, *A Walk by Faith: Founding Stories of the Law School*. Service & Integrity, Vol. 2, p. 32 (2009). http://digitalcommons.law.byu.edu/life_law_vol2/32 [https://perma.cc/WQ2Z-YQ4H].

[4] Hafen 2010 B.Y.U. L. Rev. at 804; James H. Backman, LDS Attorneys: Approaching the Modern Era, J. Reuben Clark Law Society, 2004, 7–8, http://www.jrcls.org/publications/perspectives/backman%20later%20lds.attorneys.jan9.04.pdf [https://perma.cc/4ANC-4FHS]; Dale A. Whitman, *Memories of Carl Hawkins*, 2010 B.Y.U. L. Rev. 813, n. 6 (2010).

[5] Hafen (2009).

[6] *Prof. Hawkins Joins BYU Law Faculty*, University of Michigan, 18 L. Quadrangle Notes 6 (Fall, 1973), https://www.law.umich.edu/historyandtraditions/faculty/Faculty_Lists/Alpha_Faculty/Documents/Law_Quad_Notes/Hawkins_Carl_1973.pdf [https://perma.cc/TWX4-EUH3] (hereinafter "Prof. Hawkins Joins BYU Law Faculty").

[7] Robert E. Riggs, *Carl Hawkins Tribute*, 2010 B.Y.U. L. Rev. 811 (2010).

[8] Whitman. 2010 B.Y.U. L. Rev. at 813.

[9] Backman (2004).

[10] See Laura Krugman Ray, *Clerk and Justice: The Ties That Bind John Paul Stevens and Wiley B. Rutledge*, 41 Conn. L. Rev. 211, 214 (2008).

[11] Carl S. Hawkins, University of Michigan Law, Law Quadrangle Notes, Vol. 02, Iss. 01 (November 1957), https://www.lib.umich.edu/faculty-history/faculty/carl-s-hawkins/bio [https://perma.cc/NGZ5-G8DD]; *Obituary: Hawkins, Carl, supra* note 1.

[12] Louis H. Pollak, *Aspects of Thurgood Marshall: The Lawyer-Patriot Who Repaired His Country*, 22 Del. Law. 15, 16 (2004).

[13] 343 U.S. at 667.

[14] Prof. Hawkins Joins BYU Law Faculty.

[15] 345 U.S. at 67.

[16] Laura K. Donohue, *The Shadow of State Secrets*, 159 U. Pa. L. Rev. 77, 82 (2010) (citing *Reynolds*, 345 U.S. at 7-10).

[17] *Id.*

[18] See David Rudenstine, *The Irony of a Faustian Bargain: A Reconsideration of the Supreme Court's 1953 United States v. Reynolds Decision*, 34 Cardozo L. Rev. 1283, 1385, n. 513 (2013) citing Carl Hawkins, Draft of United States v. Reynolds Opinion (Dec. 3, 1952) (unpublished draft) (on file with Margaret I. King, Special Collections Library of the University of Kentucky, Manuscript Collection).

[19] Sudha Setty, *Litigating Secrets: Comparative Perspectives on the State Secrets Privilege*, 75 Brook. L. Rev. 201 (2009)

[20] *Id.*

[21] Prof. Hawkins Joins BYU Law Faculty.

[22] Danae Friel, *Ernest L. Wilkinson, University Builder*, BYU Magazine, Fall 1999, https://magazine.byu.edu/article/ernest-l-wilkinson-university-builder/ [https://perma.cc/D2NY-CHTD]; *E. L. Wilkinson, of D.C. Law Firm, Dies*, Washington Post, Apr. 7, 1978, 1978 WLNR 210575.

[23] Prof. Hawkins Joins BYU Law Faculty.

[24] See also *Matter of Nathan*, 99 Mich. App. 492, 494, 297 N.W.2d 646, 647 (1980) and *Anthony v. Forgrave*, 126 Mich. App. 489, 493, 337 N.W.2d 546, 547 (1983) for Michigan cases citing commentary by Hawkins.

[25] Carl S. Hawkins, *Professional Negligence Liability of Public Accountants*, 12 Vand. L. Rev. 797, 811 (1959); Andrew J. Morris, *Clarifying the Imputation Doctrine: Charging Audit Clients with Responsibility for Unauthorized Audit Interference*, 2001 Colum. Bus. L. Rev. 339, 380, n. 106 (2001).

[26] Obituary: Hawkins, Carl.

[27] See Jason Ostrom, *The Competing Roles of Law Professors*, 42 S. Tex. L. Rev. 539 (2001); Nicola A. Boothe-Perry, *The "New Normal" for Educating Lawyers*, 31 BYU J. Pub. L. 53 (2016).

[28] Obituary: Hawkins, Carl.

[29] *Alexander v. Med. Assocs. Clinic*, 646 N.W.2d 74, 84 (Iowa 2002); *Jones v. Hansen*, 254 Kan. 499, 516–17, 867 P.2d 303, 315 (1994); *Sifers v. Horen*, 385 Mich. 195, 205–06, 188 N.W.2d 623, 627 (1971); *Draggin' y Cattle Co. v. Addink*, 372 Mont. 334, 343, 312 P.3d 451, 458 (2013); *Hebron Brick Co. v. Robinson Brick & Tile Co.*, 234 N.W.2d 250, 255 (N.D. 1975); *Vega by Muniz v.*

Piedilato, 154 N.J. 496, 521, 713 A.2d 442, 455 (1998); *DCR Inc. v. Peak Alarm Co.*, 663 P.2d 433 (Utah 1983).

[30] Carl S. Hawkins, *Premises Liability After Repudiation of the Status Categories: Allocation of Judge and Jury Functions*, 1981 Utah L. Rev. 15, 61 (1981).

[31] David M. King, *Training Within the Organization: A study of Company Policy and Procedures for the Systematic Training of Operators and Supervisors, Educational Methods* (London: Tavistock Publications, 1968), 126.

[32] Hafen 2010 B.Y.U. L. Rev at 803.

[33] Mary Anne Q. Wood, *Tribute to Carl Hawkins*, 2010 B.Y.U. L. Rev. 817 (2010).

[34] Tim Zinnecker, BYU Law Professor Carl Hawkins: 1926 – 2010, The Faculty Lounge, May 18, 2010, http://www.thefacultylounge.org/2010/05/byu-law-professor-carl-hawkins-1926-2010.html [https://perma.cc/6H4Y-SGNJ].

[35] Monte Stewart, *Carl Hawkins, Teacher*, Clark Memorandum, Fall 2010, 13.

[36] Ed Kimball, *Carl Hawkins*, 2010 B.Y.U. L. Rev. 809 (2010).

[37] Reese Hansen, *Tribute to Carl S. Hawkins*, 2010 B.Y.U. L. Rev. 807 (2010).

[38] J. Clifton Fleming, Jr., *Carl Hawkins: The Indispensable Player*, 2010 B.Y.U. L. Rev. 799, 802 (2010).

[39] *Id.*

[40] Hansen, 2010 B.Y.U. L. Rev at 807.

[41] Obituary: Hawkins, Carl.

[42] *Id.*

[43] Hafen, 2010 B.Y.U. L. Rev. at 805.

[44] Carl S. Hawkins, *Accreditation of Church-Related Law Schools*, 32 J. Legal Educ. 172, 184–85 & n. 38 (1982).

Chapter 8

Roger L. Hunt: Virtuous Judge in Sin City

Learning Integrity Early in Life

Las Vegas, affectionately known as "Sin City," features rampant casino gambling, adult entertainment, prostitution, alcohol consumption, and recreational drug use.[1] In some ways, the city of Las Vegas draws similarities to the cities of Sodom and Gomorrah from the Holy Bible or the city of Ammonihah from the Book of Mormon.[2] Amid the bright lights of the Las Vegas Strip and mega-casinos live a small sect of faithful saints in the Las Vegas area. Members of The Church of Jesus Christ of Latter-day Saints, who comprise approximately four percent of the Nevada population, espouse ideals of Christian faith and religious piety.[3] In fact, members of the Church founded Las Vegas with the establishment of the Old Mormon Fort in 1855.[4] Judge Robert H. Hunt, U.S. District Judge for the District of Nevada in Las Vegas, Nevada, has shined as a light unto the world and conveyed a positive influence for good to the people surrounding Clark County, Nevada.

Roger L. Hunt, a native Nevadan, was born in Overton and raised on a dairy farm in the rural town of Bunkerville, Nevada. Burnkerville is a small community located approximately 80 miles northeast of Las Vegas along I-15 near the city of Mesquite close to the Arizona border. While in high school, Hunt showed early academic prowess and popularity becoming both valedictorian and student body president. Hunt then attended the College of Southern Utah (later Southern Utah University) for one year and subsequently took a two-year hiatus from his schooling to serve a mission for the Church in New England. He served in the New England States Mission under mission president Truman G. Madsen. Madsen was a popular scholar, author, and professor of philosophy and religion at Brigham Young University. After serving as a missionary, Hunt transferred to Brigham Young University where he earned his finished his B.A. degree in history, graduating in 1966. He worked on a master's degree for one year and then entered law school at the National Law Center at George Washington University, Washington, D.C. Hunt received a Juris Doctor degree, with honors, in 1970.

While attending law school, Hunt worked as a legislative aide to Senator Howard Cannon. Cannon, a Democrat, served four terms in the Senate representing Nevada.[5] On his experience working for Senator Cannon, Hunt learned "[t]hat integrity was important, and that one must do what one thinks is right, not what others may think you should do for political or popularity reasons." Hunt recalled, "I did not always agree . . . but I was confident that he believed his course of action was correct, and he followed his heart."[6]

Gaining Confidence in the Jury System

After graduating from law school, Hunt returned west to the Silver State and worked as a trial lawyer in Las Vegas for 22 years before becoming a federal judge. He passed the Nevada Bar in 1970 and began his legal career working as a deputy district attorney for the Clark County District Attorney's Office from 1970 to 1971. In December 1971, Hunt joined the Las Vegas firm Rose & Norwood to work in private practice primarily handling the defense of civil litigation. Hunt became a partner after only 18 months with the firm. The firm name later changed to Edwards, Hunt, Hale & Hansen, Ltd. Hunt remained with the firm until his appointment to the federal bench in 1992.[7] As a lawyer in private practice, Hunt took many cases to trial. On his experience as a lawyer before becoming a judge, Hunt said, "[V]ery few experiences match the satisfaction of a successful cross-examination or of a jury verdict reflection what I believed to be the truth, which, fortunately, happened nearly always. I have a lot of confidence in the jury system."[8]

While in private practice, Hunt argued two cases before the Nevada Supreme Court. In *Hartford Ins. Grp. v. Winkler*, 89 Nev. 131, 508 P.2d 8 (1973), Hunt represented an automobile insurance company in an action brought by the driver's judgment creditors in a dispute involving automobile insurance coverage. In another case, in 1980, Hunt represented the Dunes Hotel in an action brought by an injured employee who filed suit against the hotel and the Las Vegas Convention Service. While the employee was working, employees of Las Vegas Convention Service lost control of a piece of equipment they were loading onto a freight elevator, knocking the employee through the railing to the floor below. The employee collected workers' compensation benefits but also brought a third-party action against the convention service and hotel.[9]

Serving as a U.S. Magistrate Judge

After working in private practice for more than two decades, Hunt became a U.S. Magistrate Judge in 1992, where he served for eight years until his appointment as a United States District Judge. One key difference between U.S. Magistrate Judges, also known as "Article I" Judges, and "Article III" District Judges is that Magistrate Judges do not receive life tenure. Magistrate Judges receive appointment for eight-year terms which may be subsequently renewed.[10] Article III Judges, on the other hand, serve for life or until they choose to retire. Article III judges receive appointment by the President and confirmation by the U.S. Senate. The terms "Article I" and "Article III" refer to the articles under the U.S. Constitution. Magistrate Judges play an integral part of the federal judicial system.[11]

As a U.S. Magistrate, Judge Hunt presided over both criminal and civil matters. In criminal cases, Magistrate Judges generally have authority to preside over trials in petty offense cases, misdemeanor cases, and felony preliminary proceedings. Judge Hunt also issued search warrants, including search warrants authorizing agents of the U.S. Food and Drug Administration to search three business selling nutrition products and to seize a variety of allegedly misbranded and unapproved products.[12]

In *United States v. Everett*, 972 F. Supp. 1313 (D. Nev. 1997), Judge Hunt decided a case involving the qualifications of an expert witness where the driver was charged with operating a motor vehicle under the influence of drugs and with speeding. The government called as its lead witness a ranger with the National Park Service over the defendant-driver's objection. Judge Hunt considered the parameters set forth by the landmark U.S. Supreme Court in *Daubert v. Merrell Dow Pharmaceuticals, Inc.,* 509 U.S. 579 (1993) for determining the admissibility of expert witness testimony. Under *Daubert* (pronounced Dow-burt), Judge Hunt considered whether the testimony is generally accepted in the scientific community, whether it has been subjected to peer review and publication, whether it has been tested, and whether the known or potential rate of error is acceptable.[13] Judge Hunt concluded that upon an appropriate foundation being laid, the protocol conducted by the ranger would be admissible to the extent that the witness can testify to the probabilities, based upon observations and clinical findings, but could not testify, by way of scientific opinion, that the conclusion was an established fact by any reasonable scientific standard.[14]

In civil cases, Magistrate Judges often rule on nondispositive motions and resolve pre-trial discovery disputes, including discovery matters.[15] In *Pioneer Chlor Alkali Co. v. Nat'l Union Fire Ins. Co. of Pittsburgh, Pennsylvania*, 863 F. Supp. 1226 (D. Nev. 1994), Judge Hunt presided over a case involving a chlorine gas manufacturer and insurance coverage after a gas leak. The chlorine gas manufacturer sued the insurance company for breach of the risk policy in effect at time of the gas leak, seeking coverage for damage to equipment, loss of gas, and business interruption losses. Judge Hunt ruled that the cause of the loss was a factual question precluding summary judgment and that the term "corrosion" was an unambiguous policy term. Judge Hunt ruled that Nevada's

Unfair Claim Practices statute was enacted as "part of a comprehensive plan to regulate insurance practice in Nevada" and expressly grants insureds a private right of action against insurance companies that violate the statute.[16]

A Mounting Judicial Crisis Avoided

After serving as U.S. Magistrate for eight years, a new opportunity became available for Judge Hunt. With the growing population of Nevada and increased court docket, Congress approved the creation of two new district judges in 2000 for the District of Nevada.[17] But with President Bill Clinton, a Democrat in the White House, and a Republican-controlled Senate, many judicial vacancies existed. In an address given to the American Bar Association a year earlier in 1999, President Clinton declared a "mounting vacancy crisis" in the federal courts accusing the Republican-led Senate of political foot-dragging with a slowdown of judicial confirmations.[18] Senate Judiciary Committee Chairman Orrin Hatch, a Republican from Utah, and other conservative Republicans in the Senate, blocked many of the liberal judges nominated by Clinton.[19] Senator Harry Reid, a Democrat who represented Nevada and was often at odds politically with Hatch but of the same faith, approached Hatch and asked, "What if I gave you two stake presidents?"[20] Senator Hatch agreed. Reid recommended the names of two stake presidents: Roger Hunt and Kent Dawson. Hunt was serving as stake president of the Las Vegas Nevada Warm Springs Stake. Dawson had been serving as President of the Henderson Nevada Black Mountain Stake and presided as a judge for the Henderson Justice Court.[21] Based on the recommendations from Senator Reid, President Clinton nominated Hunt and Dawson to the bench and they both received confirmation by the Senate with endorsement from Hatch.[22]

On the nomination and confirmation process, Hunt recalled, "For a position that must be absolutely non-political, the nomination and confirmation process to be become a federal judge is very political." Hunt added, "There were efforts by the

Senators to get me to state how I would rule on certain issues before those issues had come before me and without any factual foundation. It is both impossible and improper to answer such questions." Hunt found that living the standards of the Church helped him during the confirmation by the Senate—a process that sometimes blocks nominees who have engaged in certain misconduct. Hunt recalled, "It was a time when having tried to live up to the standards of the gospel and the church, and being politically boring, gave me a great advantage."[23]

Deciding Key Cases in Sin City

Naturally, as a judge in Las Vegas, Hunt decided cases involving casinos. In 2003, Judge Hunt presided over the case involving the trademarks "Colosseum" and "Empire" used by the casino Caesars Palace in *Caesars World, Inc. v. Milanian*, 247 F.Supp.2d 1171, (D. Nev. 2003). The owners of the casino brought an action against a defendant whose business model was to apply for a series of trademarks for a particular theme that he expected would become a theme for a casino or resort hotel. At the time, Caesars Palace was building its new 4,000 seat theatre on the Las Vegas Strip called The Colosseum at Caesars Palace to feature headliners such as singer Celine Dion. Judge Hunt found that the defendant's bogus intent-to-use trademark applications, filed only to reserve names so that they could be sold or licensed to unrelated third parties, were not made with bona fide intent to use in commerce, and thus were void. The usurper acted with bad faith and was ordered to pay attorneys' fees. Judge Hunt also ordered a permanent injunction and transfer of Internet domain names to Caesars Palace.[24]

Judge Hunt decided many memorable cases during his career on the bench. Hunt presided over the case involving a man who threatened to blow up Nellis Air Force Base and a case involving the development of the Yucca Mountain Nuclear

Storage facility.[25] Judge Hunt also decided cases involving defrauding elderly people of their life savings, trafficking in child pornography, armed bank robbery, shootings in armed robberies, illegal re-entry of illegal aliens with criminal convictions, and drug trafficking. Hunt recalled, "As in the cases I had as a lawyer, almost every case I tried had a meaning to me. More importantly, they all had meanings to the parties involved."[26]

In one of the most emotionally charged cases during his tenure as a judge, Judge Hunt reviewed the habeas corpus petition in 2007 asserted by Robert Hays who claimed his innocence.[27] Hays was accused of raping and sexually assaulting his eight-year-old daughter by his ex-wife. Hays was convicted of four counts of sexual assault and four counts of lewd conduct with a minor and sentenced to four sentences of life in prison to be served consecutively even though his daughter later recanted her testimony. After the Nevada Court of Appeals and the Nevada Supreme Court denied his appeal, Hays filed a federal petition for a writ of habeas corpus. Individuals convicted in state court can seek a petition for writ of *habeas corpus*, Latin for "that you have the body," in federal court but the petitions are rarely granted.[28] The daughter continued to recant her testimony and appeared on the television shows of Maury Povich and Montel Williams to plead her father's innocence.[29]

Judge Hunt reviewed the petition and concluded that Hays demonstrated many constitutional errors during his criminal trial by clear and convincing evidence. The girl tried to tell the prosecutor that the allegations against her father were false before the trial began but the prosecutor never forwarded this information to the court or the defense. The daughter said in a sworn statement, "My father Robert Hays never sexually abused me, I had to lie because [the prosecutor] threatened and scared me after I told him NO that my father never touched me." She continued in the sworn written statement, "[The prosecutor] never gave me a chance to tell him that my mother threatened to kill me and my brother and sisters if I did not tell everybody that my father sexually abused me."[30] Judge Hunt concluded the prosecutor engaged in prosecutorial misconduct. Hays also showed ineffective assistance of counsel by his court-appointed public defender. The defense lawyer failed to seek an evidentiary hearing after the girl recanted her testimony, argue at sentencing, adequately cross-examine witnesses during the trial, and object to prosecutorial misconduct. Judge Hunt concluded that the cumulative error doctrine applied. Hays was denied due process and a fair trial in violation of the guarantees of the Fifth and Fourteenth Amendments. After serving for 14 years in prison, Judge Hunt ordered the unconditional release and exoneration of Hays.[31] Hays later settled a federal civil rights lawsuit against the county, the prosecutor, the detective, the nurse, and his trial defense lawyer for an undisclosed amount.[32]

In reflecting on the Hays case, Judge Hunt found that Robert Hays had been done an injustice. The conviction of Hays had been obtained "because someone had frightened a little girl into telling a lie and who when tried to tell everyone that it had been a lie, but her pleas had been ignored or rejected." Hunt added, "Fortunately, when she became an adult, she was finally able to convince others of the truth and free her father from prison, and herself from the anguish that he false testimony had imprisoned for 14 years. I was grateful to have been able to make the decision, although I had to offend members of the legal community in doing so."[33]

In 2009, Judge Hunt presided over the high-profile sexual assault civil suit involving Nevada Governor Jim Gibbons. In *Mazzeo v. Gibbons*, 649 F.Supp.2d 1182 (D. Nev. 2009), a woman claimed that Gibbons sexually assaulted her while he was a U.S. Congressman and a candidate in the gubernatorial election. On a rainy Friday the 13th in October 2006, just a few weeks before the election, Chrissy Israel Mazzeo met up with her friend to enjoy happy hour at a restaurant in Las Vegas. Gibbons was seated at a nearby booth with his campaign manager, and two women. After sharing drinks, Mazzeo claimed that Gibbons attempted sexual assault in a parking garage.

While Judge Hunt dismissed most of the claims asserted in the complaint, he allowed some of the claims to proceed. The court concluded that Mazzeo's allegations were sufficient to sustain a claim for intentional infliction of emotional distress against the governor to survive a pre-trial motion to dismiss. Mazzeo alleged that Gibbons forcefully pinned her against a wall and told her he was going to rape her. Mazzeo also alleged that an associate made death threats that caused her to move out of her home. Judge Hunt ordered that certain portions of the complaint be stricken from the record that included "inappropriate commentary and dramatic flourishes" such as the phrase that read "like a well-deserved, public slap in the face."[34] After Judge Hunt denied the pre-trial motion to dismiss the case in its entirety, the parties reached a settlement instead of going to trial. The former cocktail waitress reached a $50,000 settlement in the civil lawsuit involving the sitting governor, an amount less than the defendants would have paid in legal costs to defend the suit if the case went to trial.[35]

In a case involving more twists than a Steven Spielberg movie, Judge Hunt presided over the discovery of a purportedly stolen Norman Rockwell painting found in the art collection of filmmaker Steven Spielberg.[36] The painting in question, *Russian Schoolroom*, appeared in *Look* magazine in 1967. The painting depicts Russian schoolchildren in a classroom with a bust of Soviet leader Vladimir Lenin. The painting was stolen from a small art gallery in Clayton, Missouri in June 1973. In 1988, the painting turned up and was sold at an auction in New Orleans for about $70,000. Spielberg bought the painting from Judy Goffman Cutler, a noted art dealer who specialized in American illustrators, in 1989 for $200,000. A member of Spielberg's staff spotted the painting on a FBI's list of stolen works of art and notified the authorities.

Las Vegas art dealer Jack Solomon then filed suit against Spielberg and Cutler with Solomon claiming ownership of the painting. Solomon was the owner of the painting at the time of the theft in 1973. During the legal joust, the painting remained in custody of the court in Las Vegas with the contesting parties splitting the cost of keeping the painting in climate-controlled storage.[37] After a bench trial, Judge Hunt ruled in 2010 that the painting belonged to Cutler rather than Solomon. Hunt ruled that Solomon, the previous owner, knew and consented to the sale of the painting in 1988. Solomon reached an agreement with the New Orleans auction house in 1988 when he received a share of the proceeds from the sale of the painting. Solomon previously received $20,000 from his insurance company in 1973 for the lost artwork. On appeal, the Ninth Circuit agreed with Judge's Hunt decision.[38] After the controversy, Cutler swapped the *Russian Schoolroom* painting with Spielberg for another Norman Rockwell painting.[39]

Judge Hunt also presided over the trial involving a Navy SEAL who stole and illegally smuggled into the United States automatic weapons, explosives, and other military items from Iraq for profit. The federal jury found Nicholas Bickle guilty of 13 federal conspiracy and arms trafficking counts in 2012. Hunt sentenced Bickle to nearly 18 years in prison finding that Bickle abused his position of trust. Judge Hunt commented, "I think he felt as a Navy SEAL he was above the law."[40] Judge Hunt denied the former Navy SEAL's motion for a new trial. Bickle argued that the admissions of character evidence of a photograph taken from Bickle's own camera denied him the right to a fair trial. Hunt concluded that the evidentiary purpose showed that the former special operations member had access to AK–47 machine guns while in Iraq, which clearly shows opportunity and feasibility. Bickle introduced the issue of his character by insisting on wearing his dress blue uniform, arrayed with medals, at each and every day of trial. Hunt found that sufficient evidence existed to support the conviction and that the evidence was "overwhelming."[41]

Based on his previous experience as a litigator before becoming a judge, Judge Hunt showed caution and even-handedness as a judge. Adam C. Anderson, a former law clerk to Judge Hunt, remarked, "He was careful. He had been a trial attorney for many years. He wanted to be a careful judge." Anderson described Judge Hunt as "unemotional but thoughtful . . . demure and quiet."[42] Calder Huntington, another former law clerk, learned the importance of taking the proper time to deliberate before making decisions while also following the axiom that "justice delayed is justice denied." Huntington recalled, "While you want to take the proper amount of time, you don't want to take too much time. You have to answer the question, so people can move forward."[43]

Judge Hunt served as chief judge from 2007 and 2011 for the District of Nevada, the top administrative position for the federal court. While serving as a District Judge, Hunt served on the Ninth Circuit Judicial Council. He also served as the judicial liaison for the Criminal Justice Act Panel for 15 years where he coordinated the Court Appointed Attorneys Panel. In addition, he served on the Ninth Circuit Model Jury Instruction Committee for seven years and on the Ninth Circuit Library Committee. He also acted as co-chair of the CM/ECF Implementation Committee and chair of the Case Management Subcommittee to help integrate the court with electronic case filing. The well-esteemed jurist assumed senior status, a form a semi-retirement, on May 26, 2011, but continued to hear cases at a reduced level.[44]

Overcoming Evil with Good

Besides his involvement as a lawyer and judge, Hunt has provided meaningful service to benefit others. Along with his service as a missionary, Hunt served in the Church as a bishop's counselor, gospel doctrine teacher, high counselor, bishop, stake president of two stakes (the Las Vegas Green Valley Stake and the Las Vegas Warm Springs Stake), regional representative, patriarch, temple ordinance worker, and a sealer in the Las Vegas Temple.[45] On his church service, Hunt said, "What I have learned most is that Jesus Christ lives and suffered to pay for my sins. I have learned that the truth is important. I have learned love, compassion, the importance of being free to, and being accountable for my own decisions." Hunt added, "I have learned that I, and everyone else I am a child of God and that he expects me to help His other children, my brothers and sisters."[46]

On the relationship between the Church members in Las Vegas and the casinos, Anderson, who grew up in Las Vegas, observed, "There have always been Mormons in Vegas. . . Mormon bankers financed the casinos. There has always been this relationship between Mormons and the mob. We live here and you guys do that."[47] Judge Hunt stated, "I found that wherever I have lived, that I have the positive influence when I try to maintain the highest level of integrity possible. A reputation for integrity will open many doors and cause others to give your counsel serious consideration as you participate in various activities and groups in any community."[48] Hunt observed, "Living in Las Vegas actually has its advantages. One cannot be apathetic about what one believes and stands for. With the opposition so blatant, it also provides opportunities to talk to my children about the influence of evil. Faith and belief in God is very strong here, which outsiders usually fail to realize."[49]

Judge Hunt has also served in a variety of community volunteer activities to help improve the lives of others and the legal profession. As a practicing lawyer, Hunt served as Chair of the Nevada Indian Commission and, later, as a member the Nevada Commission on Drug Abuse Education, Prevention Enforcement and Treatment to help address drug abuse. Judge Hunt also served as president of the Nevada American Inn of Court to improve ethics and professionalism in the legal profession. As a federal judge, he served as Chairman of the Ninth Circuit Magistrate Judges Conference, as Chief Judge of the federal court in Nevada, and as a member of the Ninth Circuit Judicial Council. Judge Hunt related, "These experiences have given me an opportunity to be a positive influence in my community and state. I can only hope that my efforts to be a positive influence has been at least partially successful."[50]

President George W. Bush appointed Judge Hunt as a member of the Board of Trustees of the Harry S. Truman Scholarship Foundation, which provides scholarship funds for those entering public service.[51] While serving on the scholarship board also requires presidential nomination and confirmation by the Senate, the position comes with less political scrutiny. Hunt described his experience in serving on the Board of the Truman Scholarship Foundation as "the opportunity to work with some wonderful people who were all interested in advancing the opportunities of people who desired to serve in the public interest."[52]

Married for more than 50 years, Hunt and his wife, Mauna, whom he met on a blind date while a student at BYU, are the parents of six children.[53] The Apostle Paul wisely taught, "Be not overcome of evil, but overcome evil with good."[54] It could be said that the Honorable Roger L. Hunt has followed that admonition and has done his part to help overcome evil with good while living in Sin City.

"Where prosecutorial misconduct violates federal constitutional rights, reversal is warranted unless the misconduct was harmless beyond a reasonable doubt. . . Hays has demonstrated with clear and convincing evidence that he is entitled to relief as a result of constitutional errors present in his criminal trial. . . He suffered convictions for a number of crimes which were never shown to have occurred. . . The court will grant the petition for writ of habeas corpus unconditionally. Hays will be granted his freedom." Roger Hunt, ordering the unconditional release and exoneration of Robert Hays after 14 years of wrongful imprisonment.[55]

---

[1] See Kurtis Lee, *Vegas' Newest Tourist Attraction, Customers Flock to Pot Dispensaries in the Party City as Nevada Starts Allowing Sales*, Los Angeles Times, Jul. 2, 2017, 8, 2017 WLNR 20241118.

[2] Paul Farhi, *Las Vegas Ads' Winning Streak*, Washington Post, Dec. 2, 2004, 2004 WLNR 24450740 (calling Las Vegas the "silicone-and-keno Sodom and Gomorrah of the 21st century"). See also Alma Chapter 14 in the Book of Mormon recounting wickedness in the city of Ammonihah.

[3] Pew Research Center, Religious Landscape Study, Adults in Nevada, http://www.pewforum.org/religious-landscape-study/state/nevada/ [https://perma.cc/A8VY-MK3H].

[4] National Park Service, The Old Mormon Fort: Birthplace of Las Vegas, Nevada, https://www.nps.gov/nr/twhp/wwwlps/lessons/122fort/ [https://perma.cc/4TBZ-CPJ4] (citing John Steele's diary reprinted in The Fortress, Vol. 1, No. 4 (Las Vegas, Nevada: Friends of the Fort, 2000)).

[5] Adam Bernstein, *Former Nevada Sen. Howard Cannon Dies,* Washington Post, Mar. 7, 2002, B06, 2002 WLNR 15328016.

[6] Roger L. Hunt, U.S. District Judge, District of Nevada, letter to the author, December 7, 2017 (hereinafter "Hunt (2017)").

[7] The Harry S. Truman Scholarship Foundation, Roger Hunt, https://truman.gov/roger-hunt [https://perma.cc/T245-5ZY7].

[8] Hunt (2017).

[9] *Ortolano v. Las Vegas Convention Serv.*, 96 Nev. 308, 608 P.2d 1103 (1980), overruled by *Harris v. Rio Hotel & Casino, Inc.*, 117 Nev. 482, 25 P.3d 206 (2001),

[10] 28 U.S.C. § 636.

[11] Hon. Lisa Margaret Smith, *Top 10 Things You Probably Never Knew About Magistrate Judges*, Federal Lawyer, 36, 38 (May–June 2014).

[12] See *In re Prop. Seized from Int'l Nutrition, Inc.*, No. CV-S-94-0304-LDG RLH, 1994 WL 16483469, at *1 (D. Nev. July 19, 1994).

[13] Michael H. Gottesman, *Admissibility of Expert Testimony After Daubert: The "Prestige" Factor*, 43 Emory L.J. 867 (1994), attorney for the plaintiffs in the Daubert case describing the correct pronunciation as "Dow-burt" rather than "Dough-bear." See also Michael Smith, *Pronouncing "Daubert": An Important Lesson You May Not Learn in Evidence Class*, Michael Smith's Law Blog, Aug. 25, 2014, https://smithblawg.blogspot.com/2014/08/pronouncing-daubert-important-lesson.html [https://perma.cc/FY2V-TX6Y].

[14] 972 F.Supp. at 1326.

[15] Hon. Dennis Cavanaugh, *Magistrate Judges Are Effective, Flexible Judiciary Resource*, 40 The Third Branch 10, at 1, 7, 9-11 (2008).

[16] 863 F.Supp. at 1241.

[17] 113 Stat. 1501.

[18] Nancy Mathis, *Clinton Attacks Confirmation Gap Senate Creating "Vacancy Crisis,"* Denver Post, Aug. 10, 1999, A04, 1999 WLNR 9228508.

[19] *Id.*

[20] Phone interview with Harry Reid, retired United States Senator, November 15, 2017.

21 *In the Spotlight,* Ensign, December 2000, https://www.lds.org/ensign/2000/12/portraits/in-the-spotlight?lang=eng [https://perma.cc/3JUM-89K7].

22 *People in the Church,* Deseret News, Aug. 5, 2000, https://www.deseretnews.com/article/805386/People-in-the-church.html [https://perma.cc/GLQ4-PCLG].

23 Hunt (2017).

24 247 F.Supp.2d at 1177.

25 *United States v. Nevada,* No. 2:00-CV-0268-RLHLRL, 2007 WL 2659984, (D. Nev. Aug. 31, 2007).

26 Hunt (2017).

27 *Hays v. Farwell,* 482 F.Supp.2d 1180 (D. Nev. 2007).

28 Black's Law Dictionary (10th ed. 2014), habeas corpus; Daniel Meltzer, *Habeas Corpus Jurisdiction: The Limits of Models,* 66 S Cal L. Rev. 2507, 2523-31 (1993).

29 The National Registry of Exonerations, Robert Hays, Aug. 2, 2015, https://www.law.umich.edu/special/exoneration/Pages/casedetail.aspx?caseid=4719 [https://perma.cc/F72N-BBSL].

30 482 F.Supp.2d at 1194.

31 *Id.* at 1201.

32 The National Registry of Exonerations.

33 Hunt (2017).

34 649 F.Supp.2d at 1202.

35 Carri Geer Thevenot, *$50,000 Settles Gibbons Lawsuit,* Las Vegas Review-Journal, Jul. 19, 2013, 2B, 2013 WLNR 17934367.

36 *Solomon v. Cutler,* No. 2:07-CV-645-RLH-PAL, 2010 WL 3909980 (D. Nev. Apr. 8, 2010), aff'd, *Solomon v. Spielberg,* 473 F. App'x 526 (9th Cir. 2012).

37 Mike Boehm, *Rockwell Exhibit, the Directors' Cut,* Los Angeles Times, Oct. 8, 2009, 15, 2009 WLNR 19816675.

38 *Solomon v. Cutler,* No. 2:07-CV-645-RLH-PAL, 2010 WL 3909980 (D. Nev. Apr. 8, 2010), aff'd *Solomon v. Spielberg,* 473 F. App'x 526 (9th Cir. 2012).

39 Boehm (2009).

40 Carri Geer Thevenot, *Former Navy SEAL Sentenced to Prison,* Las Vegas Review-Journal, Jul. 18, 2012, 1B, 2012 WLNR 15091506.

[41] *United States v. Bickle*, No. 2:10-CR-565-RLH-PAL, 2011 WL 5877486, at *3 (D. Nev. Nov. 22, 2011), aff'd, 566 F. App'x 589 (9th Cir. 2014).

[42] Phone interview with Adam C. Anderson, former law clerk to Judge Roger L. Hunt, November 22, 2017.

[43] Phone interview with Calder Huntington, former law clerk to Judge Roger L. Hunt, December 14, 2017.

[44] United States District Court, *supra* note 7.

[45] Las Vegas LDS Single Adult Conference 2017, Workshop Topics & Speaker Bios, Roger Hunt, http://www.vegassinglesconference.com/2017/workshop-topics-speaker-bios/ [https://perma.cc/FDA5-SBXY].

[46] Hunt (2017).

[47] Anderson (2017).

[48] Hunt (2017).

[49] *Id.*

[50] *Id.*

[51] The Harry S. Truman Scholarship Foundation.

[52] Hunt (2017).

[53] Las Vegas LDS Single Adult Conference 2017.

[54] Romans 12:21.

[55] *Hays*, 482 F.Supp.2d at 1201.

Chapter 9

Kent A. Jordan: Influential Judge Who Learned from a Great Mentor

Tutelage under Judge Latchum

Most successful lawyers and judges can point to one individual who served as an influential mentor during their legal training. Historically, aspiring lawyers studied the law on their own and trained under the tutelage of a mentor through an apprenticeship program. But the proliferation of law schools in the late nineteenth and early twentieth centuries, including the dominant Harvard method, began competing with the traditional law-office apprenticeship program. Even with the instruction provided in law schools, young lawyers can greatly benefit from mentors.[1] Kent A. Jordan, a federal appeals court judge on the U.S. Court for the Third Circuit, credits the strong influence of Judge James L. Latchum in his legal education and training. After earning his undergraduate degree from Brigham Young University and his law degree from Georgetown University, Jordan clerked for Judge Latchum on the U.S. District Court for the District of Delaware where he learned from one of the most respected federal judges.[2]

Jordan praised the attributes of the esteemed judge. "He was a great friend and a great mentor," said Jordan of Judge Latchum.[3] Jordan added, "The Judge's reputation was built upon his prodigious work ethic, the efficiency with which he ran his courtroom, his incisive mind and wit, the skill with which he managed the court as Chief Judge, the contribution he made to building the reputation of the District Court as a venue for resolving complex legal disputes, and his role as a remarkable mentor."[4]

Jordan said Judge Latchum taught him to administer justice impartially and to treat everyone equally. Latchum also instilled in Jordan an urgent sense of mission because of his constant question, "Got that done yet?" Jordan has kept Latchum's picture in his office ever since, perched where it could look over his shoulder and keep him on task. Jordan made a promise—to remember what it was like to be a prosecutor, to represent criminal defendants, to advocate for clients in private practice, and to be a member of an in-house legal team, all positions he held in a varied legal career.[5]

Jordan also praised Judge Latchum's role as a great teacher learning that "perhaps of most lasting importance, Judge Latchum was a teacher par excellence. He turned out well-crafted legal opinions, more than 700 in all, but he was also intent on turning out well-tutored law clerks. As one of those fortunate clerks, I can attest that learning at the Judge's elbow was an extraordinary and wonderful experience, and I've no doubt that each of my fellow Latchum alumni would say the same thing." Judge Latchum taught Jordan how to preside as a judge. Jordan learned that Judge Latchum "had no patience for arrogance, presumption or pretense. In the courtroom and in chambers he was not interested in oratory. He wanted mastery of the factual record and clear, logical thinking and expression, backed by basic fairness. The writing style he practiced and taught reflected his approach to life: do things with economy and precision."[6]

Becoming a Well-Respected Delaware Lawyer

Jordan's apprenticeship as a judicial law clerk for Judge Latchum prepared him for greater things to come in his legal career. After clerking for Judge Latchun, Jordan worked as an Assistant U.S. Attorney and then as a lawyer in private practice before becoming a judge. Jordan's extensive experience prepared him for the complex legal issues as a federal judge.

Jordan devoted his early career as a public servant working as an Assistant U.S. Attorney for the District of Delaware from 1987 to 1992, becoming Chief of the Office's Civil Division in 1991. He handled a variety of both criminal and civil matters.

His clients in civil cases consisted mainly of federal agencies with a broad array of legal disputes, from basic torts to complex federal regulatory and contractual problems. As a tough federal prosecutor, he went after those who violated federal criminal laws involving drug trafficking, environmental crime, extortion, tax violations, and fraud. He worked on some highly publicized cases, bringing criminals to justice, and also administering justice with an even hand.[7]

In one civil case involving an outrageous claim brought by a former employee of the U.S. Postal Service under the Federal Tort Claims Act, Jordan represented the United States government as Assistant U.S. Attorney. In *Ward v. United States*, 738 F. Supp. 129 (D. Del. 1990), a former postal employee claimed psychological and physical injuries caused by the allegedly "willful and outrageous" conduct of his employer, the U.S. Postal Service. The former postal employee, John A. Ward, claimed that his injuries stemmed from an interview with a postal inspector, C. Smith, who interviewed Ward during an internal investigation. The inspector told the postal worker that he had investigated the employee's claim for disability and found that the employee engaged in activities inconsistent with his claimed medical disability. The former postal employee claimed that the investigator accused him of defrauding the government and that Smith told him to sign a "confession." The interview lasted no more than five minutes and concluded without Ward making a statement or signing the "confession." In rejecting the claim brought the former letter carrier, the U.S. District Court held that "Postal Inspectors are granted broad discretion in the manner in which they investigate claims and implement public policy."[8] Jordan successfully represented the government in the frivolous claim brought by the former postal employee saving taxpayers thousands of dollars in the process.

In 1992, Jordan left the U.S. Attorney's Office and joined the Wilmington, Delaware firm of Morris James Hitchens & Williams as an associate and shortly later became a partner in 1994. His practice for one of the top law firms in Delaware focused on patent and related disputes in the U.S. District Court for the District of Delaware. From 1997 until 2002, Jordan was General Counsel and Vice President of Corporation Service Company (CSC), where he managed all of the corporation's legal affairs. CSC, in existence for more than 100 years, is known nationally as one of the leading incorporation service companies in the world.[9]

Donning a Robe to Serve on the Bench

Jordan then answered the call again to public service. In 2002, President George W. Bush nominated Jordan to the U.S. District Court for the District of Delaware to the same court occupied by his mentor, Judge Latchum. After his exemplary service for four years as a U.S. District Judge, President George W. Bush appointed Jordan to the U.S. Court of Appeals for the Third Circuit in 2006. In support of the nomination, Senator Joseph Biden praised the qualifications of Jordan in being elevated from the U.S. District Court to the Third Circuit: "During his . . . legal career, Judge Jordan has excelled at every step of the way. . . His colleagues describe him in many ways, but the adjectives that always come up are 'bright', 'hardworking', 'deep sense of integrity', 'intellectual honesty'. I do not know what else you could ask for a Judge. I must tell you, I have become convinced he is open-minded, collegial, and most of all, fair."[10]

Michael Castle, a member of the U.S. House of Representatives representing Delaware, endorsed Jordan to serve on the Third Circuit:

> Delaware, of course, is a small State, but for those who know anything about the law, it is a State which has a very highly-developed legal community and judicial community because of the incorporation statutes, and other reasons why Delaware is a central place for people to come. As a matter of fact, the Chamber of Commerce ranked Delaware's Judges the highest in all five categories they looked at across the entire United States of America. Kent Jordan came to the Delaware District Court and has just done a wonderful job there. I followed this carefully because I was involved in the initial selection process when he was nominated. I can tell you, as

one who practiced law in front of a lot of these Judges, very few do it as well as Kent has done it. He runs on time. He makes his decisions in a precise way. He has reduced the workload of that court for the other Judges. He has just done a great job—even a sensational job—on our District Court, so we are pleased that he has been nominated for the Third Circuit Court of Appeals. He did receive the unanimous vote of the Senate when he went before you for the District Court, and we hope it can be the same, and obviously swiftly, if possible, for the Third Circuit Court of Appeals. He, as Senator Biden has already indicated, was one of the top prosecutors and litigators in Delaware, and even has some corporation background, which is helpful as well. . . In my judgment, we have picked one of the best Judges you could find in the United States of America. So, we are looking forward to supporting Kent in every way we can. . . When you are in a small State like ours, Senator, you hear a lot about people. You usually get to have a pretty good idea of who they are. I have never heard a disparaging or discouraging word about Kent and the wonderful job he is doing in our District Court. So, I recommend him heartily to all of you here in the United States Senate.[11]

Jordan received other praise in support of his nomination to the Third Circuit. Senator Thomas R. Carper from Delaware also strongly supported Jordan. Carper said, "There was a litmus test of sorts that I used in nominating people. I always looked for people who were bright, I looked for people who knew the law. I looked for folks who had good judicial temperament, who treated people in the courtroom on either side with equal respect and made them feel welcome and listened to. I looked for people who had good judgment, not only who had good judgment, but were also able to make a decision. You do not always find that in everybody who serves as a Judge." Carper continued his reasons in supporting Jordan, "You never wanted to nominate anybody to the bench who was going to get on the bench and, frankly, not work very hard.

Kent Jordan meets that litmus test to a 'T.' I am proud that we were able to support his nomination four years ago. I think it speaks volumes that the entire delegation is here on his behalf, voicing our support of him and our approval."[12] After receiving unanimous approval from the Senate to serve as a U.S. District Judge, the Senate unanimously confirmed Jordan's elevation to the Third Circuit.

Deciding Key Cases for the Third Circuit

As a federal appeals court judge, Judge Jordan focuses on how each case before him impacts the parties in that particular case. "It is hard to know what the world might think is important. But for the parties themselves, their case is always number one," said Jordan.[13] Jordan has faced many varied cases sitting on the Third Circuit, which has appellate court jurisdiction over cases appealed from U.S. District Courts in Delaware, New Jersey, Pennsylvania, and the U.S. Virgin Islands.[14] Cases are usually heard by a three-judge panel. Each circuit has its own Court of Appeals that reviews cases decided in U.S. District Courts within the circuit. The U.S. Supreme Court receives approximately 7,000 to 8,000 petitions for a writ of certiorari each term, but the high court grants and hears oral argument in only about 80 cases.[15] Therefore, decisions from the U.S. Court of Appeals are the often the last word in thousands of cases.

At times, Jordan has voiced strong dissenting opinions from his colleagues on the Third Circuit. Jordan's dissenting opinion in *Conestoga Wood Specialties Corp. v. Sec'y of U.S. Dep't of Health & Human Servs.*, 724 F.3d 377 (3rd Cir. 2013), which the U.S. Supreme Court reversed in *Burwell v. Hobby Lobby Stores, Inc.*, 134 S. Ct. 2751 (2014), stands out among his opinions. When the U.S. Supreme Court took up the issue whether requiring group health plans and health insurance issuers to provide coverage for contraceptives violated the Free Exercise Clause of the First Amendment of the U.S. Constitution, the U.S. Supreme Court consolidated the *Conestoga Wood* case from the Third Circuit and the *Hobby Lobby* case from the Tenth Circuit. In the *Conestoga Wood* case, the plaintiffs, who practiced the Mennonite religion, challenged the requirement under the Affordable Care Act based on religious objections. Ultimately, the U.S. Supreme Court decided that the provision in the Affordable Care Act requiring certain employers to provide coverage for contraceptives violated the freedom exercise of religion, agreeing with Jordan's rationale.[16]

In another important case, U.S. Supreme Court validated Judge Jordan's reasoning where Jordan offered a dissenting opinion from his colleagues. Jordan issued a dissenting opinion in *Behrend v. Comcast Corp.*, 655 F.3d 182 (3rd Cir. 2011) that the U.S. Supreme Court later reversed in *Comcast Corp. v. Behrend*, 133 S. Ct. 1426 (2013). "I wrote a dissent in a case in *Comcast* [655 F.3d 182] . . . that had an impact on class-actions and the way in which expert opinions are considered in class actions. That was kind of significant when the Supreme Court opines on something," said Jordan reflecting on the case.[17] In *Comcast Corp. v. Behrend*, the U.S. Supreme Court held that the class action brought by subscribers to the cable television services provided by Comcast was improperly certified under Federal Rule of Civil Procedure 23(b)(3), which requires a court to find that the "questions of law or fact common to class members predominate over any questions affecting only individual members." The U.S. Supreme Court agreed with Jordan's dissent and held that the Third Circuit erred in refusing to decide whether the class's proposed damages model could show damages on a class-wide basis.

Jordan decides cases with far-reaching implications, but still focuses on the individual parties in each case. In *Santiago v. Warminster Township*, 629 F.3d 121 (3rd Cir. 2010), the Third Circuit decided a leading case involving the civil liability of municipalities for alleged excessive force conducted by the police. Gloria Santiago, a 60-year-old grandmother, brought an action under 42 U.S.C. § 1983 against a township and three of its senior police officers, including the police chief, alleging that she suffered a heart attack after being subjected to excessive force during a raid on her home. The woman sat with her hands tied for approximately 30 minutes as the police searched her home. Throughout that time, she was unable to interfere, was not a flight risk, and presented no danger. She continued to complain of pain and eventually told her grandson that she felt pain in her heart. The grandson told the officers that his grandmother was having a heart attack, and an ambulance was summoned to take her to the hospital.[18]

In writing the opinion of the court in *Santiago*, Jordan applied the law set forth by the U.S. Supreme Court in *Ashcroft v. Iqbal*, 556 U.S. 662 (2009) which directs that the court may disregard any legal conclusions and disregard "naked assertions devoid of further factual enhancement" in the plaintiff's complaint. The Third Circuit held that the grandmother's allegations are "naked assertion[s]" that the police chief directed that the police conduct the operation in the allegedly excessive manner.[19] As mere restatements of the elements of supervisory liability claims, they are not entitled to the assumption of truth. Therefore, the Third Circuit concluded that the district court properly dismissed the complaint against the township and the police. The *Santiago v. Warminster Township* case established an important precedent for supervisory liability that thousands of courts have since cited and applied.[20]

Jordan's experience as a former federal prosecutor and district judge prepared him for deciding difficult criminal cases as a federal appeals court judge. In *United States v. Tomko*, 562 F.3d 558 (3rd Cir. 2009), a contractor pleaded guilty to income tax evasion, and received a sentence of home confinement, probation, a fine of $250,000, and community service. The government appealed the sentence imposed by the district judge. William Tomko, the owner of a plumbing contracting business, directed numerous subcontractors, who were building his multimillion dollar home, to falsify information on billing invoices so that the invoices would show work being done at one of the company's job sites instead of at Tomko's home. The tax evasion scheme resulted in a tax deficiency of $228,557. Tomko proposed that in light of the then-recent Hurricane Katrina catastrophe and his construction expertise, the court should sentence him to probation and home detention, and require him to work for Habitat for Humanity. The Executive Director for Habitat for Humanity's Pittsburgh affiliate testified that the organization would appreciate Tomko's help in its efforts to rebuild the Gulf Coast and that Tomko had performed well in past projects, including providing onsite assistance and advice. If he were imprisoned, the company could lose its line of credit and the jobs of its 300–plus employees would be threatened.

Jordan joined the majority opinion of the court recognizing that although they might have applied the sentencing factors differently had they been the sentencing court judge, this disagreement does not, by itself, demand reversal. In affirming the sentence on appeal, the Third Circuit recognized Tomko's charitable acts and that the district court's reliance on these facts was both logical and consistent with the factors set forth in the federal sentencing statute.[21]

Serving in Street Clothes

Jordan has received numerous awards and accolades for his public service. He received the Philadelphia Intellectual Property Law Association Achievement Award in 2015, the Richard E. Kohler Civility and Ethics Award presented by the H.B. Cohen American Inn of Court in 2014, the Giles S. Rich American Inn of Court Meritorious Achievement Award in 2012, the University of Pennsylvania Law School Adjunct Teaching Award for the 2010-2011 academic year, and the Distinguished Lecturer Award presented by the Corporate Counsel Technology Institute at Widener University in 2007. Jordan also serves as a member of the Board of Directors of the Ministry of Caring, a non-profit, ecumenical organization which provides service for the low-income and homeless population, and as a member of the Board of Directors of the Sacred Heart Village, a non-profit organization providing affordable housing for senior citizens for the Wilmington, Delaware area.[22]

Along with his devoted public service as a judge and civic engagement, Jordan has fulfilled various callings and assignments in the Church, including serving as a full-time missionary in Japan and teaching early morning seminary.[23] Church leaders called Jordan, married and a father to six children, as President of the Wilmington Delaware Stake on May 31, 2015 succeeding W. Wynn John as stake president with Bruce R. Winn and Sheldon Rush Sumpter serving as counselors.[24] A stake president is the Church officer selected by the General Authority assigned by the Quorum of Twelve Apostles who presides over several wards or congregations. The stake president also presides over certain council meetings in which the spiritual welfare of church members is the focus, such as meetings to address the needs of the poor or to prepare for emergencies.[25]

Jordan, who has also taught law students as an adjunct professor at the University of Pennsylvania and Vanderbilt University, focuses on the importance of being humble in the legal profession.[26] As the keynote speaker at the BYU Law School convocation held in 2016, Jordan told graduates the importance of humility and gratitude, "A humble mind is an open mind, and an open mind is key to doing justice and preserving freedom. Humility can open our eyes not only to mistakes but also to possibilities we would otherwise probably not consider." Judge Jordan counseled that "[g]ratitude doesn't just help us enjoy what is good in our lives; it actually opens our eyes so that we can see the good things in the first place."[27]

"To recognize that religious convictions are a matter of individual experience cannot and does not refute the collective character of much religious belief and observance. Religious opinions and faith are . . . akin to political opinions and passions, which are held and exercised both individually and collectively." Kent A. Jordan, on the freedom of religion, in his dissenting opinion in *Conestoga Wood Specialties Corp. v. Sec'y of U.S. Dep't of Health & Human Servs.*, 724 F.3d 377, 390 (3rd Cir. 2013), which the U.S. Supreme Court reversed in *Burwell v. Hobby Lobby Stores, Inc.*, 134 S. Ct. 2751 (2014).

---

[1] James E. Moliterno, *An Analysis of Ethics Teaching in Law Schools: Replacing Lost Benefits of the Apprentice System in the Academic Atmosphere*, 60 U. Cin. L. Rev. 83 (1991).
[2] George W. Bush White House Archive, Judicial Nominees, Judge Kent A. Jordan, U.S. Court of Appeals for the Third Circuit, https://georgewbush-

whitehouse.archives.gov/infocus/judicialnominees/jordan.html
[https://perma.cc/4NCE-VVDG].

[3] Phone interview with Kent A. Jordan, Judge, U.S. Court of Appeals for the Third Circuit, Apr. 24, 2017 (hereinafter "Jordan (2017)").

[4] Kent A. Jordan, *Judge James L. Latchum: Practical Wisdom, Practical Jokes and a Practically Perfect Mentor*, 27 Del. Law. 32, 33 (2009).

[5] Celia Cohen, *A New Judge Jump-Starts the New Year*, Delaware Grapevine, Jan. 3, 2003, http://www.delawaregrapevine.com/jan-mar03stories/1-03%20jordan.htm [https://perma.cc/DZ7A-PZ47].

[6] Jordan, 27 Del. Law at 36.

[7] Hearing before the Committee on the Judiciary, S Hrg No. 109-397, 109th Cong, 2d Sess, 1 (2006) (statement of Sen. Joseph Biden).

[8] 738 F. Supp. at 133.

[9] Hearing before the Committee on the Judiciary, S Hrg No. 109-397, 109th Cong, 2d Sess, 1 (2006) (statement of Sen. Joseph Biden).

[10] Ibid.

[11] Hearing before the Committee on the Judiciary, S Hrg No. 109-397, 109th Cong, 2d Sess, 1 (2006) (statement of Rep. Michael Castle).

[12] Hearing before the Committee on the Judiciary, S Hrg No. 109-397, 109th Cong, 2d Sess, 1 (2006) (statement of Sen. Thomas R. Carper).

[13] Jordan (2017).

[14] 28 U.S.C. § 41.

[15] Justin Fielkow, Daniel Werly, Andrew Sensi, *Tackling Paspa: The Past, Present, and Future of Sports Gambling in America*, 66 DePaul L. Rev. 23, 49 (2016).

[16] 134 S.Ct. 2751.

[17] Jordan (2017).

[18] 629 F.3d at 126.

[19] *Id.*

[20] See KeyCite citing references on Westlaw.

[21] 562 F.3d at 558.

[22] Judge Kent A. Jordan, Curriculum Vitae, March 2016, Vanderbilt University Law School,

https://law.vanderbilt.edu/bio/kent-jordan [https://perma.cc/P9F8-WC6T].

23 Jordan (2017).

24 *New Stakes and Stake Leaders Announced during July 2015*, Church News, The Church of Jesus Christ of Latter-day Saints, Jul. 31, 2015, https://www.lds.org/church/news/new-stakes-and-stake-leaders-announced-during-july-2015?lang=eng [https://perma.cc/PN38-HZYY].

25 Don M. Pearson, *Encyclopedia of Mormonism* (New York, NY: Macmillan, 1992), 1415–1416.

26 Jordan (2017).

27 Kent A. Jordan, Graduation Speaker, BYU Law School, Apr. 22, 2016, http://www.law2.byu.edu/news2/-graduation-speaker [https://perma.cc/9Z43-PRNG].

Chapter 10

Mike Lee: Constitutional Lawyer Trained from an Early Age

Love for the Constitution Early in Life

Mike Lee learned from an early age constitutional values and principles from his father, Rex E. Lee, who served as U.S. Solicitor General under President Ronald Reagan. Mike Lee noted, "I didn't realize until I was thirty [years old] that not every family will discuss the Presentment Clause over the dinner table."[1] The Presentment Clause found in Article I of the U.S. Constitution, which requires the President to approve acts of Congress, states "Every Bill which shall have passed the House of Representatives and the Senate, shall, before it become a Law, be presented to the President of the United States."[2]

As a boy growing up in the Washington, D.C. area, Mike Lee watched his father argue many cases before the U.S. Supreme Court. While many young men spend their time playing sports or engaging in other activities, Lee watched and studied from one of the greatest lawyers to ever appear before the U.S. Supreme Court. Proverbs 22:6 reads, "Train up a child in the way he should go: and when he is old, he will not depart from it." Mike Lee's life and love for the Constitution reflects this passage from Proverbs. Perhaps Rex Lee's greatest legacy lies not in the landmark cases he argued before the U.S. Supreme Court, but rather with his family which includes Mike Lee, a U.S. Senator, and Thomas Lee, a Utah Supreme Court Justice.

Michael S. Lee, better known as "Mike Lee" when he ran for office, was elected to the U.S. Senate representing the State of Utah in 2010 amid the Tea Party movement. At age 39, Lee became the youngest Senator on the Hill when Utah voters sent him to Washington.[3] Before serving in the Senate, commonly referred to as the "world's greatest deliberative body,"[4] Lee had a distinguished career as a lawyer in both private practice and working for the government. Lee beat out three-term incumbent Senator Robert Bennett and businessman Tim Bridgewater in winning the Republican Party nomination in 2010. As a conservative, Lee called for more limited government. "We're ready to end the era thinking that the federal government can be all things to all people, that it can solve all the world's problems. It can't, it doesn't. It never will," Lee told *Politico* in an interview, "There is a groundswell grassroots movement afoot that's going to propel me to victory."[5]

Working in Private Practice for Sidley Austin

Lee, the subject of some speculation as a possible U.S. Supreme Court nominee in 2017,[6] received both his undergraduate degree and his law degree from Brigham Young University (BYU). At BYU, Mike Lee was the student body president while his father served as the university president. After law school, Lee worked as a law clerk for Judge Dee Benson of the U.S. District Court for the District of Utah and later for Judge Samuel Alito on the U.S. Court of Appeals for the Third Circuit Court. Alito previously worked with Mike Lee's father, Rex Lee, in the Office of the U.S. Solicitor General in the Reagan Administration. Mike Lee then worked in private practice in Washington, D.C. for the law firm Sidley Austin where he specialized in appellate litigation.[7]

"At Sidley Austin, I helped establish the religious practices group and we were involved in the religion practice at the time. I really enjoyed that," said Lee.[8] "I worked with some of the best lawyers in the country while I was at Sidley—men and women who truly understand how our government works. And that has helped in every job I have had since then, including here in the Senate," recalled Lee.[9]

At Sidley Austin, Mike Lee followed in his father's footsteps focusing on appellate advocacy. Mike Lee's father, Rex Lee, also focused on appellate litigation as a partner at Sidley Austin. In *Suzuki Motor Corp. v. Consumers Union of U.S., Inc.*, 330 F.3d 1110 (9th Cir. 2003), Lee represented the automobile manufacturer Suzuki Motor in a defamation case brought against the consumer group Consumers Union. In 1988, Consumers Union published an article in its magazine *Consumer Reports*, in which it rated the compact sport utility vehicle Suzuki Samurai "Not Acceptable" based on its propensity to roll over during accident avoidance tests. The article concluded that "The Suzuki rolls over too easily," starting with an incident during the vehicle's break-in period where the Samurai "flopped over on its side" during a low-speed maneuver. The Samurai did well on the standard course and then Consumers Union modified the course to make it more challenging and, as a result, the Samurai did far worse than its competitors. The automaker sought $60 million in compensation and unspecified punitive damages. The federal district court dismissed the case, but the U.S. Court of Appeals for the Ninth Circuit ruled in 2002 that a jury should hear the case. After an eight-year legal battle, Consumers Union and Suzuki Motor settled the lawsuit with no money changing hands. Rather, the settlement included a "clarification" by Consumers Union that the article about the Suzuki Samurai may have been "misconstrued or misunderstood."[10]

Mike Lee has strong family connections in the law. Besides learning from his father, Mike Lee has forged a close relationship with his older brother, Thomas, a Utah Supreme Court Justice. "My brother and I are very close. We talk all the time. Of course, we talk about the Constitution and politics all of the time," said Mike Lee. "My brother and I have even handled cases together."[11]

The Lee brothers worked together in the litigation brought by the State of Utah challenging the results of 2000 Census. After the Census Bureau tallied the numbers from the decennial census as required by the U.S. Constitution, Utah barely missed gaining a fourth seat in the U.S. House of Representatives. Utah then filed lawsuits challenging the counting methods from the 2000 Census. The State of Utah first argued that the decision by the Census Bureau to include federal employees living abroad but not enumerating Church missionaries living abroad, violated various constitutional and statutory provisions. Among those not enumerated were approximately 11,000 missionaries for Church who were overseas from the State of Utah on 18-month or 24-four-month proselytizing or service missions for their church on Census Day 2000 (April 1, 2000). As a result of the apportionment count calculated on the basis of the Census 2000, the State of North Carolina, not the State of Utah, was awarded the 435th seat in the House of Representatives.

In *Utah v. Evans*, 143 F. Supp. 2d 1290 (D. Utah 2001), the court held that the exclusion of missionaries did not mandate that federal government employees living abroad not be counted as residents of their home states. The court held that "[i]nclusion of federal employees, unlike the inclusion of various other groups of private American citizens abroad, does not invite the kind of manipulation by states or the injection of local or parochial bias which the founders wished to avoid."[12] The district court relied on the language in the U.S. Supreme Court case *Franklin v. Massachusetts*, 505 U.S. 788, 806 (1992) that the "constitutional goal" underlying the Apportionment Clause is "equal representation." The district court gave the Census Bureau broad discretion in apportionment decisions with that goal in mind.

After losing the argument about the counting of Church missionaries living overseas, Utah took the 2000 Census case to the U.S. Supreme Court on other grounds. In *Utah v. Evans*, 536 U.S. 452 (2002), Thomas "Tom" Lee, Mike's older brother, argued the case before the U.S. Supreme Court. The Court rejected the argument contended by Utah and held that the Census Bureau's use of a statistical method known as "hot-deck imputation" did not constitute sampling and did not violate the constitutional requirement found in Article I, section 2, clause 3 of the U.S. Constitution that an "actual Enumeration" be made of the population. The State of Utah ultimately lost the case and failed to gain a fourth seat from the 2000 Census. Utah later gained a fourth seat after reapportionment from the 2010 Census.

Representing the People as a Tough Federal Prosecutor

After working at Sidley Austin, Mike Lee moved back to Utah where he worked as an Assistant U.S. Attorney in Salt Lake City and later acted as Utah Governor Jon Huntsman's General Counsel. As a federal prosecutor, Lee prosecuted individuals for violations of various federal crimes, including bank robbery. In *United States v. Cooper*, 375 F.3d 1041 (10th Cir. 2004), Lee represented the U.S. government in an appeal brought by Todd Harold Cooper who was convicted of bank robbery in violation of 18 U.S.C. § 2113 and using a firearm while committing a crime of violence in violation of 18 U.S.C. § 924. Ironically, Cooper wore a Ronald Reagan mask during the armed robbery at the First Security Bank in South Ogden, Utah. Cooper did not know that the son of the U.S. Solicitor General for President Reagan would later represent the government in the case against him. Cooper argued that the bank was not insured by Federal Deposit Insurance Corporation (FDIC) at the time of the robbery. The Tenth Circuit held that testimony from a bank employee that deposits are insured by FDIC was sufficient evidence from which the jury could conclude that the bank was insured at the time of the robbery. The Tenth Circuit in *Cooper* denied the appeal and agreed with Lee's compelling argument before the court upholding the conviction.[13]

When Mike Lee was just 13 years old, his father successfully argued an important case representing the position of the federal government before the U.S. Supreme Court in *United States v. Leon*, 468 U.S. 897 (1984). In *United States v. Leon*, the high court recognized the good faith exception to the warrant requirement under the Fourth Amendment. "Years later I would rely on [*United States v. Leon*] as a federal prosecutor," said Lee.[14]

As a federal prosecutor, Lee handled many appeals in criminal cases involving application of constitutional principles. In *United States v. Ramirez*, 86 F. App'x 384, 385 (10th Cir. 2004), Lee represented the government in a case where a criminal defendant argued that evidence of methamphetamine obtained during a traffic stop violated both the Fourth Amendment prohibition against unreasonable searches and the Full Faith and Credit Clause. The Full Faith and Credit Clause provides that "Full Faith and Credit shall be given in each State to the public acts, Records, and judicial Proceedings of every other State."[15] The defendant was driving a van registered in Colorado through Utah when the van was stopped by a Utah Highway Patrol sergeant. The officer stopped the van after noticing the van front side windows had an excessive tint, in violation of the Utah statute. The Utah statute does not provide an exception for vehicles registered in other states. The van window tinting did not violate Colorado's less restrictive law. The U.S. Court of Appeals for the Tenth Circuit agreed with Lee's argument that the officer's observation of the defendant's vehicle provided him with reasonable suspicion to believe that the vehicle's windows had an excessive tint, in violation of Utah law, justifying stop of the vehicle. The Tenth Circuit also held that Utah was not required by the Full Faith and Credit Clause to apply the window tinting statute of Colorado in lieu of its own statute.[16]

During the confirmation hearing for Neil Gorsuch as a U.S. Supreme Court Justice in 2017 before the Senate, Lee recalled his experience appearing before Judge Gorsuch when Gorsuch served on the U.S. Court of Appeals for the Tenth Circuit. Lee told Gorsush, "In a former life, when I was a practicing attorney, I had the good fortune of appearing before you. So, I know from personal experience that you are one of the very best judges in the country. You come to oral argument prepared and you ask probing, fair questions that help you understand the arguments."[17]

Clerking for Justice Alito on the U.S. Supreme Court

Lee reunited with Alito and clerked for Justice Alito on the U.S. Supreme Court during the 2006–2007 Term after Alito's elevation to the nation's top court. During Lee's time as a law clerk for the U.S. Supreme Court, Alito decided several key cases interpreting the First Amendment. In *Morse v. Frederick*, 551 U.S. 393 (2007), the U.S. Supreme Court held that a high school principal at an off-campus, school-approved, activity did not violate the student's right to free speech by confiscating from him a banner bearing the phrase "BONG HiTS 4 JESUS" and suspending the young man. Justice Alito joined the majority opinion in the split 6-3 decision where the court held that the principal reasonably viewed the banner as promoting illegal drug use. Justice Alito also wrote the majority opinion in a key case involving the Establishment Clause under the First Amendment in *Hein v. Freedom From Religion Found.*, Inc., 551 U.S. 587 (2007). In *Hein*, the U.S. Supreme Court held in a split 5-4 decision that taxpayers lacked standing to challenge federal money spent on the President's faith-based initiatives as a violation of the Establishment Clause.

Moving Back to the Beehive State and Representing Utahns

After his clerkship on the U.S. Supreme Court, Lee moved back to Utah working for the law firm Howrey LLP focusing on appellate litigation. Mike Lee joined forces with his brother again in the case *Wilderness Society v. Kane County,* 632 F.3d 1162 (10th Cir. 2011) involving the use of federal lands in Utah. Mike Lee filed a brief on behalf of the Utah Association of Counties opposing the action brought by environmentalists. The U.S. Court of Appeals for the Tenth Circuit held that The Wilderness Society, a nonprofit environmental group, lacked standing to sue the county for infringing on the federal government's property rights. The county asserted a right of way over the Grand Staircase Escalante National Monument that opened up the land to off-road vehicles. The Tenth Circuit concluded that The Wilderness Society "has taken sides in what is essentially a property dispute between two landowners . . . [but] . . . lacks any independent property rights of its own."[18] Judge Gorsuch, who later became a U.S. Supreme Court Justice, filed a concurring opinion arguing that "[m]ost of [the] suit is long dead, gone, moot. What very little is left isn't redressable under the Supremacy Clause. That alone is enough to end this case."[19]

Partners at Howrey LLP, the Washington, D.C.-based law firm, dissolved in March 2011, soon after Lee's election to the Senate when Lee took the oath of office in January 2011.[20] At its peak, in 2008, Howrey had 16 offices and 743 lawyers, 304 of them in Washington, according to the legal trade publication National Law Journal. The firm was known for its litigation, antitrust, and intellectual property practices.[21] According to observers, Howrey simply expanded too much and too fast with overhead expenses growing faster than revenue. The firm opened offices in London, Paris, Madrid and Southern California that were never profitable. The firm also relied on litigation revenue which does not result in a steady flow of work from corporate clients.[22]

In the Senate, Lee's first bill was a proposed constitutional amendment to require Congress to balance the federal budget every year.[23] While the proposal failed to pass the Senate Judiciary Committee, the symbolic measure garnered the attention of Lee's Republican colleagues in the Senate receiving 19 co-sponsors.

As a Senator, Lee has also called for a repeal of the Seventeenth Amendment, ratified in 1913, which provides for the direct election of U.S. Senators. For the first 100-plus years of American history, state legislatures selected Senators with the rationale to buffer the Senate from the masses and bring an extra level of prestige and dignity to the office.[24] Delaware and Utah were the only states that affirmatively voted against ratification of the amendment.[25] The popular press, the party platforms, and the state legislative debates during ratification focused almost exclusively on expanding democracy, eliminating political corruption, defeating elitism, and freeing the states from what they had come to regard as an onerous and difficult responsibility. Almost no one paused to weigh the consequences of the amendment on federalism.[26] Interestingly, another early lawyer from Utah, Preston D. Richards, played a key role in the adoption of the Seventeenth Amendment.[27] This reflects the notion that even among lawyers of the same faith, reasonable minds can differ on fundamental constitutional questions.

Mike Lee adopts an originalist interpretation of the U.S. Constitution. While on the campaign trail, Senator Lee promised, "I will not vote for a single bill that I can't justify based on the . . . original understanding of the Constitution, no matter what the Court says you can do." Originalism is characterized by a commitment to two core principles. First, the meaning of the constitutional text is fixed at the time of its ratification. Second, the historical meaning of the text has legal significance and is authoritative in most circumstances.[28]

Since being elected to the Senate, Lee has also become a popular author, especially among conservative readers. Lee authored *Written Out of History: The Forgotten Founders Who Fought Big Government* where he tells the story of liberty's forgotten heroes such as Mercy Otis Warren and James Otis. Many judges and scholars believe that the 1761 Boston writs-of assistance case, argued by the great Boston lawyer James Otis, led to the passage of the Fourth Amendment.[29] *Written Out of History* became popular among readers and appeared on the *New York Times* hardcover nonfiction best-sellers list in 2017.[30] *Written Out of History* also received strong acclaim from reviewers, including Lee's colleagues in the Senate. Senator Ted Cruz, whom Lee backed in the 2016 presidential election, provided the following review of *Written Out of History*: "These stories have been forgotten or 'buried' by those who would like us to forget the founders' strong suspicion of centralized, unrestrained government. Any American who reads this book will find it difficult to put down, and will emerge from the experience not only inspired, but also better equipped to support, protect, and defend the Constitution." Senator Marco Rubio from Florida offered similar praise: "Power-hungry politicians and biased historians have deliberately neglected these captivating stories from America's founding era, stories that once restored to our national consciousness could help usher in a new era of American exceptionalism."[31]

Lee also authored *Our Lost Constitution: The Willful Subversion of America's Founding Document* where he argues for a return to the Constitution's original meaning. Lee previously wrote *The Freedom Agenda: Why a Balanced Budget Amendment is Necessary to Restore Constitutional Government* arguing that a balanced budget amendment is the only way to force fiscal responsibility and *Why John Roberts Was Wrong About Healthcare: A Conservative Critique of The Supreme Court's Obamacare Ruling*. Lee's books reflect his heart-felt passion for defending the Constitution and recognizing the influence of the early Founders.

Lee, a lifelong member of The Church of Jesus Christ of Latter-day Saints, served a two-year mission for the Church in the Texas Rio Grande Valley where he also learned Spanish.[32] Lee sees the value that church members can make in their communities as they defend constitutional values. "In a sense, they can do as much as anyone can. As they work hard to represent their clients and do so professionally and collegially, the more they will enhance the practice of law and strengthen our legal system." Lee added, "I also think it is important . . . given our history. As a matter of official doctrine, the Constitution was written by wise men. In light of that doctrinal belief, LDS members should do everything they can and to learn everything they can about the Constitution to strengthen it, defend it, and protect it."[33]

"The judiciary is set apart from—and, in a way, set above—the other branches of our republic because we allow it to invalidate actions of the elected branches. Our confidence in the American judiciary depends entirely on . . . judges who are independent and whose only agenda is getting the law right." Mike Lee, on the need for an independent judiciary, during the confirmation hearing for U.S. Supreme Court Justice Neil Gorsuch.[34]

---

[1] Phone interview with Mike Lee, United States Senator, April 25, 2017 (hereinafter "Lee (2017)").

[2] U.S. Const. Art. I, § 7, cl. 2.

[3] Philip Rucker, *Letting His Grass Roots Show in Hopes of Growing on the Hill*, Washington Post, Feb. 4, 2011, 2011 WLNR 2504922.

[4] J. Morgan Kousser, *The Strange, Ironic Career of Section 5 of the Voting Rights Act, 1965-2007*, 86 Tex. L. Rev. 667, 670, n. 4 (2008) (describing the origin of the phrase "world's greatest deliberative body").

[5] David Catanese, *Sen. Bennett Loses GOP Nomination*, Politico, May 8, 2010, http://www.politico.com/story/2010/05/sen-bennett-loses-gop-nomination-036960 [https://perma.cc/2JPZ-7SSM].

[6] Boyd Matheson, *The Case for Sen. Mike Lee as a Supreme Court Justice*, Deseret News, Jan. 27, 2017, 2017 WLNR 2592458.

[7] Mike Lee, US Senator for Utah, About Mike, https://www.lee.senate.gov/public/index.cfm/about-mike [https://perma.cc/A3XY-AZKH].

[8] Lee, *supra* note 1.

[9] Sidley Austin LLP, A conversation with Alumnus Mike Lee, United States Senator from Utah, October 2016, https://www.sidley.com/en/sidley-pages/conversations/a-conversation-with-mike-lee.

[10] Earle Eldridge, *Consumers Union, Suzuki Settle Suit Over Tipping Claim Automaker Gets Clarification, Not Cash, USA Today*, Jul. 9, 2004, 2004 WLNR 6668394.

[11] Lee (2017).

[12] 143 F.Supp.2d at 1301.

[13] *United States v. Cooper,* 375 F.3d at 1047.

[14] Lee (2017).

[15] U.S. Const. art. IV, § 1.

[16] 86 F. App'x at 386.

[17] U.S. Senate Judiciary Committee Hearing on Justice Neil Gorsuch's Nomination to the Supreme Court, Statement of Sen. Lee, Mar. 20, 2017, 2017 WLNR 8751432.

[18] 632 F.3d at 1171.

[19] *Id.* at 1180.

[20] Eli Segall, *Howrey Votes to Dissolve Law Firm*, Houston Business Journal, Mar. 14, 2011, 2011 WLNR 5028400.

[21] Case Sullivan, *Howrey Trustee in $4.2 Million Settlement with Former Partners, Reuters Legal*, May 6, 2014.

[22] Seven Pearlstein, *Why Howrey Law Firm Could Not Hold It Together*, Washington Post, Mar. 19, 2011, 2011 WLNR 5458078.

[23] S.J.Res. 5, 112th Congress (2011–2012).

[24] Lillian Cunningham, *Episode 6 of the Constitutional Podcast: "Senate and States,"* Washington Post, Sept. 11, 2017, 2017 WLNR 27965092.

[25] Ralph A. Rossum, *The Irony of Constitutional Democracy: Federalism, the Supreme Court, and the Seventeenth Amendment*, 36 San Diego L. Rev. 671, 711, note 213 (1999).

[26] *Id.* at 711–712.

[27] *Utah Mourns Preston D. Richards-Law-Marker, Educator, and Friend*, Deseret News, Feb. 1, 1952.

[28] Amy Coney Barrett & John Copeland Nagle, *Congressional Originalism*, 19 U. Pa. J. Const. L. 1, 12 (2016).

[29] Akhil Reed Amar, *The Fourth Amendment, Boston, and the Writs of Assistance*, 30 Suffolk U. L. Rev. 53 (1996).

[30] *New York Times Best-sellers Fiction*, Record Journal (Meriden, Conn.), Jun. 18, 2017, 2017 WLNR 18950822.

[31] Mike Lee, *Written Out of History: The Forgotten Founders Who Fought Big Government* (Sentinel, 2017), Amazon.com, Editorial Reviews, https://www.amazon.com/Written-Out-History-Forgotten-Government/dp/0399564454 [https://perma.cc/M7RH-3C7Q].

[32] U.S. Senate Judiciary Committee Hearing on Justice Neil Gorsuch's Nomination to the Supreme Court, Statement of Sen. Lee, Mar. 20, 2017, 2017 WLNR 8751432.

[33] Lee (2017). See also Doctrine & Covenants 101:80 which states "And for this purpose have I established the Constitution of this land, by the hands of wise men whom I raised up unto this very purpose, and redeemed the land by the shedding of blood."

[34] U.S. Senate Judiciary Committee Hearing on Justice Neil Gorsuch's Nomination to the Supreme Court, Statement of Sen. Lee, Mar. 20, 2017, 2017 WLNR 8751432.

Chapter 11

Rex E. Lee: Supreme Court Litigator and Advocate

Defending the Constitution

Rex E. Lee stood before the nine justices in the historic court chamber at the U.S. Supreme Court on December 7, 1982, 41 years to the day after the bombing of Pearl Harbor.[1] While American soldiers fought for American freedoms and principles following the bombing of Pearl Harbor, on this commemorative Pearl Harbor Day, U.S. Solicitor General Lee fought to preserve the sanctity of the U.S. Constitution. Standing poised before the raised mahogany bench where the justices sat in the chamber rising 44 feet to a coffered ceiling flanked by 24 marble columns, Lee passionately argued the case *INS v. Chadha* involving the constitutionality of the legislative veto on behalf of the U.S. government.[2]

Rex Lee passionately addressed the court:

> The power to legislate is the power to make law, to change people's rights and obligations. It is the most important power of government and in the view of those who wrote the Constitution it has the greatest potential for abuse. The Constitution is unusually explicit concerning how this legislating power, this power to make laws, is to be accomplished: either passage by both houses of Congress and presentation to the President for his approval or, in the event of veto by the President, passage by two-thirds of both houses of Congress over his veto. In recent times Congress

has invented a device which circumvents these basic constitutional requirements, eliminates the President from his constitutionally guaranteed participation in the lawmaking process, and switches the authority to legislate, to make changes in the legal rights and obligations that people would otherwise have, to Congress acting alone by majority vote or to a single house or committee of Congress. The legislative veto in this case suffers from the same defect as the legislative veto in any other case. Whatever labels one may choose to attach to it, no label can obscure the fact that a legislative veto is something that Congress does. It is an official governmental act by Congress. . . And if it is legislative in character, then it must comply with the constitutional prerequisites for legislation, passage by two houses and approval by the President.[3]

Even though Lee could not sway the opinion of his former mentor, Justice Byron White, seven out of the nine justices on the U.S. Supreme Court agreed with Lee's legal analysis and invalidated the legislative veto. The Court ruled that the legislative veto violated the Presentment Clause in Article I of the U.S. Constitution that "Every Bill which shall have passed the House of Representatives and the Senate, shall, before it become a Law, be presented to the President of the United States."[4] The Court noted that the records of the Constitutional Convention reveal that the requirement that all legislation be presented to the President before becoming law was uniformly accepted by the Framers. Presentment to the President and the Presidential veto were considered so imperative that the draftsmen took special pains to assure that these requirements could not be circumvented. The Court also observed that the Presentment Clause serves the important purpose of assuring that a "national" perspective is grafted on the legislative process.[5] In his dissent, Justice White noted that *Chadha* struck down "in one fell swoop provisions in more laws enacted by Congress than the Court has cumulatively invalidated in its history."[6] An article examining the impact of *Chadha* estimates that the decision invalidated "virtually every variety of more

140

than 200 congressional vetoes enacted over the span of 50 years."[7] As a result, Congress cannot utilize the legislative veto. Rex Lee later remarked that the case was "one of the half-dozen most important cases ever decided by the Supreme Court."[8]

Making His Mark

One of the greatest Supreme Court litigators of the 20th century, Rex Edwin Lee, was born in California on February 27, 1935 to Rex and Mabel Lee.[9] His father was killed in an accident before he was born, and his mother married Wilford Shumway. Rex Lee grew up in small town of St. Johns, Arizona where he lived near extended family in the small farming and ranching community. Lee's extended family believed in public service. His cousins, Mo Udall and Stewart Udall, later served in the U.S. House of Representatives and his uncle, Levi Stewart Udall, was a prominent judge and church leader in St. Johns.[10]

Rex Lee served as a missionary for the Church in Mexico "where he learned to speak the language, to love the common people, and to love the Lord and His great work."[11] He graduated from Brigham Young University in 1960 serving in his final year as student body president.[12] Lee then embarked on studying the law. He once described himself as "a pretty fair student at a pretty good law school," a profound understatement which reflects his humility.[13] Rex Lee finished first in his class from the prestigious University of Chicago Law School in 1963.

When Lee's academic credentials at the University of Chicago qualified him for a Supreme Court clerkship, Dallin Oaks, then one of Lee's professors, accompanied him to Washington. Oaks, a fellow member of the Church, previously served as a law clerk to Chief Justice Earl Warren. A few weeks later, the chief justice phoned Oaks with the news that Rex had not gone unnoticed by a fellow westerner: "Would you feel bad if I didn't hire your friend, Rex Lee? Whizzer White wants him."[14]

141

After law school, Lee accepted a prestigious clerkship on the U.S. Supreme Court where he clerked for Justice Byron "Whizzer" White during the 1963–1964 Term. President John F. Kennedy nominated Justice White just a year earlier in 1962. The Supreme Court unanimously decided the landmark First Amendment free speech case *New York Times Co. v. Sullivan*, 376 U.S. 254 (1964) during Lee's clerkship. In Justice White's most famous written opinion during the term, *McLaughlin v. Florida*, 379 U.S. 184 (1964), the Court struck down an anti-miscegenation law aimed at preventing cohabitation of interracial couples. The Court relied on the reasoning in *McLaughlin* three years later in *Loving v. Virginia*, 388 U.S. 1 (1967) holding that anti-miscegenation laws prohibiting interracial couples from marrying violated the Equal Protection Clause. Lee's time on the U.S. Supreme Court provided him with valuable training and experience as an appellate advocate in his later career.

The *McLaughlin v. Florida* case reflects a shift in the court's attitude toward civil rights. Meanwhile, Lee's religion—The Church of Jesus Christ of Latter-day Saints—continued to prohibit black men from receiving the priesthood. At the time, the Church also prevented white men from marrying black women in temples. This ban remained in place until 1978 until Church President Spencer W. Kimball announced a revelation that removed the ban.

Returning to the Grand Canyon State

Lee returned to his home state of Arizona and worked for the law firm Jennings, Strouss & Salmon in Phoenix from 1964 to 1971 after clerking for the U.S. Supreme Court. While in private practice, Lee focused on appellate litigation and further developed his appellate advocacy skills. After just three years, Lee became a partner at the firm.[15] At Jennings Strouss, Lee worked with Richard Kleindienst, who helped build and energize the Republican Party in Arizona before becoming U.S. Attorney General under President Richard Nixon.[16] Lee also taught anti-trust law at the University of Arizona Law School for several years in addition to his full-time practice.[17]

As a partner at Jennings Strouss, Lee argued his first case before the U.S. Supreme Court in 1970. In *Pike v. Bruce Church, Inc.*, 397 U.S. 137 (1970), Lee represented an official charged with enforcing the Arizona Fruit and Vegetable Standardization Act which required that cantaloupes grown in Arizona and offered for sale must be packed in closed standard containers. A grower of cantaloupes transporting uncrated cantaloupes from its Arizona ranch to a nearby California city for packing and processing argued that the Arizona law was unconstitutional. In what would become a rarity, the U.S. Supreme Court ruled against Lee's argument and found that the Arizona state law imposed a "straitjacket" on the grower and placed an undue burden on interstate commerce in violation of the Commerce Clause.[18]

Building a Law School from the Ground Up

The Board of Trustees at Brigham Young University and then-university president Dallin H. Oaks presented a new opportunity to Lee. Oaks asked Lee, his former pupil from their days at the University of Chicago, to come to Utah and serve as the founding dean of the new J. Reuben Clark Law School at BYU. Never one to reject a call to church service, Lee assumed the role as founding dean. Church President Gordon B. Hinckley later said, "His was the task of assembling a faculty and a library, the two great basic assets of any good school of law."[19] Lee played a key role in recruiting the initial faculty, including Carl S. Hawkins, a law professor at the University of Michigan. At only 36 years of age, Lee became the dean of the new law school and served as the founding dean from 1972 to 1975 and again from 1977 to 1981 where he helped build the law school from its inception. Besides recruiting faculty and overseeing construction of a new building, Lee also used his advocacy skills to recruit students.

Scott Cameron, a member of the charter class, recalled that during the first two years until the new law school building opened, the law school met in the little Catholic school, St. Francis of Assisi, on Ninth East. Cameron recalled, "I love that the Law School started there because St. Francis of Assisi had turned away from wealth to a very simple life in order to benefit others." During the first two years, the facilities were less than ideal. Instead of study carrels, students used banquet tables sectioned into four places with tape. All the books were kept in the small auditorium, which Rex Lee called "the great hall." Despite the cramped surrounding, Lee fostered a great learning environment and a great pioneering effort. Lee sold students that they were part of a great pioneering effort akin to the early pioneers in the Church.[20]

Dean Lee saw the value and opportunities that religious-based law schools could offer. Tom Shaffer, then Dean of the Notre Dame University Law School, provided guidance to Lee by incorporating faith as an integral part of the total educational program. Lee wrote that "church-related law schools . . . represent important islands of diversity in an otherwise uniformly secular sea."[21]

Lee took a leave of absence from his position as dean and accepted a position as the Assistant Attorney General for the Civil Division in the U.S. Department of Justice answering the call to public service. Lee served in the Administration of President Gerald Ford from 1975 to 1977 during the tumultuous time following the resignation of President Richard Nixon and the Watergate scandal that implicated many top lawyers in the Nixon Administration. Lee worked with Antonin Scalia, then Assistant Attorney General for the Office of Legal Counsel, who later became a U.S. Supreme Court Justice. Lee also worked with U.S. Solicitor General Robert H. Bork and Attorney General Edward Hirsch Levi. During a time of great upheaval following the Watergate scandal, Lee added integrity to the U.S. Department of Justice.

Lee joined Scalia and Bork in several cases during their time with the U.S. Department of Justice. The three government lawyers co-authored an appellate brief involving Cuban cigars in a case before the U.S. Supreme Court. In *Alfred Dunhill of London, Inc. v. Republic of Cuba*, 425 U.S. 682 (1976), Scalia presented the oral argument before the Court arguing for a strict interpretation of the U.S. Constitution. Scalia, Bork, and Lee promoted constitutional originalism supported by conservative organizations like the Federalist Society and the Heritage Foundation.[22]

As Assistant Attorney General, Lee also worked with Bork and Scalia on the U.S. Department of Justice Committee on Revision of the Federal Judicial System that examined the needs of the federal courts. The committee concluded that the swelling the size of the federal judiciary indefinitely would damage collegiality, an essential element in the collective evolution of sound legal principles, and diminish the possibility of personal interaction throughout the judiciary. The committee also concluded that large numbers dilute the great prestige and, given the low compensation provided for federal judges, that dilution will make it increasingly more difficult to attract first-rate men and women to the bench.[23]

During his time as Assistant Attorney General, Lee gained more experience arguing cases before the U.S. Supreme Court. In *Mathews v. De Castro*, 429 U.S. 181 (1976), the U.S. Supreme Court considered whether a divorced woman under 62 years of age was entitled to certain government benefits. In his oral argument before the Court, Lee pleaded, "But the point is, what you really come down to then is the question of how much leeway do we give to Congress in making these kinds of judgments."[24] The Court unanimously agreed with Lee's argument holding that governmental decisions to spend money to improve the general public welfare in one way and not another are not confided to the courts. Statutory classifications for certain government benefits do not infringe upon the Due Process Clause of the Fifth Amendment.[25]

The Solicitor General and not Pamphleteer General

Lee returned to BYU during the Carter Administration and then President Ronald Reagan asked Lee to serve as his U.S. Solicitor General. The Solicitor General oversees virtually all federal litigation in the Supreme Court.[26] Former Solicitor General Drew Days stated, "Once cases reach the Supreme Court, the Solicitor General plays an important role in the development of American law" and can have a substantial "impact upon the establishment of constitutional and other principles."[27] Lee described the position as "the greatest lawyering job in the world" because the Solicitor General "represents the world's most interesting client before the world's most interesting court."[28]

Lee left his biggest mark on the law from a national perspective during his tenure as Solicitor General from 1981 to 1985. Lee represented the U.S. Government before the Supreme Court and learned that it "accomplishes nothing" to "lecture the Justices about where they went wrong" and to urge them to overturn well-established precedent.[29] As Solicitor General, Lee won 23 out of 30 cases he argued, a remarkable rate of success.[30]

As Solicitor General, Lee argued that courts should use judicial restraint and adopt a narrow definition of the "actual case or controversy" requirement found in Article III of the U.S. Constitution. In *Valley Forge Christian Coll. v. Americans United for Separation of Church & State, Inc.*, 454 U.S. 464 (1982), an organization dedicated to separation of church and state challenged transfer of federally owned property to a religious organization without financial payment. Lee argued:

> The feature of our constitutional system that distinguishes courts from the other two branches of government is that courts perform their law interpretive function, including declarations of constitutionality, only in cases or controversies and interest of the kind that these plaintiffs are pressing in this case, an interest in seeing that a particular philosophy of government prevailed, can be carried to the elected branches, and those branches are free to entertain it. . . In contrast to the political branches of government, which are perfectly free under the Constitution to entertain any advocacy for a particular form of government, philosophy of government that is put to them, the tradition ever since Marbury versus Madison has been that courts decide only those issues as they arise in actual lawsuits brought by persons who are injured in fact, and on at least seven separate occasions, reaching all the way back to the early parts of this century, this Court has said that that injury in fact means an injury more specific than the effect that is felt by the populace as a

whole, and in our separation of powers, check and balance constitutional system, the most effective check on judicial power is the case or controversy limitation.[31]

The U.S. Supreme Court found Lee's argument persuasive and held that the Court should not adjudicate abstract questions of wide public significance which amount to generalized grievances, pervasively shared and most appropriately addressed in the representative branches.[32]

Next to the *Chadha* case, in the eyes of his son, U.S. Senator Mike Lee, Rex Lee's second most impactful case was *United States v. Leon*, 468 U.S. 897 (1984). *United States v. Leon* recognized the "good faith" exception to the Fourth Amendment exclusionary rule.[33] In his oral argument before the U.S. Supreme Court, Lee said that "the imperative of judicial integrity does not prevent the courts from considering all evidence seized in violation of the Fourth Amendment." Lee argued the imperative of judicial integrity. As a society, we "pay a price for technical rules that our citizens are unable to understand and respect." Lee also said that we demean the Fourth Amendment when its values depend on "things whose relevance the common citizen has a hard time understanding." People can understand that some useful purpose is served when evidence obtained in flagrant violation of a defendant's rights is suppressed but they have much more difficulty accepting "the validity of suppression when it is done in response to a minor departure from rather technical and unclear requirements, or when the police have acted in reasonable good faith."[34]

In a split 6-3 decision, the U.S. Supreme Court held in *United States v. Leon* that evidence seized on the basis of a mistakenly issued search warrant could be introduced at trial. Lee's former boss, Justice White, wrote the opinion of the court holding that the marginal or nonexistent benefits produced by suppressing evidence obtained in objectively reasonable reliance on a subsequently invalidated search warrant cannot justify the substantial costs of exclusion.[35]

As an advocate for conservative constitutional principles, Lee faced criticism. Harvard Law School Professor Larry Tribe, in reaction to *United States v. Leon*, was "quite struck by the fact that the Statue of Liberty was in shackles and being dismantled as the court was coming to an end."[36] In a speech delivered at the University of Georgia School of Law, Lee countered, "People who live in the United States have more rights and enjoy more freedoms because of the work of the United States Supreme Court during the October 1983 Term. Neither literally nor symbolically is the Statue of Liberty in shackles. It is simply being restored to its original condition."[37]

Continued Success Before the Supreme Court and in Higher Education

Lee resigned his position as U.S. Solicitor General after Reagan's first term amid some controversy. Some accounts say he was forced to quit by colleagues who thought he was too restrained in his advocacy of the president's social agenda. Lee remarked, "There has been this notion that my job is to press the administration's policies at every turn and announce true conservative principles through the press of my briefs. It is not. I'm the solicitor general, not the pamphleteer general."[38] After leaving the Solicitor General's Office because of philosophical differences with the polices of the Reagan Administration, Lee joined the prestigious law firm Sidley Austin as a partner focusing on appellate litigation while also teaching at BYU as the endowed George Sutherland Professor of Law.

As a man of devout faith, Lee advocated for religious freedom. In *Corp. of Presiding Bishop of Church of Jesus Christ of Latter-day Saints v. Amos*, 483 U.S. 327 (1987), the U.S. Supreme Court considered whether a faith-based organization can consider religion in employment preferences. Lee, while working for Sidley Austin, argued on behalf of The Church of Jesus Christ of Latter-day Saints and other faiths, "There is nothing in the establishment clause that prohibits churches from promoting religion. Indeed, that is the very reason for their existence. And neither does the establishment clause prohibit government from permitting churches to promote religion."[39]

In *Amos*, the Court held that the exemption for religious organizations applied to a church-operated gymnasium that terminated an employee because he failed to qualify for a temple recommendation, a certificate of eligibility to attend the temples of the Church. Justice White held that applying a religious exemption to Title VII of the Civil Rights Act's prohibition against religious discrimination in employment did not violate the Establishment Clause. The *Amos* case had monumental implications affecting the employment decisions among all religious organizations.[40] On the freedom of religion, Lee wrote "There is, I think, no area of constitutional law more in need of solid, creative examination and fresh ideas by the courts, scholars, and practitioners than the issue of what constitutes an establishment of religion."[41]

The Board of Trustees at Brigham Young University then called on Lee again. This time, top church leaders who sit on the Board of Trustees asked Lee to serve as president of the Church's flagship university. Lee accepted the academic leadership position with one condition—that he could still argue cases before the Supreme Court.[42] During his stewardship as President of BYU from 1989 until 1995, Lee argued nine additional cases before the Supreme Court.[43] Lee also wrote two books on the U.S. Constitution. In *A Lawyer Looks at the Constitution,* Lee examined the high court's rulings on school prayer, due process, equal protection and abortion during the 1960s, 1970s and early 1980s as examples of judicial excess. In *A Lawyer Looks at the Equal Rights Amendment,* Lee gave a scholarly study of the amendment which offers willing readers a perceptive, reasonable discussion of the far-reaching effects of the proposed constitutional amendment.[44]

Besides his career as a lawyer, law professor, and university administrator, Lee also served in various church callings, include service as a bishop, stake president, and Sunday School teacher. Most importantly, he taught his family. Rex Lee once said, "I want them to know the value of eternal things."[45]

In his later years, Lee's greatest fight took place not inside the courtroom, but with a bout of cancer. Lee underwent several cancer treatments, but Lee pressed forward with determination. Justice Sandra Day O'Connor remarked, "I remember an appearance at the court by Rex Lee [near the end of his 1987 hospitalization for cancer treatment]. Looking very pale and weak, he had to sit on a stool for the only time I saw him do that. I think he wore a wig. But nonetheless, [he was] effective. And we were all very moved by that." O'Connor said, "He inspired all of us with his courage in the face of a terminal illness."[46] President Hinckley added, "During a considerable part of the time that he has served as president, he has carried the terrible burden of cancer." Hinckley added, that Lee "fought this dread disease with patience, with prayer, with faith, and with the best medical care available. When many others might have quit long ago, he has gone forward quietly doing his duty."[47] Lee died in 1996 at 61 years of age, but his influence will not be forgotten.

When U.S. Supreme Court Justice David Souter was asked how advocacy before the nation's high court has changed in recent times, Souter paused for a moment to reflect and answered, "Well, I can tell you that the biggest change by far is that Rex Lee is gone. Rex Lee was the best Solicitor General this nation has ever had, and he is the best lawyer this Justice ever heard plead a case in this Court." Justice Souter added further praise, "Rex Lee was born to argue tough cases of immense importance to this nation. He set new standards of excellence for generations of lawyers and justices. No one thing has happened to change the nature of advocacy of this Court which has had as much impact as the loss of that one player."[48] Justice White echoed the sentiments expressed by Justices O'Connor and Souter in praise of Rex Lee. Justice White recalled, "He was an experienced, careful, and very brainy advocate. And he was the epitome of integrity on whom we could rely for straight talk about the cases coming before the court."[49] Justice O'Connor observed, "I can truthfully say that all of the justices enjoyed Rex Lee's presentations before us. He was a highly respected advocate, showing not only his detail of knowledge about the case and the law, but exhibiting wit and charm every time."[50]

In one empirical analysis to determine which lawyers won the most cases before the U.S. Supreme Court, Rex Lee, Archibald Cox, and Wade McCree, past U.S. Solicitors General, showed the most success. This success is even more impressive given Lee was listed as counsel of record nearly 150 times in briefs.[51] Lee was considered the most successful Supreme Court litigator in the analysis of nearly 9,500 Supreme Court merits briefs and their respective Supreme Court opinions from

1946 through 2013.[52] This study focused just on names that appeared in briefs but did not study the lawyers who presented oral arguments. McCree argued 25 cases before the high court compared to 59 cases argued by Lee.[53] While some Supreme Court litigators have argued more cases before the high court, notably Lawrence G. Wallace and Erwin N. Griswold, Lee's rate of success has few equals.[54] Based on both anecdotal evidence in the minds of U.S. Supreme Court Justices and in terms of empirical evidence, Rex Lee is arguably the greatest advocate before the U.S. Supreme Court in modern history.

While J. Reuben Clark, Jr. is the namesake for the law school at BYU, Lee arguably has made a greater impact on the American legal system than any other lawyer who belongs to The Church of Jesus Christ. Judge Thomas B. Griffith on the U.S. Court of Appeals for the District of Columbia Circuit, said, "We don't go a good enough job talking about him. He is a lion and he's not fully appreciated about it. Rex is the most influential Mormon lawyer in American history—bar none."[55] Oaks, who worked closely with Lee for many years, said, "Rex E. Lee stands out . . . because of his outstanding work as Solicitor General of the United States, his preceding service as an Assistant Attorney General, and his monumental influence on a whole generation of LDS lawyers in the founding and leading of the J. Reuben Clark Law School."[56] Judge Kent A. Jordan on the U.S. Court of Appeals for the Third Circuit added, "He was a man of monumental ability and integrity."[57]

"Constitutional defects cannot be cured by practical expediency." Rex E. Lee, in his oral argument before the U.S. Supreme Court in *INS v. Chadha,* convincing the Court to invalidate the legislative veto.[58]

[1] *Immigration and Naturalization Service v. Chadha*, 462 U.S. 919 (1983).

[2] Supreme Court of the United States, Visitor's Guide to the Court, https://www.supremecourt.gov/visiting/visitorsguide-supremecourt.aspx [https://perma.cc/8K3G-ZHJB].

[3] Transcript of Oral Argument, *Immigration and Naturalization Service v. Chadha*, 462 U.S. 919 (1983), Oyez,

https://apps.oyez.org/player/#/burger8/oral_argument_audio/18351 [https://perma.cc/E8G5-6TER].

[4] U.S. Const. art. I, § 7, cl. 2; 462 U.S. at 948.

[5] 462 U.S. at 948.

[6] *Id.* at 1002 (White, J., dissenting).

[7] Robert S. Gilmour & Barbara Hinkson Craig, *After the Congressional Veto: Assessing the Alternatives*, 3 J. Pol'y Analysis & Mgmt. 373, 373 (1984).

[8] Steven Davis, *Unconstitutionality of the Missouri Legislative Veto: An Environmental Group's Effect on the Constitutional Landscape*, 5 Mo. Envtl. L. & Pol'y Rev. 93, 102 (1998) (citing Rex Lee, Brigham Young University constitutional law lecture (March 1994)).

[9] *Great American Lawyers: An Encyclopedia*, Volume 1, edited by John R. Vile (Santa Barbara, California: ABC-CLIO), 452; *Death: Rex Edwin Lee*, Deseret News, Mar. 16, 1996, https://www.deseretnews.com/article/477068/DEATH--REX-EDWIN-LEE.html [https://perma.cc/VR3E-T8PV] (hereinafter "Death: Rex Edwin Lee").

[10] Levi Stewart Udall, 1891–1960, Biographical Sketch, University of Arizona Library, http://www.library.arizona.edu/exhibits/lsudall/index.html [https://perma.cc/J6GK-QWMK].

[11] Gordon B. Hinckley, To a Man Who Has Done What This Church Expects of Each of Us, BYU Devotional, Oct. 17, 1995, https://speeches.byu.edu/talks/gordon-b-hinckley_man-done-church-expects-us/ [https://perma.cc/34H3-DX36].

[12] Death: Rex Edwin Lee.

[13] Dallin H. Oaks and J. Frederic Voros, Jr., *Rex et Lex: A Look at Rex E. Lee*, 27 University of Chicago Law School Record, 38, 39 (Fall 1981).

[14] *Id.*

[15] *Id.*

[16] Jennings, Strouss & Salmon, PLC, History, http://www.jsslaw.com/history.aspx [https://perma.cc/6ZBL-SS9M].

[17] J. Reuben Clark Law Society, *Clark Memorandum*, Fall 1978, 10.

[18] 397 U.S. at 146.

[19] Hinckley (1995).

[20] Scott W. Cameron, *Farewell to St. Reuben's*, J. Reuben Clark Law Society, Clark Memorandum, Fall 2013, 38–39.

[21] Rex E. Lee, *Today's Religious Law School: Challenges and Opportunities*, 78 Marq. L. Rev. 255, 257 (1995).

[22] Morgan Cloud, *A Conclusion in Search of a History to Support It*, 43 Tex. Tech L. Rev. 29, 45 (2010).

[23] Judith Resnik, *Housekeeping: The Nature and Allocation of Work in Federal Trial Courts*, 24 Ga. L. Rev. 909, 964 (1990) (citing Dept. of Justice Comm. on Revision of the Fed. Judicial System, The Needs of the Federal Courts 6–7 (1977)).

[24] Transcript of Oral Argument, *Mathews v. De Castro*, 429 U.S. 181 (1976), Oyez, https://apps.oyez.org/player/#/burger6/oral_argument_audio/17369 [https://perma.cc/3AV5-PLRU].

[25] 429 U.S. at 185.

[26] Tara Leigh Grove, *The Exceptions Clause as a Structural Safeguard*, 113 Colum. L. Rev. 929, 985–86 (2013).

[27] Drew S. Days, III, *Executive Branch Advocate v. Officer of the Court: The Solicitor General's Ethical Dilemma*, 22 Nova L. Rev. 679, 680 (1998).

[28] Rex E. Lee, *Lawyering for the Government: Politics, Polemics & Principle*, 47 Ohio St. L.J. 595, 596 (1986).

[29] Seth P. Waxman, *Twins at Birth: Civil Rights and the Role of the Solicitor General*, 75 Ind. L.J. 1297, 1315 (2000).

[30] Lee Davidson, *Supreme Court Justices Pay Tribute to the Late Rex E. Lee*, BYU Magazine (Fall 1996), https://magazine.byu.edu/article/supreme-court-justices-pay-tribute-to-the-late-rex-e-lee/ [https://perma.cc/VM33-6XEV].

[31] Transcript of Oral Argument, *Valley Forge Christian Coll. v. Americans United for Separation of Church & State, Inc.*, 454 U.S. 464 (1982), Oyez, https://apps.oyez.org/player/#/burger8/oral_argument_audio/18394 [https://perma.cc/LXF4-7T5H].

[32] 454 U.S. at 475.

[33] Phone interview with Mike Lee, United States Senator, Apr. 25, 2017.

[34] Transcript of Oral Argument, *United States v. Leon*, 468 U.S. 897 (1984), Oyez, https://apps.oyez.org/player/#/burger8/oral_argument_audio/19479 [https://perma.cc/TG3T-NVD2].

[35] 468 U.S. at 922.

[36] Rex E. Lee, *The Supreme Court's 1983 Term: Individual Rights, Freedom, and the Statue of Liberty*, 19 Ga. L. Rev. 1, 2 (1984).

[37] *Id.* at 12–13.

[38] Lincoln Caplan, *Why The Law Gets No Respect; Both Left And Right Have Made It A Public Punching Bag*, Washington Post, September 20, 1987, 1987 WLNR 2240698.

[39] Transcript of Oral Argument, *Corp. of Presiding Bishop of Church of Jesus Christ of Latter-day Saints v. Amos*, 483 U.S. 327 (1987), Oyez, https://apps.oyez.org/player/#/rehnquist1/oral_argument_audio/18163 [https://perma.cc/F3JL-FEWY].

[40] Scott D. McClure, *Religious Preferences in Employment Decisions: How Far May Religious Organizations Go?*, 1990 Duke L.J. 587, 611 (1990)

[41] Rex E. Lee, *Religion and the Burger Court*, 84 Mich. L. Rev. 603 (1986).

[42] Davidson (1996).

[43] *Id.*

[44] Eric Malnic, *Rex E. Lee Dies; Solicitor General in Reagan Years*, Washington Post, Mar. 13, 1996, 1996 WLNR 6587399.

[45] Oaks and Voros (1981).

[46] Davidson (1996).

[47] Hinckley (1995).

[48] Theodore B. Olson, *In Memory of Rex E. Lee (1937-1996) Rex E. Lee Conference on the Office of The Solicitor General of the United States*, 2003 B.Y.U. L. Rev. 1, 183 (2003).

[49] Davidson (1996).

[50] *Id.*

[51] Adam Feldman, *Who Wins in the Supreme Court? An Examination of Attorney and Law Firm Influence*, 100 Marq. L. Rev. 429, 457–58 (2016).

[52] *Id.*

[53] Tony Mauro, *A Year in the Life of the Supreme Court*, 6 J.L.: Periodical Laboratory of Leg. Scholarship 115, 122 (2016).

[54] Joan Biskupic, *Deputy Solicitor Heads for New Bench Mark; 127th Case Will Tie Supreme Court Record*, Washington Post, Oct. 31, 1994, A21, 1994 WLNR 5490780.

[55] Phone interview with Thomas B. Griffith, Judge, U.S. Court of Appeals for the District of Columbia Circuit, Sept. 1, 2017.

[56] Dallin H. Oaks, former Utah Supreme Court Justice, letter to the author, May 12, 2017.

[57] Phone interview with Kent A. Jordan, Judge, U.S. Court of Appeals for the Third Circuit, Apr. 24, 2017.

[58] Transcript of Oral Argument, *Immigration and Naturalization Service v. Chadha*, 462 U.S. 919 (1983).

Chapter 12

Monroe G. McKay: Innovator in the Law

Silencing Criticism

While having a family member in Congress would normally help a lawyer's chances to become a federal judge, for Monroe G. McKay, the influence of his brother, Gunn McKay, ironically almost stalled his nomination.[1] When a vacancy for the U.S. Court of Appeals for the Tenth Circuit arose after Chief Judge David Thomas Lewis took senior status in 1977, the judicial nominating and screening committee unanimously recommended Monroe McKay. Monroe McKay, at the time a law professor at Brigham Young University who previously worked as a successful lawyer in private practice in Arizona and law clerk for the Arizona Supreme Court, was known as a constitutional expert. Utah Governor Scott Matheson, on the other hand, lobbied strongly for David Watkiss, a Salt Lake attorney, for the judicial vacancy.[2] Watkiss successfully defended Boeing Aircraft Co. after a 727 jet crashed in 1965, at the Salt Lake Airport, claiming the lives of 43 passengers. At the time, the case against Boeing was the first ever lawsuit to go to trial involving the 727 aircraft that rolled out in 1962 and was once considered "very risky."[3]

The feud involved Utah's top two Democrats. The Utah Governor charged U.S. Representative Gunn McKay with abusing the judicial nominating process by exerting congressional pressure on the White House to have his brother appointed to the bench. Matheson said, "I have no criticism with respect to the personalities involved in the selection process. Those are all qualified persons. But President [Jimmy] Carter established the nominating process and it has been abused. I'm very displeased about that part of it." In a scathing telegram sent to President Jimmy Carter, Governor Matheson wrote that Watkiss "was the only recommendation from Atty. Gen. (Griffin) Bell. Mr. Watkiss was also the overwhelming choice of the Utah State Bar. He was my personal choice, based on my experience as past bar president and upon a close association in the practice of law for nearly 25 years. Your decision to personally intervene outside the rules you have established for judicial selection is crushing and disheartening." Matheson wired the President, "It violates the integrity of your recent comment that the process 'gives the public legitimate, assurance that selections are made on the basis of merit.' "[4] Matheson charged Gunn McKay with violating the integrity of the judicial nominating process by lobbying House Speaker Thomas "Tip" P. O'Neill directly for his brother.

With strong support from the Utah State Bar Association and the instrumental political assistance of Speaker O'Neill, President Carter ultimately choose McKay over Watkiss.[5] McKay quickly silenced any criticism. Only a few days after blasting the selection, one leading opponent emerged from a meeting with Monroe McKay saying, "This guy may turn out to be the best circuit judge we've got."[6]

Embarking on a Career in the Law

Born in Huntsville, Utah in 1928, Monroe Gunn McKay came from a devout family. His cousin, David O. McKay, served as President of The Church of Jesus Christ of Latter-day Saints from 1951 to 1970. A graduate of Weber High School in Ogden, Utah, Monroe McKay enlisted in the U.S. Marine Corps where he served from 1946 until 1948. After serving his country in the military, Monroe McKay served as a missionary for the Church in South Africa from 1950 to 1953, following in his father's footsteps. His father, James Gunn McKay, previously served as a missionary in South Africa from 1906 to 1910.[7] After devoting years of service to his country and his faith, McKay embarked on educational pursuits graduating from Brigham Young University in 1957 and then from the prestigious University of Chicago Law School in 1960.

While in Chicago, McKay received guidance from Chicago lawyer John K. Edmunds. As President of the Chicago Stake for over 20 years, Edmunds saw the Church grow from a few small branches to a great stake. As an outstanding lawyer in a mid-sized firm and a law professor at Northwestern University, Edmunds also provided mentorship to many other up-and-coming lawyers who attended the University of Chicago Law School, including Dallin H. Oaks (1957), C. Keith Rooker (1961), and Rex E. Lee (1963).[8]

After graduating from law school, McKay began his legal career as a law clerk for Arizona Supreme Court Justice Jesse Addison Udall from 1960 to 1961.[9] Because of his dedicated military and missionary service, McKay, at age 32, brought years of life experiences to his work on the Arizona Supreme Court. At the time, Udall, served as the Vice Chief Justice of the Arizona Supreme Court. As a law clerk, McKay learned how to apply and interpret the U.S. Constitution in individual cases that he would later use during his many years as a federal appeals court judge.

In *State v. Locks*, 91 Ariz. 394, 372 P.2d 724 (1962), the Arizona Supreme Court considered whether the Arizona state obscenity statute prohibiting the sale of obscene and indecent pictures violated the First Amendment freedom of speech. The defendant argued that the decision by the U.S. Supreme Court three years earlier in *Smith v. California*, 361 U.S. 147 (1959) rendered the Arizona obscenity statute unconstitutional because the statute lacks a "scienter" requirement. Scienter, Latin for "knowingly," is a "degree of knowledge that makes a person legally responsible for the consequences of his or her act or omission."[10] The Arizona Supreme Court recognized that the U.S. Supreme Court allows state courts to interpret their own state laws. In the decision, Justice Udall wrote, "we hold that the element of scienter is implicit in the Arizona obscenity statute" and upheld the indictment for obscenity.[11]

McKay then joined the Phoenix law firm Lewis, Roca, Scoville, Beauchamp & Linton working as an associate from 1961 to 1966 where he handled both civil and criminal cases.[12] In private practice, McKay returned to argue cases before the Arizona Supreme Court where he previously clerked. In *State*

158

v. LeVar, 98 Ariz. 217, 403 P.2d 532 (1965), McKay represented a man convicted of first-degree murder before the Arizona Supreme Court. The court held that the trial court did not abuse its discretion in refusing the defense counsel's motion for mistrial because the defendant, due to his mental condition, was unable to communicate with counsel in time to permit counsel sufficiently to prepare for trial. The court observed that the defense counsel conducted the defense with the highest degree of professional skill and that no counsel with unlimited time for preparation could legitimately have done more for the defendant.

McKay represented another criminal defendant before the Arizona Supreme Court in *State v. Bird*, 99 Ariz. 195, 407 P.2d 770 (1965). The defendant sought post-conviction relief after being found guilty of robbery and kidnapping with intent to commit the crime of robbery. McKay argued that the trial court improperly gave a jury instruction on circumstantial evidence. The court held, however, that the instruction on circumstantial evidence, though not couched in language ordinarily used, was not an incorrect statement of law. Even though it might not have been necessary, in view of substantial direct testimony sufficient to support the conviction, the defendant, who had requested the circumstantial evidence instruction, could not complain.

Returning to the African Continent

McKay took a leave of absence from private practice and returned to the African continent from 1966 to 1968 where he previously served as a missionary. McKay relied on his experience in the Marine Corps and missionary experience to direct another corps—the Peace Corps—in Malawi. McKay accepted President John F. Kennedy's now famous challenge to Americans in his inaugural address to "Ask not what your country can do for you, ask what you can do for your country." President Kennedy established the Peace Corps to provide young Americans an opportunity to serve in Africa, Asia, and Latin America in the fields of education, public health, community development, agriculture, and construction, among other areas.[13]

Malawi, a small landlocked country in southeastern Africa, remains one of the poorest nations in the world. McKay oversaw 160 Peace Corps volunteers who helped improve education and public health for the Malawi people. At the time, more than half the children in Malawi died of malnutrition before they reached five years of age. McKay told the *Salt Lake Tribune*, "Our presence there has made possible a secondary school system in each of the 23 districts of the country." McKay added, "And besides teaching and training future Malawi teachers, the Peace Corps is conducting an extensive health program with emphasis upon tuberculosis control and childcare clinics. This is such a beautiful country it has been called the Alps of Africa. The climate is fine, we have some nice game parks and even a few elephants left." Joined by his wife, Lucy, and their four children, the McKay family lived in Blantyre, the economic center of the country named after the birthplace in Scotland of explorer David Livingstone.[14]

Working in Private Practice and Academia

McKay returned to Phoenix after his service in the Peace Corps and re-joined the law firm Lewis Roca where he became a partner in 1968 and continued working at the firm until 1974. McKay sought out additional opportunities to provide community service to those in need. He served a member of the Phoenix Community Council Juvenile Problems from 1968–1974, President of the Arizona Association for Health and Welfare from 1970–1972, and President of the Maricopa County Legal Aid Society from 1972–1974.[15]

As a law partner, McKay engaged in zealous advocacy for the legal rights of his clients. In *Dodge v. Nakai*, 298 F. Supp. 17 (D. Ariz. 1968), McKay worked on the first case under the Indian Civil Rights Act (ICRA) of 1968.[16] McKay represented the executive director of a nonprofit legal services corporation, which was organized to provide legal assistance for indigent Indians, and indigent members of the Navajo Tribe who sought legal assistance from the organization. The federal district court first held that the court had proper jurisdiction to consider the action brought against the superintendent of the Navajo police department and area director of the Indian reservation for the Bureau of Indian Affairs who barred the executive director from the reservation.[17] The court then held that the Navajo Tribal Council order to exclude the executive director of the legal services corporation violated due process. The Tribal council order was considered a "legislative act" and the court concluded that the order of exclusion constituted an unlawful bill of attainder.[18] A bill of attainder, prohibited by the U.S. Constitution, is a special legislative act prescribing punishment, without a trial, for a specific person or group.[19]

McKay then left private practice to join the new BYU Law School in 1974 as a member of the faculty where he became a popular teacher using innovative teaching methods. In a contracts class, McKay taught the principle under common law contracts that "even a peppercorn is sufficient consideration" to bind a party to a contract. Professor McKay once laid down on the long bench in the moot court room and ruminated about peppercorns for an entire class period.[20]

McKay also learned from other faculty members, including Carl Hawkins. McKay recalled:

> When I left the practice to take up teaching at the then-new BYU Law School, my mentor was Carl Hawkins who came to the new faculty from his endowed professorship at Michigan. He told me he had learned to play pool at the faculty lounge and thought he had become fairly good. One table was reserved for four of the university's distinguished college deans. One summer day one of them was away, and they told Carl they needed another stick in the game. Carl was flattered. After the break, it was his shot. When he had it lined up, one of the deans said: "Carl, what is your theory of this shot?" Puzzled, Carl said: "What do you mean 'what is my theory'?" The dean replied: "If you don't have a theory, you are just rattling the balls hoping something good will happen."[21]

McKay also had a sense of humor. One Halloween, Professor McKay arrived at his class dressed as the "Great Pumpkin" and proceeded to give his lecture on contracts.[22]

Deciding Key Cases on the Tenth Circuit

As a federal appeals court judge, McKay decided many important cases interpreting the U.S. Constitution, including the First Amendment. In *Lanner v. Wimmer*, 662 F.2d 1349 (10th Cir. 1981), McKay considered a case involving the constitutionality of the released time program at public schools in Logan, Utah permitting students to attend church-operated seminaries during regular school hours. Except for some occasional enrollment in released-time classes sponsored by several Protestant churches, the overwhelming use of the program attending released-time classes were operated by The Church of Jesus Christ of Latter-day Saints, the same faith as McKay. While the court found a First Amendment violation with the gathering of attendance slips prepared by school officials, the Tenth Circuit generally upheld the constitutionality of the other aspects of the release time program. McKay wrote the opinion of the court holding, "It is clear that released-time programs permitting attendance at religious classes off school premises do not per se offend the establishment and free exercise clauses."[23] In recognizing the constitutionality of release time for religious education, McKay and the Tenth Circuit observed, "The conflicts between public school curricula and religious doctrines cannot be avoided by simply declaring that everything public schools teach is 'secular' and therefore not religious." The court continued, "Such a shallow definitional approach ignores the role that religion has historically played, and will likely continue to play, in the development of belief systems."[24]

As a result of the *Lanner v. Wimmer* decision, students in Utah and other states benefit from release time for religious education combined with secular education. In 2012, 31 years after the landmark decision handed down by the Tenth Circuit, more than 250,000 children in 32 states participated in released-time programs. In 2012, more than 84,000 students in

Utah in grades 9-12 participated in the Church's seminary program, the vast majority of which involved release time at public high schools.[25] The U.S. Court of Appeals for the Fourth Circuit upheld the constitutionality of a similar off-campus religious instruction program in 2012 applying the precedent established in *Lanner v. Wimmer*.[26]

In *Roberts v. Madigan*, 921 F.2d 1047 (10th Cir. 1990), the Tenth Circuit considered another case involving the wall of separation between church and state in schools. In *Roberts v. Madigan*, a fifth-grade elementary school teacher challenged a decision by school officials who ordered removal of the Bible from the school library, removal of religiously oriented books from a classroom library, and a directive to the teacher that he keep his Bible out of sight during classroom silent-reading time. The Tenth Circuit found no violation of the Establishment Clause with the decision by school officials. McKay, writing the opinion of the court, held, "We believe . . . that [the teacher's] actions, when viewed in their entirety, had the primary effect of communicating a message of endorsement of a religion to the impressionable ten-, eleven-, and twelve-year-old children in his class."[27]

In his judicial philosophy as a conservative judge, McKay showed restraint rather than activism. In *Allen v. United States*, 816 F.2d 1417, 1424 (10th Cir. 1987), the Tenth Circuit considered claims brought by nearly 1,200 plaintiffs who sued the United States government under the Federal Tort Claims Act, alleging some 500 deaths and injuries as a result of radioactive fallout from above ground atomic bomb tests held in Nevada from 1951 to 1962. The trial lasted thirteen weeks with more than 54,000 pages of exhibit evidence. The district court deliberated for 17 months and ruled against the Government on nine of the claims. On appeal, after reviewing the case for more than 15 months, the three judges ruled unanimously that the Government could not be held liable for injuries suffered as a result of discretionary decision-making powers given the Atomic Energy Commission (AEC). McKay joined the three-judge panel in denying the claims but sympathized with the injured residents who lived downwind from the Nevada test sites. McKay wrote, "While we have great sympathy for the individual cancer victims who have borne alone the costs of the AEC's choices, their plight is a matter for

Congress." The court held that "[o]nly Congress has the constitutional power to decide whether all costs of government activity will be borne by all the beneficiaries or will continue to be unfairly apportioned, as in this case."[28]

Judge McKay also showed the ability to use sarcasm and humor. For example, in *Mescalero Apache Tribe v. New Mexico*, New Mexico claimed the right to enforce its game laws against nonmembers of the tribe on the reservation.[29] The Tenth Circuit rejected the claim, holding that the tribe had sovereignty over hunting and fishing on its territory. Astonishingly, the state argued that the tribe had no traditional territory, and therefore no rights associated with territory, because the Mescaleros were being swept from their lands by a tide of white settlers. Writing for the court, Judge McKay opined, "If we were to accept the State's argument, we would be enshrining the rather perverse notion that traditional rights are not to be protected in precisely those instances when protection is essential, i.e., when a dominant group has succeeded in temporarily frustrating exercise of those rights." McKay added, "We prefer a view more compatible with the theory of this nation's founding: rights do not cease to exist because a government fails to secure them. See The Declaration of Independence (1776)."[30]

Thirty-three years after McKay took the bench over Governor Scott Matheson's objection, President Barack Obama appointed the Utah Governor's son, Scott Matheson, Jr., in 2010, to the Tenth Circuit where McKay and Matheson decided several cases together. In *Awad v. Ziriax*, 670 F.3d 1111 (10th Cir. 2012), McKay and Matheson, acting as part of a three-judge panel, granted an injunction invalidating a proposed constitutional amendment approved by voters in Oklahoma to prevent courts from considering or using international law or Shari'a law. The Tenth Circuit held that the proposed constitutional amendment violated the Establishment Clause of the First Amendment. In granting the injunction brought by the Muslim Oklahoma resident, Matheson wrote the opinion of the court, joined by McKay, that "[f]ederal courts should be wary of interfering with the voting process, but we agree with the district court and the Sixth Circuit that 'it is always in the public interest to prevent the violation of a party's constitutional rights.' "[31] Any division between the Mathesons and McKays diminished.

Innovations in the Classroom and Courtroom

As a judge and legal scholar, McKay also engaged in ground-breaking legal scholarship. Judge McKay delivered an address at the sixth annual Foulston-Siefkin Lecture at Washburn University School of Law in Kansas in 1983 discussing the Double Jeopardy Clause. Kansas is one of the states in the territorial jurisdiction of the Tenth Circuit, along with Colorado, New Mexico, Oklahoma, Utah, and Wyoming.[32] Each year since 1978, the Wichita law firm of Foulston Siefkin has sponsored the lecture series to bring a prominent legal scholar to Washburn University to challenge and enhance the legal thinking of students and faculty. McKay's speech, later published in the Washburn Law Journal entitled "Double Jeopardy: Are the Pieces the Puzzle?," has been cited extensively.[33] The Fifth Amendment provides that no person shall "be subject for the same offense to be twice put in jeopardy of life or limb."[34] McKay traced the history of the double jeopardy doctrine and recognized that the doctrine is in "a state of disarray."[35] Because American courts have struggled to interpret the language and meaning of the language, McKay proposed the radical suggestion that the solution to the ill-fitting puzzle of judicial opinions is to set aside past precedent and start from scratch.[36]

Under the leadership of Judge McKay, the Tenth Circuit employed a variety of innovations to increase the efficiency of the court, including judicial screening. With the collegiality and willingness of the individual judges to participate in the spirit of innovation, the court produced extraordinary results in a very short time despite an increased court docket. He served as Chief Judge for the Tenth Circuit, the top administrative position for the court, from 1991 to 1993. McKay noted in 1993 that, "Even faced with an increased filing rate, the court is so current at the present time that four of twenty panels at a recent oral argument session were cancelled because there were not enough cases at issue to conduct hearings."[37] Other courts would benefit from utilizing the innovative techniques utilized by the Tenth Circuit and the wisdom of McKay. After all, the legal axiom that "justice delayed is justice denied" rings true.[38]

After 16 years of active service, including two years as Chief Judge, McKay assumed senior status, a form of semi-retirement, on December 31, 1993.[39] Even after taking senior status, McKay continued to decide many noteworthy cases in his reduced role. McKay left a lasting impact on many people and cases in his total service spanning more than four decades as a federal appeals court judge. In one of his most cited opinions, *United States v. Cockerham*, 237 F.3d 1179 (10th Cir. 2001), McKay wrote the opinion for the court where the Tenth Circuit applied the rules when a criminal defendant expressly waives the right to appeal as part of a negotiated plea agreement. The defendant's waiver of the statutory right to direct appeal contained in a plea agreement is enforceable if the defendant has agreed to its terms "knowingly and voluntarily."[40]

In deciding cases, Judge McKay also exhibited an ability to make helpful comparisons—even drawing a football analogy in one case. In *Moore v. Guthrie,* 438 F.3d 1036 (10th Cir. 2006), the Tenth Circuit decided a case involving a police chief's directive to wear riot helmets, rather than a more protective face mask, during police training exercises. A police officer was injured when a bullet flew up beneath his "riot helmet" during an intense "live fire" training exercise with other police officers, causing him to lose 57 percent of his vision in one eye. The police officer sued the police chief and the city for violation of his Fourteenth Amendment right to bodily integrity. In upholding dismissal of the case, McKay wrote that the plaintiff "is asking us to play Monday-morning quarterback about a decision (providing riot helmets rather than more protective face gear) that seems, at most, negligent."[41]

McKay left a mark not just on the lives of the people in individual cases he decided as a judge, but also with his former law students and law clerks. James W. Parkinson, who worked on the *Ellis v. R.J. Reynolds Tobacco Company* (Tobacco Master Settlement Agreement) case and the action involving American soldiers used as slave laborers in World War II, praised the lessons he learned as a research assistant for

Professor McKay at BYU. "He has been a lifetime mentor and role model to me. I am very close to him," said Parkinson. "He is extraordinarily accomplished. He believes in doing it right."[42] Charles F. Wilkinson, a former law clerk, said, "After understanding Monroe McKay, I knew with absolute clarity all that a lawyer should be, and that ideal has stayed with me for my entire legal career." Wilson added, "I wish . . . we could . . . declare Monroe a national monument, for he embodies the highest of our profession's and nation's aspirations."[43] Deborah A. Geier, another former law clerk to McKay, lauded, "To this day, my year in Salt Lake City clerking for 'the Judge,' as he is known affectionately by his legion of devoted former clerks, was the most rewarding year of my professional life."[44]

———————

"It undoubtedly will come as a surprise to many that two hundred years after we threw out King George III, the rule that 'the king can do no wrong' still prevails at the federal level in all but the most trivial of matters." Monroe McKay, on the Federal Tort Claims Act and state sovereignty.[45]

———————

[1] Marcus G. Faust, *Lawyer, Lobbyist, and Latter-Day Saint*, 27 Tex. Tech L. Rev. 1117, 1129 (1996).
[2] *Id.*
[3] David B. Watkiss. *S.L. Services to Honor Lawyer David K. Watkiss,* Deseret News, Apr. 30, 1997, https://www.deseretnews.com/article/557892/SL-services-to-honor-lawyer-David-K-Watkiss.html [https://perma.cc/KL92-RMYH]; Boeing, 727 Commercial Transport Historical Snapshot, http://www.boeing.com/history/products/727.page [https://perma.cc/KP6F-C6QL].
[4] UPI, *McKay's Brother Chosen; Matheson Sore*, Ogden Standard-Examiner, Sept. 23, 1977, 8.
[5] Faust, 27 Tex. Tech L. Rev. at 1117.
[6] *Thanks, Judge Monroe McKay*, Deseret News, Nov. 24, 1993, https://www.deseretnews.com/article/322555/THANKS-JUDGE-MONROE-MCKAY.html [https://perma.cc/K96D-Q6PR].
[7] Terry L. Givens and Philip L. Barlow, *The Oxford Handbook of Mormonism* (Oxford: Oxford University Press, 2015), 372.

[8] James H. Backman, LDS Attorneys: Approaching the Modern Era, J. Reuben Clark Law Society, 2004, 2, http://www.jrcls.org/publications/perspectives/backman%20later%20lds.attorneys.jan9.04.pdf [https://perma.cc/4ANC-4FHS]; Dallin H. Oaks, *The Beginning and the End of a Lawyer*, J. Reuben Clark Law Society, Clark Memorandum, Spring 2005, 8.

[9] Historical Society of the Tenth Judicial Circuit, Table II: Judges of the Tenth Circuit Court of Appeals, The Federal Courts of the Tenth Circuit: A History, p. 463, https://static1.squarespace.com/static/54170cd0e4b00eba52a2db00/t/54243c81e4b0a1a24669ea4e/1411660929287/13Appdx-Table2.pdf [https://perma.cc/5L9E-LYN7] ("hereinafter "Historical Society of the Tenth Judicial Circuit").

[10] Black's Law Dictionary (10th ed. 2014), scienter.

[11] 372 P.2d at 725.

[12] Historical Society of the Tenth Judicial Circuit.

[13] David M. Johnson, *Service Is Its Own Reward*, 38 Colo. Law. 5 (2009) (citing Arthur M. Schlesinger Jr., *A Thousand Days: John F. Kennedy in the White House*, Houghton Mifflin Co., 1965).

[14] Phil Hewlett, *Cousin to LDS Leader Likes Africa Peace Job*, Salt Lake Tribune, Jan. 7, 1968, 78.

[15] *Id.*

[16] Robert J. Mccarthy, *Civil Rights in Tribal Courts: The Indian Bill of Rights at Thirty Years*, 34 Idaho L. Rev. 465, 471 (1998); Indian Civil Rights Act, Pub. L. No. 90-284, Tit. II-VII, §§ 201-701, 82 Stat. 77 (codified as amended at 25 U.S.C. §§ 1301-1341).

[17] 298 F. Supp. 17.

[18] *Dodge v. Nakai*, 298 F. Supp. 26, 33 (D. Ariz. 1969).

[19] U.S. Constitution art. I, § 9, cl. 3; art. I, § 10, cl. 1; Black's Law Dictionary (10th ed. 2014), bill of attainder.

[20] Val Ricks, *Assent Is Not an Element of Contract Formation*, 61 U. Kan. L. Rev. 591, 639 (2013).

[21] The Honorable Monroe G. McKay, *Retrospective on the Career of Judge William J. Holloway, Jr. Holloway Lecture, Oklahoma City December 2, 2014*, 40 Okla. City U. L. Rev. 173, 174 (2015).

[22] Deseret News, *supra* note 6.

[23] 662 F.2d at 1357.

[24] *Id.* at 1532.

[25] Joseph Walker, *Released-time Academic Credit Upheld by Federal Court,* Deseret News, Jul. 5, 2012, https://www.deseretnews.com/article/865558570/Released-time-academic-credit-upheld-by-federal-court.html [https://perma.cc/2LSV-HAXK].

[26] *Moss v. Spartanburg Cty. Sch. Dist. Seven,* 683 F.3d 599, 608 (4th Cir. 2012).

[27] 921 F.2d at 1057.

[28] 816 F.2d at 1427.

[29] 630 F.2d 724 (10th Cir.1980), vacated, 450 U.S. 1036 (1981), decision on remand, 677 F.2d 55.

[30] 630 F.2d at 730; See also James D. Gordon III, *Humor in Legal Education and Scholarship*, 1992 B.Y.U. L. Rev. 313, 322 (1992).

[31] 670 F.3d at 1132.

[32] 28 U.S.C. § 41.

[33] Honorable Monroe G. McKay, *Double Jeopardy: Are the Pieces the Puzzle?*, 23 Washburn L.J. 1 (1983).

[34] U.S. Const. amend. V.

[35] McKay, 23 Washburn L.J. at 16.

[36] See also Craig Albee, *Multiple Punishment in Wisconsin and the Wolske Decision: Is It Desirable to Permit Two Homicide Convictions for Causing A Single Death?*, 1990 Wis. L. Rev. 553, 556 (1990).

[37] Honorable Monroe G. McKay & John K. Kleinheksel, *The Decisional Process Within the Tenth Circuit--A Panoramic View of Its Internal Operations and Recent Innovations*, 33 Washburn L.J. 22, 39 (1993).

[38] *George Walter Brewing Co. v. Henseleit*, 132 N.W. 631, 632 (Wis. 1911).

[39] U.S. Court of Appeals for the Tenth Circuit, Senior Judge Monroe G. McKay, https://www.ca10.uscourts.gov/judges/senior-judge-monroe-g-mckay [https://perma.cc/XGP4-UDFN].

[40] 237 F.3d at 1181.

[41] 438 F.3d at 1041.

[42] Phone interview with James Parkinson, California lawyer, Jun. 9, 2017.

[43] Charles F. Wilkinson, *Home Dance, the Hopi, and Black Mesa Coal: Conquest and Endurance in the American Southwest*, 1996 B.Y.U. L. Rev. 449, 482 (1996).

[44] Deborah A. Geier, *Tribute to Professor Erik Jensen*, 67 Case W. Res. L. Rev. 649, 651 (2017).

[45] *Allen v. United States*, 816 F.2d 1417, 1424 (10th Cir. 1987) (Monroe, concurring).

Chapter 13

Michael W. Mosman: Fighter Against Terrorism

Small Town Roots

From his small-town roots and humble beginnings growing up in Lewiston, Idaho, Michael W. Mosman has decided some of the most important cases affecting the lives of millions of people in the nation's capital as a member of the top-secret U.S. Foreign Intelligence Surveillance Court. As one of the select judges on the top-secret court, Mosman makes critical decisions to promote national security and combat terrorism while preserving privacy rights. Mosman was raised in the small town of Lewiston, located about 270 miles north of Boise at the confluence of the Clearwater and Snake rivers. Lewiston served as the first Territorial Capital of Idaho when the newly formed Idaho Territory first organized in 1863 breaking off from the Washington Territory.[1]

Mosman chose a career in the law following the footsteps of his father, Roy, who worked as a local prosecutor, judge, and lawyer in private practice in northern Idaho.[2] Roy Mosman engaged in conflict with a stalwart passion for justice. When speaking about his father, Michael Mosman said, "At his funeral, I remarked that if there had been more early Christians like my father, there would have been fewer martyrs and more dead Roman soldiers."[3] Mosman also learned the value of hard work as a youth working in a lumber yard in northern Idaho and as a missionary for the Church in Spain.[4]

After attending Ricks College, later renamed Brigham Young University-Idaho, in rural Rexburg, Idaho, Mosman received his undergraduate degree from Utah State University where he achieved recognition as valedictorian. Mosman

171

planned to work as a marriage counselor but after completing his undergraduate psychology degree, he decided to embark on a career in the law following his father's profession. "I had seen the law through my father's career and others as an honorable career," he said. "I still think it's an honorable career. On average, I think lawyers pay more attention to honesty than most people because they have to confront it regularly with their clients."[5]

Supreme Court Clerkship

Mosman attended law school at Brigham Young University where he became editor-in-chief of the Brigham Young University Law Review. After law school, Mosman worked as a law clerk for Judge Malcolm Wilkey with the influential U.S. Court of Appeals for the District of Columbia Circuit and then clerked for Justice Lewis Powell, Jr. on the U.S. Supreme Court during the 1985–1986 Term.[6] "At the Supreme Court, I did a lot of death penalty cases. . . which were wrenching and dramatic cases . . . Those were a lot of last minute things where [Justice Powell] and I got involved. We were minutes away from a scheduled execution and trying to figure out the right thing to do."[7]

At the time, Justice Powell was the key "swing" vote in many cases decided by the U.S. Supreme Court involving the death penalty along with issues involving affirmative action, equal protection, and abortion.[8] Under the "rule of four," four out of the nine justices that sit on the U.S. Supreme Court are needed to grant a writ of certiorari for review, but five justices are needed to reverse the decision by a lower court and grant a stay.[9]

During Mosman's time as a U.S. Supreme Court law clerk, the court held in *Ford v. Wainwright*, 477 U.S. 399 (1986) that the "Eighth Amendment prohibits the State from inflicting the penalty of death upon a prisoner who is insane." While Justice Powell joined with the majority opinion in *Ford v. Wainwright*, Powell wrote a concurring opinion where he voiced different reasoning than the opinion of the court. Justice Powell wrote that in determining sanity of a person facing the death penalty "a constitutionally acceptable procedure may be far less formal than a trial. The State should provide an impartial officer or board that can receive evidence and argument from the prisoner's counsel, including expert psychiatric evidence that may differ from the State's own psychiatric examination."[10] After his retirement, Powell expressed regret for some of the death penalty cases he decided and stated that he felt the death penalty was unconstitutional as a matter of law.[11]

Fighting Crime

Mosman had a distinguished career in private practice with the law firm of Miller and Nash in Portland, Oregon after clerking on the nation's highest court. But Mosman felt a calling to public service and sought a position as a federal prosecutor. He worked as an Assistant U.S. Attorney from 1988 to 2001 and then as U.S. Attorney for the District of Oregon from 2001 to 2003.[12] "I worked for a long time handling violent crimes on Indian reservations. They weren't famous [cases] and didn't make the newspapers. That was my most rewarding experience to vindicate the rights of crime victims who often didn't have much of a voice," Mosman recalled. "It was difficult emotionally and draining but, in the end—very rewarding."[13]

As a federal prosecutor, Mosman helped fight terrorist activities in the Pacific Northwest. He oversaw prosecution of the "Portland Seven" terrorism case in 2003— two years after the terrorist attacks on September 11, 2001.[14] Defendants Jeffrey Leon Battle (a/k/a Ahmad Ali and Abu Isa), Patrice Lumumba Ford (a/k/a Larry Ford), Ahmed Ibrahim Bilal, Muhammed Ibrahim Bilal, October Martinique Lewis (a/k/a Khadijah), and Maher Mofeid Hawash (a/k/a Mike Hawash) pled guilty to various charges in the case. Battle and Ford pled guilty to conspiracy to levy war against the United States and were sentenced to 18 years in prison. Ahmed Bilal and Muhammed Bilal pled guilty to conspiracy to contribute services to Al-Qaeda and the Taliban and conspiracy to possess and discharge firearms in furtherance of crimes of violence and were sentenced respectively to ten years and eight years in prison. October Lewis pled guilty to four counts of money laundering and was sentenced to three years in prison. The charges against Al Saoub were dismissed after he was killed in Pakistan by Pakistani troops in 2003.[15]

Mosman's work fighting terrorism caught the attention of key people in the administration of President George W. Bush. When a vacancy arose on the court in 2003, President Bush nominated Mosman to serve as a U.S. District Judge for the District of Oregon. Attorney General John Ashcroft said that Mosman "has been important in the Department of Justice in securing justice in these cases."[16] During his confirmation hearing before the Senate, Mosman told Senators how his experience as a federal prosecutor prepared him to serve as a federal court judge. "I think the principal thing about my career in the U.S. Attorney's Office that has helped me prepare for this nomination is my experience with many different criminal trials," said Mosman. "I've had the opportunity perhaps in this kind of career to try more cases than I might otherwise have done. And so seeing those trials, participating in them, watching how that unfolds in Federal court has been very beneficial to me." Mosman continued, "I think also it's given me an opportunity to watch Federal judges in action and, as you have said, to ponder what it means to be a Federal judge, what those qualities are that make for a good Federal judge." Mosman added how his experience as a law clerk on the U.S. Supreme Court prepared him to serve on the bench. He told the Senators, "I think I would go back to the time I had with Justice Lewis Powell, where I first really saw in action the kind of civility and decency and respect that he manifested constantly to litigants that really for me are the primary hallmarks of a great judge."[17] With his stellar resume, the Senate unanimously confirmed Mosman.

Deciding Key Cases in Oregon

As a federal district judge in Oregon, Mosman has presided over a variety of both civil and criminal cases. In one important case involving privacy and email under the Fourth Amendment, *In re U.S.*, 665 F.Supp.2d 1210 (D. Or. 2009), Mosman rejected the claim that acquisition of email from a service provider without notice to the subscribers violated the Fourth Amendment. The court held that subscribers voluntarily exposed the contents of their emails to the service provider. The government was not required to serve notice of a search warrant to subscribers who sent or received e-mails, which warrant was served on the internet service providers (ISPs), for electronic information stored on the providers' servers, since the e-mails to be seized were in possession of the ISPs.[18] Mosman held that subscribers were, or should have been, aware that their personal information and contents of their online communications were accessible to the ISPs and their employees, and could have been shared with the government under appropriate circumstances.[19]

Mosman is probably best known for his decision in *Lemons v. Bradbury*[20] involving a voter initiative in Oregon to overturn the recognition of same-sex domestic partnerships adopted by the Oregon State Legislature. Mosman denied the request for an injunction brought by voters who argued that the Oregon Secretary of State's signature verification procedures violated due process and equal protection rights. In the decision, Mosman compared due process rights to obtaining a driver's license: "If you give a 16–year–old a driver's license and then arbitrarily take it away without any warning, that might violate the due process clause." Judge Mosman further explained that a 14–year–old can't come forward and say, I can prove I'm just as good a driver as anybody else, so you should give me a license, it's not fair if you don't, because the 14–year–old doesn't come within that property line, doesn't come within the original entitlement granted by the State. Mosman reasoned, "It sounds, certainly to the 14–year–olds I know, it sounds perhaps cruel to say it, but they simply have no due process rights in the decision of the State not to initially grant them a driver's license."[21]

The U.S. Court of Appeals for the Ninth Circuit agreed with Mosman's reasoning when the voters appealed the decision. The federal appeals court affirmed Judge Mosman's ruling that the Oregon Secretary of State's procedures did not violate constitutional rights.[22]

Top-Secret Surveillance Court

With ten years of experience as a district judge, U.S. Supreme Court Chief Justice John G. Roberts, Jr. asked Mosman to serve on the Foreign Intelligence Surveillance Court in 2013. Under the Foreign Intelligence Surveillance Act (FISA), the Chief Justice appoints judges to sit on the influential court. "When I was first asked by the Chief Justice, I went to my wife and I explained it and she said, 'Let me get this straight. This is a job where get no additional pay with significant extra work with no help for your work back home and it's controversial. Yeah, that sounds like something you would do.' " While Mosman recognizes some challenges with the court, he sees the value of the court compared to systems in other countries. "It has been very rewarding and very challenging. There is not a lot I can say about it. It is interesting to talk about the balance between liberty and security and not just in an abstract view." Mosman's accepted the call to serve on court with a seven-year term running from 2013 until 2020.

Congress created the Foreign Intelligence Surveillance Court in 1978 with passage of the Foreign Intelligence Surveillance Act (FISA).[23] The Court entertains applications submitted by the United States Government for approval of electronic surveillance, physical search, and other investigative actions for foreign intelligence purpose to promote national security and combat terrorism. Most of the Court's work is conducted ex parte with no adversary party and just the government lawyers present. The top-secret proceedings are needed to protect classified national security information.[24]

Judges on the court sit in a locked, windowless room with walls of corrugated steel, in a restricted area of a Justice Department building in Washington, D.C. Conducting proceedings completely hidden from the public, the court grants government agents permission to surveil targets if probable cause exists that the targets are foreign powers or agents of foreign powers.[25]

Decisions of the Foreign Intelligence Surveillance Court are subject to review by the Foreign Intelligence Surveillance Court of Review, a panel of three senior federal circuit court judges appointed by the U.S. Supreme Court Chief Justice. Decisions of the Foreign Intelligence Surveillance Court of Review are then subject to review by the U.S. Supreme Court although the U.S. Supreme Court has declined to reconsider any decisions to date.[26]

In the first four-decade history since the enactment of the Foreign Intelligence Surveillance Act in 1978, the Foreign Intelligence Surveillance Court of Review has only issued three published decisions from the Foreign Intelligence Surveillance Court. In 2016, the Foreign Intelligence Surveillance Court asked the Foreign Intelligence Surveillance Court of Review for guidance on an issue involving the use of a "pen register" in a certified question. A "wiretap" involves voice communications being heard and recorded, whereas a "pen register" is a mechanical device attached to a telephone line which deciphers the numbers being dialed.[27] The Foreign Intelligence Surveillance Court of Review held that under the section in the Foreign Intelligence Surveillance Act (FISA) governing pen register/trap-and-trace authorization orders, a court could authorize the use of a pen register to collect post-cut-through digits, as long as the collecting agency was directed to take all reasonably available steps to minimize collection of content information and the agency was prohibited from making use of any content information that might be collected.[28]

The Foreign Intelligence Surveillance Court sits in the nation's capital composed of 11 federal district court judges designated by the Chief Justice of the Supreme Court. Each judge serves for a maximum of seven years and their terms are staggered to ensure continuity. Three judges come from the District of Columbia. The other eight judges come from other places around the country.

The Foreign Intelligence Surveillance Court came under increased scrutiny in 2013 after media reports of government surveillance programs conducted by the National Security Agency (NSA) and the Central Intelligence Agency (CIA). The British newspaper, *The Guardian*, published an article in 2013 detailing the NSA's efforts to collect millions of telephone records from Verizon, an American telecommunications company. The public's indignation focused not on the mere existence of these programs, but rather on the federal judges serving on the Foreign Intelligence Surveillance Court who had seemingly approved many of the most controversial programs, including the bulk collection of telephone records and Internet metadata.[29]

Some members of Congress have called for a change in the selection process for judges who sit on court to provide for more accountability and legitimacy. Under the law originally passed by Congress, other than the geographic requirements set forth in the statute, the Chief Justice's authority to appoint judges remains unconditional and unconstrained. To strengthen the legitimacy of the court, Rep. Adam Schiff, a Democrat from California, introduced H.R. 2761: The Presidential Appointment of FISA Court Judges Act in 2013. The proposal sought to "ensure that the Foreign Intelligence Surveillance Court remains a truly independent check on the executive branch." The proposal from Rep. Schiff would require a separate nomination by the President followed by Senate confirmation for all judges who sit on the court. Other proposals would divide the power of appointment between the different branches of the federal government.[30] To date, all proposals to change the selection process for judges who sit on the Foreign Intelligence Surveillance Court have failed as the U.S. Supreme Court Chief Justice wields unilateral appointment power.

Judges typically spend several weeks per year in Washington, D.C. away from their families on a rotating basis deciding cases and then return to their local chambers. "You spend a week there, do your work, and go home. Someone else takes your place the next week," said Mosman.[31] Judges who sit on the court sacrifice their time doing extra work without any extra compensation while facing strong criticism from outsiders trying to achieve a proper balance between the competing interests of national security and privacy rights.

Balancing Responsibilities

Prior to his work as a federal judge, Mosman faced some challenges as a young lawyer trying to find the proper balance between fulfilling his work obligations and living his religious convictions. Mosman considers keeping the sabbath day holy one challenge he faced early in his legal career. "I was at a pretty young age in my career where I didn't have a lot of institutional power," recalled Mosman. "I had to essentially say—I am not available."[32]

In speaking to a group of law students, Mosman offered suggestions on ways to cope with conflicts in the legal profession after administering a questionnaire to attorneys and judges who have been exposed to substantial conflict in legal practice. Mosman said, "Almost uniformly my respondents said that the most confrontational lawyers they deal with are young ones." Because young attorneys tend to become more aggressive when nervous or scared, they come across as less professional. Reading from his responses, Judge Mosman advised, "Make it about issues, not egos. Don't personalize it. Make it about the dispute that you have with the other side, not their personalities." Judge Mosman also counseled not to respond with threatening behavior, but rather to respond in a non-confrontational way for as long as possible. "Know your limits," Judge Mosman counseled. "Humor can help. . . The practice of law has been hard in many ways, confrontation is hard." Judge Mosman reflected, "And it's a dark world. I cannot deny that it has changed me, changed my relationship with the world, the church, and other people. But I don't really regret any of it. I am grateful for what conflict and confrontation have taught me."[33]

As a bishop, primary teacher, and working with the young men's youth organization, Mosman has predominantly worked with the youth in church callings. "I have taught young people most of my life. What I have learned most is loving people is the most important part of church teaching."[34]

As a judge, Mosman sees the individual worth of each person, especially in criminal cases when sentencing defendants convicted of federal crimes. "The thing that comes up the most in my work in day to day life is my belief in the infinite worth of each person that comes before you" said Mosman, in seeing the value of each individual. "My interaction with them are deeply driven that they are my brother. They are my sister. There is a loving God who knows them."[35]

"[S]ubscribers are, or should be, aware that their personal information and the contents of their online communications are accessible to the ISP and its employees and can be shared with the government under the appropriate circumstances. Much of the reluctance to apply traditional notions of third party disclosure to the e-mail context seems to stem from a fundamental misunderstanding of the lack of privacy we all have in our e-mails. Some people seem to think that they are as private as letters, phone calls, or journal entries. The blunt fact is, they are not." Judge Michael W. Mosman on the limitations of digital privacy.[36]

---

[1] Amasa M. Eaton, *Recent State Constitutions*, 6 Harv. L. Rev. 53, 54 (1892); Shelle Jennsen, Idaho History: Idaho's First Capital, Go Idaho, July 22, 2016, https://goidaho.com/idahos-first-capital/ [https://perma.cc/79JL-SVYJ].

[2] Fred Leeson, *The Monday Profile Aspiring Federal Judge Michael Mosman*, The Oregonian, May 12, 2003, 2003 WL 15798368.

[3] Judge Michael Mosman, Spirit in the Law Series, BYU Law Newsroom, Apr. 2, 2015, http://law.byu.edu/news2/spirit-law-judge-michael-mosman [https://perma.cc/TA4H-3GEW] (hereinafter "Mosman (2015)").

[4] Phone interview with Michael W. Mosman, United States District Judge, District of Oregon, Jul. 6, 2017 (hereinafter "Mosman 2017").

[5] Leeson (2003).

[6] Hearing before the Committee on the Judiciary, S Hrg No. 108-135, 108th Cong, 2d Sess, 4 (2003) (statement of Michael W. Mosman).

[7] Mosman (2015).

[8] Richard H. Fallon, Jr., *A Tribute to Justice Lewis F. Powell, Jr.*, 101 Harv. L. Rev. 399, 401 (1987).

[9] James F. Fagan, Jr., *When Does Four of a Kind Beat a Full House? The Rise, Fall and Replacement of the Rule of Four*, 25 New Eng. L. Rev. 1101, 1111 (1991).

[10] 477 U.S. 427.

[11] Margareth Etienne, *Introduction: Tinkering with Death in Illinois*, 2003 U. Ill. L. Rev. 1073, 1073–74 (2003) (citing John C. Jeffries, Jr., Justice Lewis F. Powell, Jr. 451-52 (1994)).

[12] Leeson (2003).

[13] Mosman (2017).

[14] Bryan Denson, *Local Judge Will Sit on Secretive Wiretap Panel,* The Oregonian, Jun. 8, 2013, 2013 WLNR 14154465.

[15] John C. Richter, *Counter-Terrorism: A Federal Prosecutor's View,* 33 Okla. City U. L. Rev. 297, 329 (2008).

[16] Brigham Young University-Idaho, Alumni News, Fall 2003, http://www.byui.edu/upward/archive/summit/fall2003/alumninews [https://perma.cc/9JGC-5V7D].

[17] Mosman (2017).

[18] 665 F.Supp.2d at 1224.

[19] *Id.*

[20] *Lemons v. Bradbury,* No. CV–07–1782–MO, 2008 WL 336823 (Feb. 1, 2008), aff'd 585 F.3d 1098 (9th Cir. 2008).

[21] 2008 WL 336823 at *5.

[22] 585 F.3d at 1102.

[23] Foreign Intelligence Surveillance Act of 1978 § 105(a)(3)(A), codified, as amended, at 50 U.S.C. §§ 1801-1885c.

[24] *Id.*

[25] Nola K. Breglio, *Leaving FISA Behind: The Need to Return to Warrantless Foreign Intelligence Surveillance,* 113 Yale L.J. 179 (2003).

[26] *Id.*

[27] 68 Am. Jur. 2d Searches and Seizures § 353.

[28] *In re Certified Question of Law,* 858 F.3d 591 (Foreign Intel. Surv. Ct. Rev. 2016).

[29] *The Power to Appoint FISA Judges: Evaluating Legislative Proposals to Reform 50 U.S.C. S 1803 and Improve the Surveillance Court,* 51 Harv. J. on Legis. 365, 367–68 (2014).

[30] *Id.*

[31] Mosman (2017).

[32] *Id.*

[33] Mosman (2015).

[34] Mosman (2017).

[35] *Id.*

[36] *In re U.S.,* 665 F. Supp. 2d 1210, 1224 (D. Or. 2009).

Chapter 14
Dallin H. Oaks:
Defender of Religious Liberty

Following in Lincoln's Footsteps

Dallin H. Oaks, one of the foremost defenders of religious liberty, considers arguing a case before the Illinois Supreme Court at the Old State Capitol in Springfield as one of his fondest memories from his illustrious legal career. Even though he lost the case, Oaks recognized the great privilege to argue in the same courtroom where Abraham Lincoln appeared in a record 175 cases.[1] Lincoln also delivered his famous "House Divided" speech in Representatives Hall in 1858 at the Old State Capitol in Springfield where he declared "A house divided against itself cannot stand. I believe this government cannot endure, permanently, half slave and half free."[2]

In *People v. Tranowski*, 20 Ill. 2d 11, 169 N.E.2d 347 (1960) on appeal before the Illinois Supreme Court decided in 1960, Oaks took on a pro bono case and represented Stanley Tranowski, who had been convicted of armed robbery as a habitual defender. Oaks recalled, "In the *Tranowski* case, I knew from the beginning that I had a case that was a loser. At the same time, I felt an obligation to do my best for the client, a poor Polish boy." Ultimately, the Illinois Supreme Court rejected Tranowski's appeal and sustained the criminal conviction holding that evidence of other robberies was admissible where the evidence served to place the defendant in the area at a correct time to establish a scheme or design which was strikingly similar to the offense charged in the indictment.[3] Oaks later wrote, "What I *learned* from the defeat was very little, but what I *experienced* was very precious to me.

I love arguing a case before the court where Abraham Lincoln still holds the record of the lawyer who appeared most frequently. It was very sweet to me to represent a poor Polish boy." Oaks added, "And there was a sweet aftermath to my representation: after the case was lost, this boy's brother, a poor blue-collar worker in Chicago, came to my law firm office with several hundred dollars for the service I had given to his brother and their family. When I refused (of course), he thanks me and said, 'that means that my wife and I can use this money to buy a washer.' "[4]

Oaks's recollection of the *Tranowski* case reflects his lifelong passions for the law, history, and service to others. Oaks recalled, "As I reflected on the satisfaction I had handling that case for that indigent Polish boy and compared it to the level of satisfaction I was experiencing representing large corporations, it turned my thinking around on how I wanted to spend my life."[5]

Clerking for the Chief Justice in Washington

After graduating from the University of Chicago Law School, one of the nation's most prestigious law schools, Oaks clerked for U.S. Supreme Court Chief Justice Earl Warren during the 1957–1958 Term. "My year clerking for the chief justice was challenging, satisfying, and far-reaching. . . I was allowed to see and participate in the work of the nation's highest court and to work side by side with lawyers who were the present and future leaders of the bench, the bar, and the nation."[6]

Oaks worked on many important cases as a U.S. Supreme Court law clerk. In *Sherman v. United States*, 356 U.S. 369 (1958), the U.S. Supreme Court set forth the modern standard for the entrapment defense in criminal cases. Justice Warren, who wrote the opinion of the court with the assistance of his clerk Oaks, held that "[e]ntrapment occurs only when the criminal conduct was "the product of the creative activity" of law-enforcement officials. . . To determine whether entrapment has been established, a line must be drawn between the trap for the unwary innocent and the trap for the unwary criminal."

Justice Warren continued, "On the one hand, at trial the accused may examine the conduct of the government agent; and on the other hand, the accused will be subjected to an 'appropriate and searching inquiry into his own conduct and predisposition' as bearing on his claim of innocence."[7]

In reflecting on his time clerking for the Chief Justice in a speech given to the J. Reuben Clark Law Society at the Church Conference Center in Salt Lake City, Utah, in 2005, nearly five decades later, Oaks recalled:

> Chief Justice Earl Warren was an unlikely mentor and boss for a conservative lawyer like me. As you know, he and others on the so-called "Warren Court" are the authors of many opinions that represent and set the direction for what is now known as judicial activism. In my view this judicial activism has worked far-reaching mischief in the law. Whether one agrees or disagrees with the outcome of these activist decisions, they are unfortunate precedents because they are matters that should be decided by elected lawmakers, not life-tenured federal judges. For this and other reasons my confidential personal year-end tally shows that I disagreed with the chief justice's votes on 40 percent of the cases decided on the merits that year. The 60 percent in which I agreed with him were obviously more comfortable for me, especially in cases where he was writing the opinion for the Court. Many of these were very satisfying to me personally.[8]

The exactness by Oaks in recording and maintaining that personal tally of decisions for nearly five decades also reflects his meticulous character.

Lessons Learned in the Competitive Atmosphere of Private Practice

After graduating from one of the nation's top law schools and clerking for the Chief Justice on the U.S. Supreme Court,

Oaks had many opportunities available to him. He decided to return to Chicago after clerking on the nation's high court and worked in private practice for Kirkland, Ellis, Hodson, Chaffetz & Masters (now Kirkland & Ellis LLP), one of the world's most elite law firms.[9] During this time in private practice, Oaks worked on the *Tranowski* case as a pro bono matter appearing before the Illinois Supreme Court.

Oaks learned a valuable lesson working at a large law firm in private practice in the highly competitive atmosphere in Chicago. Oaks credits the influence of his church leader and stake president, John K. Edmunds, a prominent lawyer in Chicago. Oaks said, "This was a time for further decisions on the relative priorities of family, Church, and profession. Soon, at a time when I was handling a heavy load of cases and working four evenings a week, President Edmunds called me as a stake missionary. He told me this calling would require about 40 hours of missionary time each month, which meant three to four evenings per week. I couldn't see how I could accept this calling and still keep up with my law practice." Determined to follow the admonition of his church leader, Oaks said, "I could not say no to a calling that I knew to be from the Lord, especially when that calling came through a servant of the Lord who had wielded such a powerful influence in my life. Gathering all my faith, I accepted the call." Oaks recognized that this one decision became a significant turning point in his life. Oaks stated, "I reduced the time spent in my law practice, almost entirely omitting night work, and devoted that time to missionary activity. Yet I observed no reduction in my performance or advancement in the profession. I was seeking first to build up the kingdom of God, and all those other things were added to me . . . This proved to be a crucial decision in my life."[10] Oaks demonstrated his commitment to living his faith and following the inspiration from his church leaders.

Returning to the University of Chicago

Oaks returned to his alma mater and joined the faculty at the University of Chicago Law School. Edward Levi, Dean of the University of Chicago Law School, recruited Oaks in 1961 and encouraged his former pupil to leave behind private practice as a lawyer and embark on a career as a scholar and teacher.[11] Levi later served as the U.S. Attorney General for President Gerald Ford following the Watergate scandal and set the modern standard for the attorney general with a reputation clearly "above politics"—a standard that Oaks also followed.[12] Oaks left behind the competitiveness of private law practice to pursue loftier professional goals.

As a young professor at the University of Chicago, Oaks conducted a groundbreaking and comprehensive study in conjunction with the American Bar Foundation on the effects of the exclusionary rule under the Fourth Amendment to the U.S. Constitution in search and seizure cases.[13] The exclusionary rule is a rule that excludes or suppresses evidence obtained in violation of an accused person's constitutional rights.[14]

In 1961, the U.S. Supreme Court decided the landmark case *Mapp v. Ohio*, 367 U.S. 643 (1961) which imposed the exclusionary rule upon all the states as a requirement of due process. Previously, the exclusionary rule was only a rule of evidence applicable in about half the states and in the federal courts.[15] In his study on the exclusionary rule, Oaks observed that "[a] prime defect of the exclusionary rule is that police who have been guilty of improper behavior are not affected in their person or their pocketbook by the application of the rule. . . The immediate impact of the exclusionary rule falls not upon the police but upon the prosecutor who is attempting to obtain a conviction." Oaks concluded that the exclusionary rule is "well tailored to deter the prosecutor from illegal conduct. But the prosecutor is not the guilty party in an illegal search and seizure, and he rarely has any measure of control over the police who are responsible."[16]

Fourteen U.S. Supreme Court opinions, scores of lower court opinions, and hundreds of scholarly articles have subsequently cited the landmark research conducted by Oaks.[17] U.S. Supreme Court Justice William Rehnquist declared in an opinion, "The most comprehensive study on the exclusionary rule is probably that done by Dallin Oaks in 1970."[18] The article written by Oaks on the exclusionary rule is the second most cited of those published by The University of Chicago Law Review.[19] Oaks also established a modern standard for empirical research in the law. Prior to his study, legal scholarly rarely utilized empirical research. In looking back at the study, Oaks said, "What I see now as the lasting impact of my exclusionary rule study and article is that it was the best statement of a position now rejected by a majority of legal scholars and courts that is still desired by a small minority, of which I am one."[20]

As a law professor, Oaks also focused his research agenda on the intersection between law and religion foreshadowing his future zealous advocacy for religious freedom as a member of the Quorum of the Twelve Apostles of the Church of Jesus Christ of Latter-day Saints. In his first book, *The Wall between Church and State* published by the University of Chicago Press, Oaks examined religious freedom in the context of government aid to private schools, the school prayer issue, tax concessions to religious organizations, and other issues involving religion, law and public affairs.[21]

During his ten years as a professor at the University of Chicago Law School, Oaks also served as assistant state's attorney for Cook County, Illinois. Oaks further served as associate dean and acting dean of the law school. Oaks took a hiatus as a visiting professor at the University of Michigan Law School in Ann Arbor during the summer of 1968. He won praise for service as legal counsel to the Bill of Rights Committee of the Illinois Constitutional Convention in 1970. From 1970 to 1971, he also served as executive director of the American Bar Foundation.[22]

As a law professor at the University Chicago, Oaks examined the events surrounding the assassination of Joseph Smith, Jr. who founded The Church of Jesus Christ of Latter-day Saints. In an article entitled "The Suppression of the *Nauvoo Expositor*" published in the Utah Law Review, Oaks recounted the decision by the Nauvoo City Council, with Joseph Smith, acting as mayor, to order the suppression of the *Nauvoo Expositor* which led to his martyrdom. Oaks concluded that there was "considerable basis in the law of their day for their action in characterizing the published issues of the *Nauvoo Expositor* as a nuisance."[23]

Oaks followed up his research in this law review article with a full-length and award-winning book of the historical events surrounding the criminal case of the accused assassins of Joseph Smith. In *Carthage Conspiracy: The Trial of the*

Accused Assassins of Joseph Smith published by the University of Illinois Press, Oaks tells the dramatic story surrounding the martyrdom of Joseph Smith, and his brother, Hyrum, at the Carthage jail and the subsequent murder-conspiracy trial of the accused assassins. The book also deals with the question of achieving justice when crimes are politically motivated and popularly supported.[24]

In *Carthage Conspiracy,* Oaks and co-author Marvin S. Hill, a history professor at Brigham Young University, meticulously examined trial transcripts and other historical documents surrounding the murder-conspiracy trial held in Hancock County, Illinois in the context of Church and American history.

In his analysis of the acquittal by the jury in the Smith murder case, Oaks recognized that "[t]he jury's sovereign power to nullify the written law can be used to shield a person who has committed a morally reprehensible act that is approved by the community from which the jury is drawn."[25] Oaks also pointed out that jury nullification requires that the composition of the jury be reasonably representative of the entire community, but the jury of the accused Joseph Smith assassins excluded all members of the Church, even though they comprised at least half the population of the county.[26] *Carthage Conspiracy* received praise from many readers, including scholars and laypersons. One reviewer with the *Journal of American History* described the book as "One of the best books to appear on Mormon history in years. . . . An illuminating study of authority in a democratic society." Another review lauded "*Carthage Conspiracy* is a superb work of historical analysis and reconstruction."[27] The Mormon History Association selected *Carthage Conspiracy* for the Best Book of the Year Award in 1976.[28]

Heading Home to Utah

Oaks left the University of Chicago Law School and accepted a position as president of Brigham Young University at age 39, a remarkably young age for the head of a major university. Oaks accepted the call to return to his birth state of Utah. During his tenure as president of Brigham Young

University from 1971 until 1980, Oaks helped establish the J. Reuben Clark Law School. He worked closely with the appointment of a law school dean in Rex Lee, the recruitment of faculty, the assembling of a library, and the construction of the law school building.[29]

After serving as president of Brigham Young University for nine years, Oaks became as an Associate Justice on the Utah Supreme Court in 1980. Oaks preferred this post to any other office in government. He said, "I can't think of anything in public life I'd rather do than be an appellate judge."[30] Oaks served from 1980 until his resignation in 1984 when he answered the call to serve as a member of the Quorum of Twelve Apostles for the Church. Oaks wrote 148 opinions during his five years on the state's highest court.[31]

Among the decisions that Oaks wrote, the case *Leigh Furniture & Carpet Co. v. Isom*, 657 P.2d 293 (Utah 1982) involving business unfair trade practices has garnered the most attention from subsequent courts. In *Leigh Furniture*, the Utah Supreme Court set forth what is now known as the "Leigh Furniture test" used in cases involving the intentional interference with economic relations, a common tort action brought by businesses for unfair trade practices.[32] While the holding in Leigh Furniture was overruled in 2015 by a subsequent decision for one element, the *Leigh Furniture* test established an important precedent in the law of unfair trade practices.[33]

As a Utah Supreme Court Justice, the court faced difficult questions involving broad legal issues. In one case, *In re J. P.*, 648 P.2d 1364 (Utah 1982), the Utah Division of Family Services filed a petition with the juvenile court asking that the parental rights of the natural mother of J. P., then four years old, be terminated in the best interest of the child under the Utah statute. The mother filed a motion to dismiss the petition, alleging that the statute relied upon by the state was unconstitutional. After a hearing, the presiding judge granted the mother's motion to dismiss, holding the amended statute to be a violation of the mother's substantive right to "liberty, privacy, and family integrity" as guaranteed by the Ninth and Fourteenth Amendments to the United States Constitution, and void on its face for vagueness in contravention of procedural due process of law as guaranteed by the Fourteenth

Amendment to the United States Constitution and Article I of the Constitution of Utah.

In discussing the importance of preserving family bonds, Oaks wrote the opinion of the Utah Supreme Court recognized that "the recognition of the due process and retained rights of parents promotes values essential to the preservation of human freedom and dignity and to the perpetuation of our democratic society." As a passionate defender of traditional family values, Oaks wrote, "The family is a principal conservator and transmitter of cherished values and traditions." The judicial opinion written by Oaks continued, "Any invasion of the sanctity of the family, even with the loftiest motives, unavoidably threatens those traditions and values."[34] The Utah Supreme Court affirmed with the trial court decision and granted the mother's motion to dismiss the petition seeking to terminate her parental rights.

In another case before the Utah Supreme Court involving procedural due process guaranteed under the Fifth and Fourteenth Amendments to the U.S. Constitution, *Nelson v. Jacobsen*, 669 P.2d 1207 (Utah 1983), Oaks wrote "[t]imely and adequate notice and an opportunity to be heard in a meaningful way are the very heart of procedural fairness." Justice Oaks wrote that Due Process "is not a technical concept that can be reduced to a formula with a fixed content unrelated to time, place, and circumstances."[35]

Oaks also examined due process rights in *Codianna v. Morris*, 660 P.2d 1101 (Utah 1983) where the prosecution withheld evidence from the defendant in a criminal case. The evidence withheld consisted of eleven witness depositions, four written witness statements, and the unrecorded statement of one witness to a prosecution investigator. In the decision by the Utah Supreme Court, Oaks wrote, "A prosecutor violates due process . . . if he fails to reveal voluntarily evidence which, viewed in the context of the entire record, creates a reasonable doubt about defendant's guilt." The court ruled, "There is no violation of due process if the evidence demonstrates only a 'mere possibility that an item of undisclosed information might have helped the defense, or might have affected the outcome of the trial.' "[36]

Oaks decided an important case involving the discovery rule involving Utah's two-year statute of limitations for a wrongful death action in *Myers v. McDonald*, 635 P.2d 84 (Utah 1981). In *Myers*, the plaintiffs, husband and wife, were guardians of 14-year-old Bobbie Menzies, the wife's brother, who was killed in an automobile accident.[37] The plaintiffs were unable to discover that the youth died until after the statute of limitation for wrongful death had run. Oaks and the other justices on the Utah Supreme Court held that the discovery rule should be applied where "[t]he hardship the statute of limitations would impose on the plaintiff in the circumstances of [the] case outweighed any prejudice to the defendant from difficulties of proof caused by the passage of time."[38] The *Myers* case established an important legal precedent setting forth the requirements for the discovery rule in statute of limitations cases.[39]

Answering the Highest Call and Defending Religious Freedom Across the Globe

Oaks resigned from the Utah Supreme Court when he received the highest call for any priesthood holder in the Church—serving as a member of the Quorum of the Twelve Apostles. In the lifetime call to serve as a special witness of Jesus Christ, Oaks has passionately advocated for religious liberty. In giving speeches, attending conferences, and participating in other activities throughout the world, Oaks has defended the fundamental right to religious freedom. For example, Oaks signed the Williamsburg Charter in 1988 on behalf of The Church of Jesus Christ of Latter-day Saints.[40] The Williamsburg Charter was written by a group of farsighted U.S. religious, political, and community leaders, that charter celebrates and reaffirms religious liberty as the foremost freedom of the First Amendment of the United States Constitution.[41] In 2016, Oaks delivered a resounding speech at the University of Oxford speaking on the importance of religious freedom. Oaks stated, "Understanding religion and its relationship to global concerns and to governments is essential to seeking to improve the world in which we live." He added, "None of us can ignore the importance of religion globally—in politics, conflict resolution, economic development, humanitarian relief, and more." Oaks further explained that "[u]nderstanding religion its relationship to global concerns at to governments is essential to seeking to improve the world in which we live."[42]

Always willing to impart his knowledge stemming from his days as a law professor, Oaks shared his insights with readers in his autobiography entitled *Life's Lessons Learned*. Imparting his personal experiences that helped shape his life and teachings, Oaks divided his memoir into three major sections: childhood and youth, his years as BYU president and a justice of the Utah Supreme Court, and his service in the Quorum of the Twelve Apostles. Oaks overcame great challenges in life growing up without a father and losing his wife to cancer.[43] Yet through that adversity, Oaks has continued to press forward and steadfast while assuming the mantle of leadership for the Church and inspiring millions of people around the globe.

Oaks has received well-deserved recognition for his years of service in promoting religious freedom and public service. The Becket Fund for Religious Liberty awarded Oaks the prestigious Canterbury Medal in 2013 for his lifetime of service in promoting the cause of religious freedom. The medal recognizes individuals who demonstrate courage in the defense of religious freedom and is named for Canterbury Cathedral, where Thomas Becket stood in defense of religious freedom against King Henry II.[44] In 2012, Oaks also received another distinction with the Lee Lieberman Otis Award for Distinguished Service to honor his years of dedicated public service.[45]

Oaks has left an enduring legacy in the law not just with his opinions and scholarship, but with the student organization that bears his name. The Dallin H. Oaks Society, a student organization at the University of Chicago Law School, increases awareness within the law school community of the presence, beliefs and concerns of law students who are members of The Church of Jesus Christ of Latter-day Saints. The Society also assists in recruiting students and those of similar beliefs to attend the law school, provide fellowship for these students as they make their transition into the law school community, and develop networking opportunities between current students and graduates of the law school who are members of the Church.[46]

Throughout his life as a lawyer, law professor, author, university president, state supreme court justice, and disciple of Jesus Christ, Oaks has inspired countless persons to pursue careers in the law and to preserve legal and constitutional rights in the face of opposition.

———————

"[T]he right of a parent not to be deprived of parental rights without a showing of unfitness, abandonment, or substantial neglect is so fundamental to our society and so basic to our constitutional order that it ranks among those rights referred to in . . . the Ninth Amendment of the United States Constitution as being retained by the people." Dallin H. Oaks, in a Utah Supreme Court decision, on the fundamental right of parents to raise their children.[47]

———————

[1] Illinois Courts, Abraham Lincoln's Cases: The History of the Illinois Supreme Court, http://www.illinoiscourts.gov/SupremeCourt/Historical/Lincoln2.asp [https://perma.cc/5QY6-L33C].

[2] Abraham Lincoln Online, Old State Capitol, http://www.abrahamlincolnonline.org/lincoln/sites/capitol.htm [https://perma.cc/75NP-KYHF].

[3] 169 N.E.2d 347.

[4] Dallin H. Oaks former Utah Supreme Court Justice, letter to the author, May 12, 2017 (hereinafter "Oaks (2017)").

[5] Sarah Galer, *Federalist Society honors Elder Dallin H. Oaks, JD'57,* The University of Chicago News, May 15, 2012, https://news.uchicago.edu/article/2012/05/15/federalist-society-honors-elder-dallin-h-oaks-jd-57 [https://perma.cc/4THR-BC6U].

[6] Dallin H. Oaks, *The Beginning and the End of a Lawyer,* J. Reuben Clark Law Society, Clark Memorandum, Spring 2005, 8.

[7] *Sherman v. United States,* 356 U.S. 369, 372–73 (1958).

[8] *Id.*

[9] *Id.*

[10] *Id.*

[11] *Id.*

[12] Scott Horton, *Responses to the Ten Questions,* 35 Wm. Mitchell L. Rev. 5051, 5053 (2009).

[13] Dallin H. Oaks, *Studying the Exclusionary Rule in Search and Seizure*, 37 U. Chi. L. Rev. 665 (1970).

[14] Black's Law Dictionary (10th ed. 2014), exclusionary rule.

[15] Fred E. Inbau, *Public Safety v. Individual Civil Liberties: The Prosecutor's Stand*, 89 J. Crim. L. & Criminology 1413, 1414 (1999).

[16] Oaks, 37 U. Chi. L. Rev. at 725–726.

[17] Albert W. Alschuler, *Studying the Exclusionary Rule: An Empirical Classic*, 75 U. Chi. L. Rev. 1365, 1365–66 (2008).

[18] *California v. Minjares,* 443 U.S. 916, 926 (1979).

[19] Alschuler, 65 U. Chi. L. Rev. at 1366.

[20] Dallin H. Oaks, *The Suppression of the Nauvoo Expositor*, 9 Utah L. Rev. 862, 890-891 (1965).

[21] Dallin H. Oaks, *The Wall between Church and State*, 1st ed., (Chicago: University of Chicago Press, 1963).

[22] President Dallin H. Oaks, First Counselor in the First Presidency, The Church of Jesus Christ of Latter-day Saints, https://www.lds.org/prophets-and-apostles/what-are-prophets/bio/dallin-h-oaks?lang=eng [https://perma.cc/ST7Y-PL8U].

[23] Oaks, 9 Utah L. Rev. at 890–891.

[24] Dallin H. Oaks and Marvin S. Hill, *Carthage Conspiracy: The Trial of the Accused Assassins of Joseph Smith*, 1st ed. (Champaign, IL: University of Illinois Press, 1979).

[25] *Id.* at 212.

[26] *Id.* at 213–214.

[27] University of Illinois Press, *Carthage Conspiracy: The Trial of the Accused Assassins of Joseph Smith*, http://www.press.uillinois.edu/books/catalog/66efg9nm9780252007620.html [https://perma.cc/7JR9-7SP3].

[28] *Id.*

[29] Oaks (2017).

[30] *Id.*

[31] Results conducted from a Westlaw search on September 23, 2017 (within Utah state cases, search for: "ju(oaks)" without quotation marks).

[32] *Garth O. Green Enterprises, Inc. v. Harward*, No. 2:15-CV-00556-DN-EJF, 2017 WL 914611, *4 (D. Utah Mar. 7, 2017).

[33] *Id.*

34 648 P.2d 1375–1376.

35 669 P.2d 1211, 1213.

36 660 P.2d 1101 at 1106 (citing *United States v. Agurs*, 427 U.S. 97, 109-110 (1976)).

37 653 P.2d 84.

38 *Id.* at 87.

39 See *Klinger v. Kightly*, 791 P.2d 868, 872 (Utah 1990).

40 Dallin H. Oaks, *Religion in Public Life*, Ensign, July 1990.

41 *Id.*

42 Elder Dallin H. Oaks, The Complementary Functions of Religion and Government in a Global Setting, Lecture given Jun. 9, 2016 at St. Johns College at the University of Oxford, Mormon Newsroom, The Church of Jesus Christ of Latter-day Saints, https://www.mormonnewsroom.org/article/transcript-elder-oaks-university-oxford [https://perma.cc/HY3B-D8WG].

43 Dallin H. Oaks, *Life's Lessons Learned* (Salt Lake City, Utah: Deseret Book, 2011).

44 Elder Dallin H. Oaks Honored for Championing Religious Freedom, Mormon Newsroom, The Church of Jesus Christ of Latter-day Saints, May 16, 2013, http://www.mormonnewsroom.org/article/elder-oaks-becket-fund-canterbury-medal [https://perma.cc/7MYF-5SA].

45 Galer (2012).

46 University of Chicago Law School, Dallin H. Oaks Society, https://www.law.uchicago.edu/studentorgs/dhos [https://perma.cc/C5MB-AMJ7].

47 *In re J. P.*, 648 P.2d 1364, 1375–76 (Utah 1982).

Chapter 15

Preston D. Richards: Hard-Working Educator, Lawyer, Public Servant

A Presidential Candidate Sparks a Flame

Preston D. Richards developed an interest in law and politics early in life. During the presidential election of 1896, the Democratic and Populist leader Williams Jennings Bryan made a stop to Utah to garner votes. When Bryan visited the local school yard, young Preston, then age 13, engaged the presidential candidate in intelligent conversation for 10 minutes, while the other youngsters stood around and stared in amazement.[1] While Bryan narrowly lost the election in 1896 to William McKinley, and also ran unsuccessfully in 1900 and 1908 for the presidency, Richards later reunited with Bryan. Seventeen years after the school yard encounter, with Bryan serving as the U.S. Secretary of State for President Woodrow Wilson, Richards worked with Bryan as assistant solicitor in the U.S. Department of State.[2]

Richards was born in 1881 in Mendon, Utah in Cache Valley as one of 11 children in his family and grew up in Utah. Life his father, Willard B. Richards, and his grandfather, Dr. Willard Richards, the first Secretary of State of Utah, Preston was a tireless worker. It was not unusual for him to work at his desk until 2 or 3 in the morning. His friends said he had to work late because he loved people so well and spent time during the day in conversation with them. He devoted his time on earth as a devoted educator, lawyer, and public servant.[3]

Preston D. Richards worked as an educator for many years in Utah before deciding to attend law school. After his cousin, Stephen L. Richards, graduated from the University of Chicago Law School in 1904, Preston followed suit. Preston graduated from the University of Chicago while also studying at Columbia University in New York.[4] Stephen L. Richards later served in the First Presidency of the Church. Other Church members have followed both Preston Richards and Stephen L. Richards in attending the top-ranked law school in the Windy City. The University of Chicago Law School remains the top choice for many aspiring lawyers in the Church.

Serving in the State Department

After graduating from the University of Chicago, Richards served as assistant solicitor in the U.S. Department of State in the nation's capital from 1910 until 1913 working alongside J. Reuben Clark, Jr. in the administration of President William Howard Taft and later in the administration of President Wilson. Richards first attended law school at Columbia University in New York, the alma mater of Clark, before graduating from the University of Chicago. While working for the U.S. Department of State, Richards authored the proclamation of statehood for Arizona issued by President Taft.[5] Arizona was proclaimed the 48th State by President Taft on February 14, 1912—the last state in the continental United States admitted to the Union. The presidential proclamation that Richards drafted states in part, "I, William Howard Taft, President of the United Stated of America, do in accordance with the provisions of the Act of Congress and the joint resolution of Congress herein named, declare and proclaim the fact that the fundamental conditions imposed by Congress on the State of Arizona to entitle that State to admission have been ratified and accepted, and that the admission of the State into the Union on an equal footing with the other States is now complete."[6]

As assistant solicitor in the U.S. Department of State, Richards also prepared the official proclamation for the Seventeenth Amendment to the U.S. Constitution. Playing a key role in the adoption of a constitutional amendment, Richards passionately defended constitutional principles and shared his abiding love for the Constitution throughout his life.[7] Richards drafted the statement of populist leader Bryan, the U.S. Secretary of State, proclaiming the ratification of the Seventeenth Amendment for the direct election of U.S. Senators. Before the adoption of the Seventeenth Amendment, the state legislatures selected U.S. Senators. Bryan strongly supported direct election of Senators. As Secretary of State on May 31, 1913, he announced "And, further, that the states whose legislatures have so ratified the said proposed amendment, constitute three-fourths of the whole number of states in the United States. Now, there, be it known that I, William Jennings Bryan Secretary of State of the United States, by virtue and in pursuance of section 205 of the Revised Statutes of the United States, do hereby certify that the amendment aforesaid has become valid to all intent and purposes as a part of the Constitution of the United States."[8]

Assisting Colonist Claims in Mexico

Richards resigned his position with the U.S. Department of State in 1913 and went to Mexico and El Paso, Texas to assist with colonist claims against the government of Mexico arising out of the Orosco and Madero rebellions.[9] Colonists who were members of The Church of Jesus Christ of Latter-day Saints first settled Colonia Juárez located in the northern part of Chihuahua, Mexico, in 1885. The early pioneers in Colonia Juárez faced many hardships. They lived out of wagon boxes and helped chisel irrigation canals along the sides of the valley to plant apple orchards. Water, an absolute necessity for growing crops in the arid region, was scarce. When the river ran dry, the colonists prayed for water. By divine providence, the 1887 Sonora earthquake displaced large boulders and ruptured an aquifer upriver. The earth tremors opened hot springs twenty miles up the river that provided a source of irrigation water to the valley. The water source has flowed reliably through the valley ever since. After the miraculous earthquake provided a water source, the colonies in Colonia Juárez thrived with rich orchards, cattle ranches, gardens, and a tannery that supplied leather for a shoe factory and for the manufacturing of harnesses and saddles.[10]

With the outbreak of the Mexican Revolution in 1910, the colonists of northern Mexico were forced to flee abandoning their comfortable homes and prosperous businesses as refugees yet again amid persecution. Mitt Romney's ancestors, who helped settle Colonia Juárez, were among the families displaced by the Mexican Revolution. While Mitt Romney's grandfather fled Mexico, some of the Romney cousins stayed in Mexico.[11]

Richards worked with Clark and the U.S. Department of State in filing claims against the Mexican government on behalf of the pioneers displaced by the Mexican Revolution. Clark served as the U.S. Ambassador to Mexico to assist the displaced colonists. For years, repeated efforts were made to reach a settlement for claims arising from the Mexican Revolution. Finally, on September 8, 1923, the United States and Mexico entered into the Treaty on General Claims involving claims under the jurisdiction of the General Claims Commission and the Special Claims Commission. A General Claims Commission was intended to deal with any outstanding matters dating from the previous claims agreement of 1868, while a Special Claims Commission was empowered to hear claims arising from the Mexican Revolution.[12] The treaty, which took effect on March 1, 1924, was intended to improve relations between the countries by forming a commission to settle claims arising after July 4, 1868, to "settle and adjust amicably claims by the citizens of each country against the other" and "for losses or damages originating from acts of officials or others acting for either Government and resulting in injustice."[13] The Commission was directed to quantify the number and size of the claims, and to the extent the aggregate claims of the citizens of one nation exceeded the other nation's claims, the difference would be paid sovereign to sovereign. The total amount of claims released against Mexico exceeded $193 million.[14]

A total of 385 residents of northern Mexico filed formal clams for loss of property. The commission ultimately awarded more than $1.1 million to the colonists who settled the states of Chihuaha and Sonora between 1885 and 1912 for their losses from uprisings between 1910 and 1920. George W. Bartch, Don P. Skousen, and Vernon Romney also assisted with claims asserted by the colonists.[15]

Overcoming Legal Hurdles with the Los Angeles Temple

After working for the U.S. Department of State and helping colonists in Mexico, Richards returned to his Utah roots. Richards partnered with J. Reuben Clark, Jr. to form the law firm Clark & Richards in Salt Lake City. The firm later maintained offices in Los Angeles, New York, and Washington, D.C. Hugh B. Brown and Albert E. Bowen, both members of the Quorum of the Twelve Apostles for the Church, worked alongside Richards as law partners at the firm Clark & Richards.[16]

Richards spent several years in California overseeing the firm's Los Angeles office living in Beverly Hills.[17] While in California, Richards served as a member of the presidency of the Los Angeles Stake of the Church and played an instrumental role in acquiring the land and government permits for the Los Angeles Temple located on a 13-acre site on Santa Monica Boulevard in the Westwood district of Los Angeles.[18] Richards worked at no expense to the Church in contacting the planning, safety, engineering, and many other government bureaus to obtain permits necessary for the temple's construction.[19]

Church officials faced one significant challenge during the planning stages in construction of the Los Angeles Temple. The government had placed limits on the purchase of structural steel imposed by the Korean War. Church President David O. McKay sent Richards and Edward O. Anderson, to plead with the National Production Authority (NPA) in Washington, D.C. for an exemption. With the help of Utah Senator Arthur V. Watkins, Richards and Anderson successfully argued their case to the NPA. Richards used his advocacy skills as a lawyer to explain that because the construction project involving a complex of buildings, including the California Mission home and the Westwood Ward chapel, started before restrictions were placed on churches, the project should continue with the other building projects, including the temple construction. The very next day after meeting with Richards and Anderson, the office of the NPA drafted a letter granting the exemption.[20]

Richards also helped the Church overcome zoning problems by contacting various government bureaus and explaining the purposes of the temple to them. "When these men realized the importance of the temple and reviewed the record of Latter-day Saints living in California," they were pleased to help "in every way to obtain the necessary permits."[21] All told, it took 15 years from the time the temple was first announced before construction actually began in 1952 because of delays caused by World War II, the Korean War, zoning problems, and changes in the temple plans.[22] While Richards did not live to see the temple dedicated, he played a key part in overcoming the legal hurdles for construction. At the time of its construction, the Los Angeles California Temple—dedicated in 1956 by President McKay—was the largest temple of the Church. The Salt Lake Temple later reclaimed the title with its additions and annexations.[23]

In one important case while in California, Richards represented a client, Theodore P. Lamb, who held mining rights. In *Bender v. Lamb*, 133 Cal. App. 348, 24 P.2d 208 (Cal. Ct. App. 1933), the California Court of Appeals affirmed the dismissal by the trial court in a case brought by the plaintiff who claimed a competing interest in the mining rights held by Lamb. The mining rights at issue involved the Sheep Creek Mine located just outside the southern boundary of what is now designated as Death Valley National Park. The location held certain lime and talc deposits of commercial quantity and value.[24] Richards successfully represented his client to secure valuable mining rights in the area amid the height of the Great Depression in 1933.

Advocating for the Right of Publicity and Constitutional Freedoms

Richards also left an impact in the law governing publicity rights. Richards scored a major legal victory in a key invasion of privacy case before the U.S. Court of the Appeals for the Tenth Circuit in 1952. In *Donahue v. Warner Bros. Pictures*, 194 F.2d 6 (10th Cir. 1952), Richards represented Alice M. Donahue, the widow of Jack Donahue, and her daughters, who brought an action against Warner Brothers Pictures. Warner Brothers produced the 1949 movie *Look for the Silver Lining*, a musical biopic that chronicles the vaudeville-to-Broadway story of 1920s' star Marilyn Miller portrayed by June Haver. From her start on the boards in Findlay, Ohio, Marilyn sings and dances her way to Broadway stardom, frequently in company with her mentor, dancer Jack Donahue played by Ray Bolger.[25] Bolger is best known for his portrayal of the Scarecrow in the 1939 MGM picture *The Wizard of Oz*.[26]

The Donahue family claimed that Warner Brothers purposely depicted the career and used the name of Donahue as the leading male star without consent. Jack Donahue was a dancer, singer, and comedian that starred in productions in New York and throughout the country. The U.S. District Court for the District of Utah entered summary judgment dismissing the action with prejudice, and the family of Donahue appealed. The U.S. Court of Appeals for the Tenth Circuit reversed the trial court decision and held that the case against Warner Brothers could proceed. Judge Sam Gilbert Bratton, in writing the opinion of the court, concluded "We find ourselves unable to share the view that Donahue's accomplishments as a dancer, singer, comedian, entertainer, and writer, made him such a public figure that his name, picture, or career could be dramatized in a motion picture photoplay based primarily upon fiction . . . without violating the right of privacy."[27]

Following Richards' death, the federal appeals court sent the case back to the Utah state court. The Utah Supreme Court considered in *Donahue v. Warner Bros. Pictures Distributing Corp.*, 2 Utah 2d 256, 272 P.2d 177 (1954) whether the showing in the State of Utah of the motion picture based partially on the life of Jack Donahue gave rise to a claim for relief in favor of his heirs on the theory that the motion picture was shown "for purposes of trade." The Utah Supreme Court rejected the contention that the Utah statute at the time proscribed the publication of a name or picture in all cases when a profit motive is present, and held that the statute proscribed only such use "for advertising or exploitation of the name or picture or for the promotion of the sale of some collateral commodity."[28] While the Donahue family ultimately lost the case after the death of Richards, the *Donahue* case decided by the Tenth Circuit created an important legal precedent in the law of publicity rights and invasion of privacy rights that many subsequent courts have cited. The estates of top-earning dead celebrities, including Michael Jackson, Charles Schultz, and Elvis Presley, and others benefit from the legal contributions of Richards who helped fight for individual privacy and publicity rights.[29]

In his last case before dying of a sudden heart attack in 1952 at age 70, Richards argued a vehicle negligence case before the Utah Supreme Court. The Utah Supreme Court issued the decision in his client's favor just a few weeks after his death. Richards represented a client injured in an automobile collision. The driver, Archie Poulsen, sought to recover damages to his car and for personal injuries sustained in an intersection collision. The plaintiff-driver stopped and looked to the east at a point where he could see 400 feet on the highway from the direction which defendant's car was coming and that at the time defendant's car was not within his vision. The court held that based on the evidence presented during the trial, the jury could reasonably find that the defendant's car was traveling unreasonably fast for the existing conditions. Richards won his last case posthumously on behalf of his client.[30]

Besides his busy law practice, Richards maintained an active presence in politics. He served in the Utah State Legislature from 1907–1908 and was an alternate delegate to the Republican National Convention held in Chicago in 1908. Richards also played a key part in the designation of the state park around the "This is the Place Monument" at the mouth of Emigration Canyon in Utah.[31]

Later in life, Richards campaigned for the Republican nomination to the U.S. Senate representing Utah in the election of 1950. In vying to serve in the Senate, the *Salt Lake Tribune* published a campaign statement by Richards that read, "Our heritage of freedom, opportunity and all the things we hold most dear are threatened by internal and external forces as they have never before been threatened since Lexington and Bull Run. The evils and dangers confronting us are too numerous to detail but as Americans we must not take them lying down." Richards continued, "We might fight. We must fight to restore constitutional principle of high dignity of the individual and the sanctity of his God-given right to be free—free to choose his own calling and to work at it when and where he will without interference by or dictation of any government or man or body of men whomsoever: to restore the principle of equal rights for all and special privilege for none."[32]

Wallace F. Bennett defeated Richards and secured the Republican nomination. Bennett then defeated incumbent Democrat Elber D. Thomas in the 1950 general election and the Senate seat remained in Republican control for decades. Wallace C. Bennett served from 1951 until 1974 in the Senate and his son, Robert Bennett, also served in the U.S. Senate. Despite working on passage of the Seventeenth Amendment, Richards could not muster the votes from Utah voters.

Richards strongly supported education. As a legislator, he worked on legislation to improve Utah schools, including the establishment of the state teacher retirement law. Before becoming a lawyer, Richards worked as a principal of four different schools in Salt Lake County and as superintendent of Granite School District in Salt Lake City.[33] Richards later taught at the University of Utah law school as a lecturer from 1919 to 1926.[34]

Like his grandfather, Willard Richards—who served as a counselor to prophet Brigham Young—Preston believed in church service. Along with his service in California as a member of the stake presidency and as a missionary in England, Preston Richards served as a member of the general board of the Church's Young Men's Mutual Improvement Association for 15 years.[35] While attending law school at Columbia University, Richards spoke at the semi-annual conference of the Eastern States Mission held in Boston. Speaking to a large audience at the conference, Richards referred to the Savior's parable of the ten talents. Richards told the congregation: "Not the least, but the greatest of all talents in man is the spiritual talent, which, if cultivated, will awaken us to an ever-growing knowledge of God and his righteousness. This talent is implanted and inherent in every man, and hence the divine injunct, 'Seek ye first the Kingdom of God.' " In conclusion, Richards appealed to each person present and asked if they were using their talent to seek out the kingdom of God and its righteousness, and he enjoined all, the necessity of doing so.[36] Richards heeded his own counsel and used his talents throughout his life to enrich the lives of others.

"We must fight to restore the constitutional principle of the high dignity of the individual and the sanctity of his God-given right to be free—free to choose his own calling and to work at it when and where he will without interference by or dictation of any government or man or body of men whomsoever; to restore the principle of equal rights for all and special privilege for none. . . We must fight to restore the purchasing power of the dollar now being destroyed by deficit spending which is now overwhelming us with debt and plunging us headlong into bankruptcy. . . By wise and courageous statesmanship and diplomacy, we must and we can establish peace in the world and peace between labor and industry at home. We must fight to restore constitutional government to America. In this fight, we call upon all good Americans, Republicans and Democrats alike, to help. It can be done, it must be done." Preston D. Richards, in a campaign statement in his failed bid for the U.S. Senate.[37]

---

[1] *Utah Mourns Preston D. Richards-Law-Maker, Educator, and Friend*, Deseret News, Feb. 1, 1952, 2B.

[2] *Id.*

[3] *Id.*

[4] Sheri L. Dew, *Go Forward With Faith: The Biography of Gordon B. Hinckley* (Salt Lake City, Utah: Deseret Book, 1996), 6.

[5] *Id.*

[6] William H. Taft, Proclamation by the President of the United States of America for Admission of Arizona, 37 Stat. 1728.

[7] *Utah Mourns Preston D. Richards-Law-Maker, Educator, and Friend* (1952).

[8] Notification of the Ratification of the 17th Amendment to the Constitution, by Secretary of State William Jennings Bryan, May 31, 1913; various papers of the 63rd Congress (SEN 63-M4); Records of the United States Senate, Record Group 46, National Archives Building, Washington, DC.

[9] *Id.*; History of the Bench and Bar of Utah (Salt Lake City, UT: Interstate Press Association, 1913), 190. Princeton University Library, Digitized by Google,

https://books.google.com/books?id=HBFLAAAAYAAJ&pg=PA177
&source=gbs_selected_pges&cad=2#v=onepage&q&f=false
[https://perma.cc/9N53-2K9T].

[10] E. LeRoy Hatch, *Mormon Colonies: Beacon Light in Mexico*, Ensign, Sept. 1972.

[11] Nick Miroff, *South of Border, Romney's Mexican Roots Run Deep,* Seattle Times, Jul. 25, 2011, A3, 2011 WLNR 14881635.

[12] David J. Bederman, *The United Nations Compensation Commission and the Tradition of International Claims Settlement,* 27 N.Y.U. J. Int'l L. & Pol. 1, 42 (1994).

[13] Treaty on General Claims, Sept. 8, 1923, United States—Mexico, 43 Stat. 1730, T.S. No. 678.

[14] *Asociacion De Reclamantes v. United Mexican States*, 561 F. Supp. 1190, 1192 (D.D.C. 1983), aff'd, 735 F.2d 1517 (D.C. Cir. 1984).

[15] Thomas Cottam Romney, *The Mormon Colonies in Mexico* (Salt Lake City, UT: University of Utah Press, 2005), 306.

[16] Edwin Brown Firmage, *Elder Hugh B. Brown, 1883–1975: In Memoriam,* Ensign, January 1976.

[17] "United States Census, 1940," database with images, FamilySearch (https://familysearch.org/ark:/61903/1:1:K97C-WPL : accessed 8 October 2017), Preston D Richards, Tract 382, Beverly Hills, Beverly Hills Judicial Township, Los Angeles, California, United States; citing enumeration district (ED) 19-45, sheet 15B, line 63, family 387, Sixteenth Census of the United States, 1940, NARA digital publication T627. Records of the Bureau of the Census, 1790 - 2007, RG 29. Washington, D.C.: National Archives and Records Administration, 2012, roll 221.

[18] *Utah Mourns Preston D. Richards-Law-Maker, Educator, and Friend* (1952).

[19] Richard O. Cowan, *Temples to Dot the Earth* (Springville, UT: Cedar Fort, 2011), 171.

[20] Gregory A. Prince and William Robert Wright, *David O. McKay and the Rise of Modern Mormonism* (Salt Lake City, UT: University of Utah Press, 2005), 257.

[21] Edward O. Anderson, *The Los Angeles Temple*, Improvement Era 56 (April 1953): 225–26; 58 (November 1955): 804.

[22] Los Angeles Temple, Ensign, May 1977, https://www.lds.org/ensign/1977/05/los-angeles-temple?lang=eng [https://perma.cc/CJX5-X4LD].

[23] LDS Church Temples, Los Angeles California Temple, http://ldschurchtemples.org/losangeles/ [https://perma.cc/LE88-4J72].

[24] See also the companion case *Pidgeon v. Lamb*, 133 Cal. App. 342, 344, 24 P.2d 206, 207 (Cal. Ct. App. 1933).

[25] Look for the Silver Lining, Plot Summary, IMDB, http://www.imdb.com/title/tt0041599/plotsummary?ref_=tt_ov_pl [https://perma.cc/LH9F-NXHY].

[26] Glenn Folwer, *Ray Bolger, Scarecrow in "Oz," Dies*, New York Times, Jan. 16, 1987, D19.

[27] 194 F.2d at 14.

[28] 272 P.2d 177; *Jeppson v. United Television, Inc.*, 580 P.2d 1087, 1088 (Utah 1978).

[29] See Zack O'Malley Greenburg, *The Highest-Paid Dead Celebrities of 2016*, Forbes, Oct. 12, 2017, https://www.forbes.com/sites/zackomalleygreenburg/2016/10/12/the-highest-paid-dead-celebrities-of-2016/#4c105d711b1b [https://perma.cc/W9Z3-PRBF].

[30] *Poulsen v. Manness*, 121 Utah 269, 241 P.2d 152 (1952).

[31] *P. D. Richards, Noted Lawyer, Dies in S.L.*, Deseret News, Feb. 1, 1952.

[32] *Id.*

[33] *Id.*

[34] University of Utah S.J. Quinney College of Law, Faculty History, http://www.law.utah.edu/library/digital-collections_trashed/faculty-history/ [https://perma.cc/STF7-A25K].

[35] *Id.*

[36] *Liahona: The Elders' Journal*, Volume 6, Issue 30, p. 728-729, [https://perma.cc/QZ4H-HTR9].

[37] *P. D. Richards, Noted Lawyer, Dies in S.L.* (1952).

Chapter 16

Milan D. Smith, Jr.: Federal Judge Epitomizing the Wisdom of Solomon

Overcoming the Blue Slip

When the name of Milan D. Smith, Jr. came before the U.S. Senate to serve as a judge on the influential U.S. Court of Appeals for the Ninth Circuit, Senator Gordon Smith, a Republican from Oregon, voiced staunch support for his older brother drawing similarity to Solomon from the Holy Bible. Senator Gordon Smith praised his older brother's qualifications to serve as a judge:

> Mr. Chairman, without equating Milan to Solomon, I can, without equivocation, speak to his many Solomon-like qualities. Milan, Jr., is the eldest of Milan and Jessica Udall Smith's ten children. I am the eighth in that number and Milan's youngest brother. In my 54 years of life, Milan has been an example and force for good in our family and, since the death of our parents, has been truly a family leader and friend to us all, through times of tears and times of cheers. For as far back as my memory serves, I have been witness to a concourse of people who have sought him out for wisdom and judgment, for counsel and comfort, on matters great and small. These have included my parents, myself, and all of my brothers and sisters, cousins and kinsmen from far and wide, his own six children, and, of course, his legions of legal clients over many decades. Without respect of persons, he has been a wise friend and a good shepherd to all. His academic

preparations and provident life speak for themselves. But, in sum, what I can say is that he is one of the wisest men I have ever known. He has an understanding heart, a heart for judgment. He is possessed of the spirit of discernment between good and bad, right and wrong, the just and the unjust. I cannot think of a time or a court when a man of his quality and preparation are more sorely in need than this one and in our time. While I doubt that Milan's fame as a judge will spread Solomon-like throughout the world, I do predict that those who come before his court will find his judgments will mean the world to them. His judgments do mean the world to me. So, my Senate colleagues, I commend to you a man who has dusted me off many times, as a boy and as a man when I have fallen, and showed me the way to better paths, to life's sunny uplands--my brother, Milan Dale Smith, Jr. I urge his confirmation to the Ninth Circuit Court of Appeals.[1]

While confirmation of federal judges can sometimes involve boisterous challenges, Senator Barbara Boxer, a long-time serving Democrat from California, voiced strong support for Smith, a conservative nominated by Republican President George W. Bush. Boxer's support stemmed in large part to a decision by Milan Smith 20 years earlier to resign in protest from the California Fair Employment and Housing Commission. During the summer of 1968 in his second year of law school, Smith clerked for the prestigious law firm Covington & Burling in the nation's capital. Smith learned an important lesson as a young apprentice studying the law: if you are ever serving in a government position and find it immoral—resign in protest.[2] Dean Acheson, while acting as Undersecretary of the Treasury, resigned in protest and opposition to President Franklin D. Roosevelt's plan to deflate the dollar by controlling gold prices and going off the gold standard.[3] Acheson, a partner at Covington & Burling, later served as Secretary of State to President Harry Truman.[4] Smith learned from Acheson's example and resigned in protest because California's Fair Employment and Housing

Commission failed to provide adequate legal remedies to women who were the victims of sexual harassment in the workplace.

Smith related, "Twenty years later, I went into Senator Barbara Boxer's office with my brother and my wife. [Senator Boxer] had used the blue slip on a number of nominees. She was just knocking off people right and left."[5] Senators can use the "blue slip" to block or delay the confirmation of judges with whom they disagree ideologically.[6] Senator Boxer pulled out a copy of Smith's resignation letter from the California Fair Employment and Housing Commission. Senator Boxer told the judicial nominee, "I wish that you were a liberal Democrat. What you showed me is fairness, compassion, integrity—just the kind of thing I would like to see in a judge."[7]

In recommending Smith to the Ninth Circuit, Senator Boxer told her colleagues in the Senate that "[t]hroughout his work for the citizens of California, Mr. Smith has demonstrated compassion, courage, and understanding of the hardships faced by average citizens. He has shown a willingness to examine all sides of an issue and to develop thoughtful and balanced solutions to problems." Boxer, a liberal Democrat, found that Smith "has fought for those who have been discriminated against, and he has added his strong voice to them, and he has shown courage. And I now know why he is such a strong supporter of equal rights for women, because I have met many of the women in his family." Boxer found that Smith "has earned the admiration of his colleagues, and today Mr. Smith has come to Washington. . . He is an individual of great character, an independent thinker. I have profound respect for him, and it is a very happy day for me."[8] With support across the aisle from Senator Boxer, Smith received unanimous approval from the Senate.

Following the Family Tradition of Public Service

Milan Smith credits the influence of his maternal grandfather, Jesse Addison Udall, and his uncle, Rex E. Lee, who served as U.S. Solicitor General, in his decision to pursue a career in the law. While less known nationally, the Udall-Lee family is arguably one of the most prominent and influential political families in U.S. history drawing similarities to the Kennedy family and the Bush family. Levi Stewart Udall served as Chief Justice of the Arizona Supreme Court and his brother, Jesse Addison Udall, also served on the Arizona Supreme Court. Other individuals in the Udall-Lee family that have served in public office include Mo Udall, a U.S. Congressman for 30 years, Stewart Lee Udall, Secretary of the Interior to presidents John F. Kennedy and Lyndon B. Johnson, Tom Udall, a U.S. Senator from New Mexico, and Mark Udall, a U.S. Senator from Colorado. U.S. Senator Mike Lee, a Republican from Utah, is also Smith's second cousin.

"I am very much aware of the distinct obligation toward public service in part because I have four generations who have served in public office, many of whom have served as judges, starting with Levi Stewart Udall," recognized Smith. "The bottom line is, I am very much aware that I have a sacred responsibility to faithfully discharge my office and the family has sacrificed a lot for the public good and in conjunction with [Doctrine & Covenants] Section 98."[9] Doctrine & Covenants Section 98, canonized scripture for members of The Church of Jesus Christ of Latter-day Saints, reaffirms that church members should remain faithful to the U.S. Constitution. The passage reads: "I say unto you concerning the laws of the land, it is my will that my people should observe to do all things whatsoever I command them. And that law of the land which is constitutional, supporting that principle of freedom in maintaining rights and privileges, belongs to all mankind, and is justifiable before me." The scripture counsels, "Therefore, I, the Lord, justify you, and your brethren of my church, in befriending that law which is the constitutional law of the land."[10]

After graduating from Brigham Young University, Smith enrolled at the prestigious University of Chicago Law School at the urging of his uncle, Rex Lee. Lee, an alumnus of the University of Chicago, told Smith that the University of Chicago was the "only true and living law school."[11]

As a law student at the University of Chicago, Smith took classes from fellow Church member Dallin H. Oaks, including a course on the law of trusts. When Smith struggled with the difficult concept of the "throwback rule" relating to the taxation of trusts, he visited then-Professor Oaks seeking assistance. The throwback rule is "a rule requiring that an amount distributed in any tax year that exceeds the year's distributable net income must be treated as if it had been distributed in the preceding year."[12] After diligent study, Smith still failed to understand the intricacies of the complex rule telling Professor Oaks "I don't understand it. I don't get it." Professor Oaks, who wrote one of the leading casebooks on trust law used in law schools, reassured his pupil and said, "I don't understand it either, but it won't be on the exam."[13] Professor Oaks later became President of Brigham Young University, a Utah Supreme Court Justice, and a member of the Quorum of the Twelve Apostles in the Church.

Dealmaker

After graduating from the University of Chicago Law School in 1969, Smith moved to California to embark on an impressive legal career working in private practice. He first joined the top law firm O'Melveny & Myers in Los Angeles. Smith then started his own firm—Smith, Crane, Robinson & Parker— where he engaged in a wide-ranging legal practice in business and real estate law. "I practiced for 37 years before I went to the bench. Like my grandfather [Jesse Addison Udall], I had a lot of opportunities to do different things. Primarily, I was a transaction lawyer and put deals together."[14]

While in private practice in California, Smith accepted an appointment from Governor George Deukmejian in 1984 to serve on the Governing Board of the Los Angeles State Building Authority, where he served as president until 1992. In 1987, Smith accepted an appointment to the California Fair Employment and Housing Commission, where he served for three years until resigning in protest.

Smith's attributes his experience raising seven children as preparation to making fair and balanced decisions as a judge.

During the confirmation hearing, Smith told the members of the Senate Judiciary Committee, "I believe that being the father now of seven wonderful children, having practiced law for 37 years and dealing with a wide variety of issues, will enable me, if confirmed, to bring a lot of what I guess my Grandmother Udall would call 'common sense' to the decisions that are brought before me. People all have aspirations. Every human being wants what is good for his or her children, his or her business, his or her country." Smith stated that if confirmed, he would work to "do in the Ninth Circuit Court of Appeals what I believe my brother has done in the Senate, which is to get to know individuals personally, become their friend, and whether you always agree with them is not necessarily the point but, rather, that you can disagree without being disagreeable. And I think that that comity among your colleagues can help bring a result that is more fair, more balanced, more appreciated by the lower courts, by the public, and others who must understand and implement the policies— or not policies, but the rulings that the court issues."[15]

Even-Handed Decisions

As one of the select federal appeals court judges just below the U.S. Supreme Court, Smith makes decisions affecting the lives of millions of American citizens, including decisions affecting environmental law. In one key environmental case, *Karuk Tribe of California v. U.S. Forest Service*, 681 F.3d 1006 (9th Cir. 2012), Judge Smith wrote a bitter dissenting opinion where he drew an analogy to Gulliver's Travels by Jonathan Swift and even included an image of Gulliver being tied down in his formal opinion. Smith wrote: "In my view, decisions such as this one, and some other environmental cases recently handed down by our court . . . undermine the rule of law, and make poor Gulliver's situation seem fortunate when compared to the plight of those entangled in the ligatures of new rules created out of thin air by such decisions."[16] Smith argued that the Ninth Circuit improperly created, rather than interpreted law "stray[ing] with lamentable frequency from its constitutionally limited role" in environmental cases, and, in so doing, threatening the independence of the judiciary.[17]

In *Karuk Tribe*, the en banc panel of the Ninth Circuit reversed a three-judge panel decision and held that the U.S. Forest Service must consult with wildlife agencies under the Endangered Species Act before issuing a notice of intent authorizing mining on national forest lands. According to one law review article, the language, tone, and far-ranging scope of Judge Smith's dissent reflects a deep divide over the function of judicial review in environmental cases in the nation's largest appellate court.[18] Smith's criticism attracted the attention of the U.S. Supreme Court that ultimately led to a change in environmental law in the Ninth Circuit, the largest federal circuit that represents 20 percent of the total population of the United States.[19]

Smith has also used his position as a federal appeals court judge to recognize constitutional rights in the face of opposition. In *United States v. Alvarez*, 617 F.3d 1198 (9th Cir. 2010), the Ninth Circuit examined the constitutionality of the Stolen Valor Act of 2005 which criminalized the act of lying about military service, either verbally or in writing.[20] The case arose from a false statement made by Xavier Alvarez in a public meeting when he served as an elected member of the board of directors of a water district in Southern California. Alvarez had a habit of lying. Alvarez lied when he said that he played hockey for the Detroit Red Wings and that he once married a starlet from Mexico. But Alvarez crossed the line when he said during a public meeting: "I'm a retired marine of 25 years. I retired in the year 2001. Back in 1987, I was awarded the Congressional Medal of Honor. I got wounded many times by the same guys."[21] A member of the public knew these claims were false and pressed the issue. Alvarez was prosecuted under the Stolen Valor Act for lying about receiving the Congressional Medal of Honor at the meeting. Alvarez pleaded guilty to one count while reserving the right to appeal on his First Amendment claim. In the appellate decision in *Alvarez*, Smith wrote the majority opinion for the Ninth Circuit holding that "[i]t has long been clear that First Amendment protection does not hinge on the truth of the matter expressed."[22]

The *Alvarez* decision by the Ninth Circuit received strong criticism from many groups, including veterans. The American Legion filed an amicus or "friend of the court" brief when the government appealed the case to the U.S. Supreme Court. Ultimately, the U.S. Supreme Court affirmed the decision of the Ninth Circuit holding that the Stolen Valor Act of 2005 infringed upon the freedom of speech protected by the First Amendment.[23]

Many groups voiced protest over the *Alvarez* case and called for a revised Stolen Valor Act. President Barack Obama signed into law an amended version, the Stolen Valor Act of 2013.[24] Despite the enactment of a constitutional Stolen Valor Act, the federal government has only rarely prosecuted offenders under the new watered-down Stolen Valor Act of 2013.[25]

In the aftermath of *Alvarez*, Smith recognized the importance of an independent judiciary. U.S. Supreme Court Justice Sandra Day O'Connor recognized two of the primary grievances that the colonists listed against King George in the Declaration of Independence involved the absence of judicial independence in colonial America.[26] The Declaration of Independence charged that the King had "obstructed the Administration of Justice, by refusing his Assent to Laws establishing Judiciary Powers" and he had "made Judges dependent on his will alone, for the tenure of their offices, and the amount and payment of their salaries." The U.S. Constitution guarantees lifetime tenure to Article III judges appointed by the President and confirmed by the Senate to maintain an independent federal judiciary as designed by the Founding Fathers to insulate the federal judiciary from political influences so that judges could apply the law fairly and without prejudice. "[*Alvarez*] was an important lesson to me on the importance of life tenure," reflected Smith. "In order to be faithful to the Constitution, I went the way the law says under *New York Times v. Sullivan* [a landmark U.S. Supreme Court First Amendment case]."[27] Akin to the wisdom of Solomon, Smith demonstrated courage to uphold the U.S. Constitution and apply the law fairly in the face of political and public opposition.

Forging a Passion for the Law and His Fellow Citizens

Smith has a passion for the law and what the law can accomplish. "I love the law as a human thing. I love legal issues and legal history. The Lord works on eternal legal principles. I look at law as stories. It is a way for people to resolve issues in a peaceful way." Smith added, "Honesty, to be on the second highest court is such a rare privilege. It's like being struck by lightning. I am amazed to be involved in fascinating issues and the privilege to deal with these cases. Finishing my career in this position is about as good at is gets."[28]

The legal community has recognized Smith as one of the top legal writers among all federal court judges. The Green Bag, a legal periodical famous during the Progressive Era and revived as a publication focused on quality legal writing, recognized Judge Smith's dissenting opinion in *Lane v. Facebook*, 709 F.3d 791 (9th Cir. 2013) in questioning an expansion of the cy pres doctrine as applied to class action lawsuits. The "cy pres doctrine" allows a court to alter a charity's objective if the original objective can no longer be achieved.[29] While some judges' opinions often read like "long-winded impromptu sermons" with the point being only faintly discernible, Smith's concise two-page opinion received recognition as a "model of economy and precision."[30]

Through his service as a full-time missionary in Argentina and other positions serving in the Church, including bishop, a counselor in a bishopric, and stake high councilor, Smith has learned the value of service. "I think the main thing that I see is the value of service," observed Smith. "That is extremely important in fulfilling the Lord's plan in helping each other solve problems. I treasure the thousands of experiences in doing my best to help relieve the burdens of others."[31]

"[T]he right to speak and write whatever one chooses— including, to some degree, worthless, offensive, and demonstrable untruths—without cowering in fear of a powerful government is . . . an essential component of the protection afforded by the First Amendment." Milan D. Smith, Jr., on the

First Amendment freedom of speech, in *United States v. Alvarez*.[32]

[1] Hearing before the Committee on the Judiciary, S Hrg No. 109-397, 109th Cong, 2d Sess, 4 (2006) (statement of Senator Gordon Smith).

[2] Phone interview with Milan D. Smith, Jr. Judge, U.S. Court of Appeals for the Ninth Circuit, Jun. 9, 2017 ("hereinafter Smith (2017)").

[3] Kenneth W. Dam, *From the Gold Clause Cases to the Gold Commission: A Half Century of American Monetary Law*, 50 U. Chi. L. Rev. 504, 513 (1983).

[4] Daniel Horowitz, *David Riesman: From Law to Social Criticism*, 58 Buff. L. Rev. 1005 (2010).

[5] Smith (2017).

[6] Ryan J. Owens, *Ideology, Qualifications, and Covert Senate Obstruction of Federal Court Nominations*, 2014 U. Ill. L. Rev. 347 (2014).

[7] Smith (2017).

[8] Hearing before the Committee on the Judiciary, S Hrg No. 109-397, 109th Cong, 2d Sess, 4 (2006) (statement of Senator Barbara Boxer).

[9] Smith (2017).

[10] Doctrine & Covenants 98:4-6.

[11] See Doctrine & Covenants 1:30 whereby church members believe The Church of Jesus Christ of Latter-day Saints is the "only true and living church upon the face of the whole earth."

[12] Black's Law Dictionary (10th ed. 2014), throwback rule.

[13] Smith (2017).

[14] *Id.*

[15] Hearing before the Committee on the Judiciary, S Hrg No. 109-397, 109th Cong, 2d Sess, 4 (2006).

[16] 681 F.3d at 1031.

[17] *Id.* at 1041.

[18] Michael C. Blumm & Maggie Hall, *Lands Council, Karuk Tribe, and the Great Environmental Divide in the Ninth Circuit*, 54 Nat. Resources J. 1, 3–4 (2014).

[19] *Id.* at 38–39; See 162 Cong. Rec. S698 (2016) (statement of Senator Sullivan).

[20] 18 U.S.C. § 704.

[21] 617 F.3d at 1200.

[22] *Id.* at 1198.

[23] *United States v. Alvarez*, 567 U.S. 709 (2012).

[24] 18 U.S.C. § 704.

[25] Mary E. Johnston, *Combating Thieves of Valor: The Stolen Valor Act of 2013 Is Constitutional Yet Unenforced*, 25 Wm. & Mary Bill Rts. J. 1355, 1392 (2017).

[26] Sandra Day O'Connor, *Judicial Independence and Civics Education,* Utah Bar Journal, September/October 2009, 10.

[27] Smith (2017) (referencing *New York Times v. Sullivan*, 376 U.S. 254 (1964)).

[28] *Id.*

[29] *Wellpoint, Inc. v. C.I.R.,* 599 F.3d 641 (7th Cir. 2010).

[30] Bryan A. Garner, *The Deep Issue: A New Approach to Framing Legal Questions*, 5 Scribes J. Legal Writing 1 (1995); Thomas Greene, Thomas A. Papageorge, *California Antitrust and Unfair Competition Law and Federal and State Procedural Law Developments*, 24 Competition: J. Anti. & Unfair Comp. L. Sec. St. B. Cal. 1, 49 (2015).

[31] Smith (2017).

[32] 617 F.3d at 1205.

$$\underline{\underline{\text{⊥}}}$$

Chapter 17

Levi Stewart Udall: Patriarch Who Launched a Political Family Dynasty

Deciding the Fate of Indian Voters

In 1948, Levi Stewart Udall faced what would become the biggest decision during his 29 years as a judge, including 13 years on the Arizona Supreme Court. Frank Harrison and Harry Austin, members of the Mohave-Apache Indian Tribe, simply wanted to exercise their constitutional right to vote. They resided on the Fort McDowell Indian Reservation located in Maricopa County northeast of Phoenix. Harrison even fought for the United States during World War II and received an honorable discharge. But Roger G. Laveen, the county recorder for Maricopa County, denied the voter registration applications submitted by Harrison and Austin.

Harrison and Austin filed a complaint in the Superior Court of Maricopa County seeking a court order, or a "writ of mandamus," compelling the recorder to register them on the voting rolls. The complaint alleged that the plaintiffs possessed all the qualifications for suffrage as set forth in the United States Constitution and the laws of the State of Arizona. The Native Americans asserted that if they were denied the right to register and vote, they would be deprived of the franchises, immunities, rights, and privileges of citizens guaranteed to them under the both the United States Constitution and the Arizona Constitution. The trial court dismissed the complaint agreeing with the county recorder. The Indians appealed the case to the Arizona Supreme Court. The United States Government, the National Congress of American Indians, and the American Civil Liberties Union (ACLU) all filed briefs with the Arizona Supreme Court in the closely watched case known as *Harrison v. Laveen*.[1]

Justice Levi Stewart Udall and the other justices on the Arizona Supreme Court considered the controlling legal authority on the issue, including the U.S. Constitution, federal statutes, the Arizona Constitution, Arizona statutes, and previous cases. In 1924, Congress declared all Indians to be citizens of the United States.[2] And just prior to World War II, Congress declared that Tribal Indians were subject to the military draft under the Selective Training and Service Act of 1940.[3] Justice Udall recognized that many Native Americans from Arizona served in the armed forces during World War II with pride and distinction, including Ira Hamilton Hayes. Hayes, a Pima Indian and a United States Marine, was one of the six flag raisers immortalized in the iconic photograph of the flag raising on Iwo Jima during World War II.[4]

Justice Udall wrote in the opinion, "The right of American Indians to vote in Arizona elections for state and federal officers has after two decades again arisen, like Banquo's ghost, to challenge us." The Arizona Constitution treated reservation Indians as "persons under guardianship." An earlier decision by the Arizona Supreme Court in 1928, *Porter v. Hall*, 34 Ariz. 308, 271 P. 411 (1928), denied Indians the right to vote based on this guardianship status. Justice Udall recognized similarly that "members of the armed services, federal employees, veterans, and even beneficiaries or recipients of social security payments or other Federal payments have all been referred to loosely, from time to time, as 'wards of the government', yet no one has had the temerity to suggest that such persons, when otherwise qualified, were ineligible to vote."[5] In writing the opinion of the court, Udall overruled the holding of the *Porter* case and concluded that the term "persons under guardianship" has no application to the plaintiffs or to the federal status of Indians in Arizona as a class. The Arizona Supreme Court reversed the decision of the trial court and granted Harrison and Austin, along with all other Native Americans in Arizona, the right to vote.[6] Udall corrected years of injustice denying Indians the right to vote.

Even though Native Americans in Arizona gained the constitutional right to vote in *Harrison v. Laveen*, Arizona continued to utilize other voter oppression methods, such as literary tests, which denied Native Americans the right to vote for decades. It was not until the 1970s, after federal law prohibited the use of literacy tests, that Arizona Indians finally achieved full voting rights.[7]

Establishing a Pattern of Public Service for the Udall Clan

Although he was not part of a Native America tribe, Levi Stewart Udall was a member of another "tribe"—the well-known Udall family. Church Prophet Brigham Young sent David King Udall to settle northern Arizona in the church's 19th-century days of polygamy. Born on January 20, 1891, in St. Johns, Arizona, Levi Stewart Udall was the son of David King Udall and his first wife, Ella. David King Udall was a prominent pioneer who served as a representative of Apache County on the Council of the Twentieth Territorial Legislature for Arizona and also served as President of the St. Johns Stake for the Church.[8]

David King Udall's first wife, Ella Stewart Udall, was a Democrat while his second wife, Ida Hunt Udall, was a Republican. Gordon Smith, the great-grandson of David King Udall and Ida, who represented Oregon from 1997 until 2009 in the U.S. Senate as a Republican, said that the great-grandmothers' party ties continue. "Their branch was Democratic, and my branch was on the other side," he said.[9]

Levi grew up in the small agricultural community in St. Johns where he attended public school and learned the value of hard work. St. Johns is the county seat of Apache County located in the northeast corner of Arizona. Levi completed his secondary education at Gila Academy in nearby Thatcher from 1910 to 1911 and briefly attended the University of Arizona in Tucson. In 1914, he married Louise Lee of Thatcher and they became the parents of six children: Inez, Elma, Stewart, Morris (Mo), Eloise, and Burr Udall.

As the son of Ella, Levi Stewart Udall was part of the Democrat branch of the family. Levi Stewart Udall was the first of David King Udall's children to run for political office, running for clerk of the Apache County Superior Court in 1914 as a Democrat. Levi Udall, however, lost the race to John H. Udall, a Republican, his brother and the son of Ida from the Republican side of the family. But like Abraham Lincoln, Levi refused to let political defeat deter him.[10]

Levi Udall worked as the clerk for the County Board of Supervisors from 1915 to 1918. He ran again for clerk of the Apache County Superior Court in 1918. This second time, he won the race and he held the position from 1919 to 1922. While working as court clerk, Udall studied the law through correspondence from LaSalle Institute of Chicago under the tutelage of Apache County Superior Court Judge A.S. Gibbons. Before the rise of law schools, many lawyers, such as Abraham Lincoln, learned the law through personal study and apprenticeship.[11] "We had three little children [when Levi was studying law]," recalled his wife, Louise, "and it was my duty to shoot them out of the room so their father could work." Although he never earned a law degree, Udall passed the bar exam and gained admission to the Arizona bar in 1922 finishing second among all test takers. Later in life while serving as Chief Justice of the Arizona Supreme Court and attending conferences, when graduates of Harvard or Yale asked him where he obtained his law degree, they were surprised when Udall said by correspondence from LaSalle Institute. Indeed, Udall had come a long way from his humble beginnings in St. Johns to the highest court in the state.[12]

After gaining admission to practice law, Udall ran for the office of Apache County Attorney. He served as county attorney for two terms, first from 1923 to 1924, and then from 1927 to 1928, representing the county in a variety of civil and criminal matters. In *Navajo County v. Apache County,* 26 Ariz. 74, 221 P. 837 (1924), Udall successfully represented Apache County in a boundary line dispute brought by Navajo County in a case before the Arizona Supreme Court. The dispute involved a narrow strip of land designated by an imaginary line determined by the legislature. Both counties claimed the town of McNary. The Arizona Supreme Court dismissed the complaint holding that range lines cannot become the official and recognized boundaries of public lands by the United States until such boundaries have been established by a government survey. Based on Udall's efforts, Apache County retained McNary.[13]

Udall also represented the county in the federal courts as county attorney. In *United States v. Porter*, 22 F.2d 365 (9th Cir. 1927), the U.S. Court of Appeals for the Ninth Circuit examined the power of the county to impose taxes on property owned by Indians outside the reservation. The taxing officers of Apache County sought to collect taxes on about 1,000 head of sheep and 100 head of cattle, owned by Indians belonging to the Navajo Tribe. The Ninth Circuit held that because the Indians lived under the protection of the state, the state could impose taxes on any property outside the reservation.

As county attorney, Udall also prosecuted persons who violated criminal laws. In *Fears v. State*, 33 Ariz. 432, 265 P. 600 (1928), Udall charged a forest ranger in the Apache National Forest, Jess T. Fears, with the offense of maliciously killing a mare in violation of the Arizona Penal Code that mandates "[e]very person who maliciously kills . . . any animal the property of another, . . . is . . . guilty of a misdemeanor."[14] The trial court found the forest ranger guilty and imposed a fine of $1. The forest ranger appealed the conviction. The Arizona Supreme Court tossed out the conviction and ruled that because the forest ranger killed the animal in his official duty as a forest ranger pursuant to a regulation of the U.S. Secretary of Agriculture for impounding of livestock, he did not kill the animal "maliciously."[15]

Serving as a Judge Amid the Great Depression

Levi Stewart Udall used his experience and name recognition as county attorney and decided to run for Superior Court Judge. In this race, he faced his mentor Judge A.S. Gibbons. When Arizona became a state in 1912, the Arizona Constitution called for the direct election of judges rather than merit-based selection.[16] Voters of Apache County selected Udall over Judge Gibbons with Udall winning 59 percent of the vote.[17] Udall served as judge of the Superior Court from 1931 to 1946 which provided his family steady income during the Great Depression.[18] By the town's standards, the Udalls were considered well to do, which caused some resentment among the people in St. Johns.[19] As Superior Court Judge, Levi traveled the county and he also presided in other cases throughout the state. His family remembers him being home only rarely. "He was not an at-home father," recalled daughter Elman. Once he presided in Tucson for six months, returning to St. Johns only on the weekends. Tucson is located 236 miles from St. Johns, a significant distance to travel even by modern standards. When he was home in St. Johns, Udall dealt with many church responsibilities as stake president. But when he held court in the Apache County courthouse, or "Daddy's Courthouse" as his children called it, he walked home every day for lunch.[20]

His most notable case as Superior Court Judge was *Arizona v. Southern Pacific Railroad* which ultimately made its way to the U.S. Supreme Court.[21] The case, involving Arizona's 1912 Train Limit Law, established an important precedent under the dormant Commerce Clause. The Commerce Clause of the U.S. Constitution in Article I grants Congress with the power "[t]o regulate Commerce with foreign Nations, and among the several States, and with the Indian Tribes."[22] The dormant Commerce Clause prohibits the states from directly regulating interstate commerce, and from discriminating against or unduly burdening it.[23]

In an effort to promote safety, Arizona's statute prohibited trains larger than 70 freight cars (exclusive of caboose), or passenger trains larger than 14 cars. The State of Arizona initiated a test case, seeking to enforce the law against Southern Pacific once the railroad company admittedly ran trains exceeding the statutory limit-and became subject to a $500 fine. Judge Udall conducted a 46-day bench trial, one without a jury, comprising 18 volumes of transcripts, 73 witnesses, and over 400 exhibits. After hearing the evidence, Judge Udall firmly believed that certain matters fell within the exclusive domain of Congress. Therefore, he found that the train length requirements were a national matter and not local matters. Judge Udall concluded that the evidence established a heavy and unreasonable burden on interstate commerce, examining for himself whether the law promoted safety.[24]

The Arizona Supreme Court reversed the decision by Judge Udall and Southern Pacific appealed the case all the way to the U.S. Supreme Court. The nation's top court agreed with Judge Udall's reasoning and found that the Arizona Train Limit Law unconstitutionally burdened interstate commerce. Justice Harlan Stone, writing the opinion of the court in 1945, held that "a state may not regulate interstate commerce so as substantially to affect its flow or deprive it of needed uniformity in its regulation."[25]

As a Superior Court Judge, Udall also decided cases outside Apache County sitting by designation. In *State v. Jobin*, Udall presided over a case in Pinal County Superior Court involving the validity of an ordinance again proselytizing by Jehovah's Witnesses who went from house to house preaching the gospel. Charles Jobin was convicted of violating an ordinance of the City of Casa Grande, Arizona.[26] The U.S. Supreme Court ultimately vacated the conviction holding that the freedoms of the First Amendment are protected by the Fourteenth Amendment from impairment by the states.[27]

Making His Mark on the Arizona Supreme Court

With 15 years of experience as a Superior Court Judge, in 1945, Udall decided to run for a seat on the Arizona Supreme Court. Udall previously filled in for the Arizona Supreme Court when members of the court faced illness or disqualification.[28] At the time, judicial candidates were selected in partisan primaries but appeared without partisan designation on the general election ballot.[29] Louise, said, "He had it in his mind all the time." Louise added, "We'd save up $5,000, and by cracky, that's all we spent. It was a tough decision to make at the time—but it was what he wanted. He'd say, 'I'm just a country boy—in the Supreme Court.' I'd say, 'Where do you think our presidents come from?' "[30] Udall's gamble to run paid off. Udall defeated incumbent Joseph H. Morgan winning 52 percent of the final vote tally by the slim margin of 3,150 votes.[31]

Arizona replaced the direct election judges to the Arizona Supreme Court with a merit selection system when voters approved a constitutional initiative in 1974 known as Proposition 108. The judicial appointment commissions comprised of lawyers and lay persons, forward a politically-balanced list of candidates that includes at least three names for each vacancy to the governor, who appoints from the list submitted. Judges then face retention in noncompetitive elections.[32]

After winning the election to the Arizona Supreme Court, Udall moved his family from the small community of St. Johns to the Phoenix area where he lived the remainder of his life. In winning the campaign, Levi Stewart Udall became the first of many future members of the Udall-Smith-Lee political family to win a statewide election.

Levi Stewart Udall served on the Arizona Supreme Court from 1946 until his death in 1960 writing 375 opinions during his tenure as a justice on the court.[33] Besides the *Harrison v. Laveen* case which recognized the right to vote for Indians, Udall decided many other important cases for the court of last resort in the Grand Canyon State.

Udall decided key cases interpreting constitutional law and the validity of ordinances. In a case involving validity of a county ordinance, Udall analyzed the principles of separation of powers and due process. The Arizona Supreme Court held that "it is not necessary, in order to provide due process, that interested parties be present at all stages of the legislative deliberations. Such a requirement is properly applicable only to adversary proceedings."[34] The court invalidated the county ordinance for failure to comply with the procedural requirement of the Arizona Zoning Act which required "strict compliance."[35] The case established an important precedent in Arizona that ordinances must "strictly comply" with applicable statutory requirements.[36]

The Arizona Supreme Court under Udall also established standards for malpractice and professional negligence. In a malpractice case against a dentist, the court affirmed a judgment in favor of the patient who alleged that the dentist was negligent in leaving two small pieces of metal from dental instruments in the patient's jaw after extracting a wisdom tooth. One of the patient's experts testified that the pieces of metal would have been readily observable in an X-ray taken of the area, which violated the standard of care. The court concluded there was sufficient evidence of a violation of standards of medical practice to sustain the verdict in the malpractice case. Justice Udall wrote that under the circumstances as shown by the record, the dentist engaged in "fraudulent concealment amounting to legal or constructive fraud."[37]

As Chief Justice of the Arizona Supreme Court, Udall decided matters involving legal ethics. In one case, *In re Wein*, 73 Ariz. 225, 240 P.2d 183 (1952), the Arizona Supreme Court decided the appropriate discipline for a lawyer who violated ethical rules in bribing the prosecutor to dismiss a case for one of the firm's clients. The lawyer paid $500 to the county attorney to secure dismissal of a criminal case. The lawyer argued that this was merely a "fee splitting arrangement" and he simply carried out the directions of his senior partner. In holding that the lawyer warranted disbarment for his unethical conduct, Udall wrote, "There can be no temporizing with an offense so serious and destructive of all order and justice as bribery of a public official. One of the highest duties we owe to society is to keep clean the course of justice in the courts, for when this is corrupted there is nothing left to justify the existence of courts or the practice of the legal profession."[38]

Udall abided by the ethics of the legal profession and he also lived his religion. As a faithful Latter-day Saint, Levi Stewart Udall dedicated years of service to the Church. His father, David King Udall, helped establish the Church presence in St. Johns and served as President of the St. Johns Stake in Arizona for 35 years. Levi succeeded his father as President of the St. Johns Stake and served for 23 years resulting in 58 years of continuous leadership for father and son.[39] At the time of his appointment in 1922, at age 31, he was the youngest stake president in the Church.[40] In a letter signed by George Albert Smith, J. Reuben Clark, Jr., and David O. McKay upon his release, the First Presidency of the Church wrote, "With our hearty approbation and full appreciation of your watchful guidance of Stake affairs, and your deep concern for the welfare of the people, we now extend to you, and to your worthy counselors, an honorable release from your positions."[41] Ezra Taft Benson reorganized the St. Johns stake presidency following Udall's election to the Arizona Supreme Court. In a letter to Levi and his wife, Louise, Benson wrote, "You and your family are greatly loved by the people over whom you have been privileged to presidency for twenty-three years." Benson, who later served as U.S. Secretary of Agriculture under President Dwight D. Eisenhower and then became

President of the Church added, "It must be a great satisfaction to all of you to know that through the blessings of the Lord and your own efforts you have discharged a great responsibility with honor, and that the Lord and the people over whom you presided have accepted your labors."[42]

Udall also served as a Sunday School teacher, high councilman, and high priest group leader in the Church. Besides being patriarch of the Udall family following the death of his father, Levi Udall also served as patriarch for the Phoenix North Stake.[43] Udall recalled the lessons he learned as a Sunday School teacher, "After nearly twenty years of teaching a Sunday School Gospel Doctrine class, I can testify that it has been a most stimulating and rewarding experience. . . Teaching Sunday School has given me a better understanding and appreciation of my fellow man. A teacher must be somewhat of a diplomat; hence, I have learned how to get along with people and how to tactfully meet difficult situations involving sharp differences of opinions."[44]

Although he never earned a formal law degree, the University of Arizona conferred upon Udall an honorary doctor of laws degree recognizing his years of public service. In the ceremony held just three months before his death, John D. Lyons, Dean of the College of Law, presented Udall with the honorary degree: "During his 29 years as a member of the Arizona judiciary, Justice Udall has been respected throughout the state for his learning and integrity. As a trial judge none was more sought after, and none more ready, for assignment to difficult and important cases beyond his home county. As an appellate justice, he has striven by precept and example to promote the just and speedy disposition of cases." The commendation further stated, "No Arizonan of his generation has better exemplified the ideal of able and devoted public service."[45]

Levi Stewart Udall established a standard for public service that many members of his family have followed. Following Levi's death on May 30, 1960 at a family picnic on Memorial Day, his brother, Jesse Addison Udall, took his place on the Arizona Supreme Court.[46] Two of Levi Stewart Udall's sons, Mo Udall and Stewart Udall, served for years in the U.S. House of Representatives. And two of his grandsons, Tom Udall and Mark Udall, became U.S. Senators. Many others in the family have also served in public office creating a political family dynasty. Stewart Udall said that his father left a modest estate because he did not expect wealth, but "he left us the best name in Arizona."[47] Senator Gordon Smith recognized, "The Udalls are to the American West, and to Arizona specifically, what the Kennedys are to Massachusetts."[48] The Udall family name and legacy will continue for generations due in large part from the pattern of service set forth by the family patriarch— Levi Stewart Udall. The Book of Mormon teaches that King Levi of ancient time on the American continent "did that which was right in the sight of the Lord."[49] The same could be said of another Levi in modern time.

"In a democracy suffrage is the most basic civil right, since its exercise is the chief means whereby other rights may be safeguarded. To deny the right to vote, where one is legally entitled to do so, is to do violence to the principles of freedom and equality." Levi Stewart Udall, recognizing the right to vote for Native Americans in Arizona.[50]

---

[1] *Harrison v. Laveen*, 67 Ariz. 337, 196 P.2d 456 (1948).

[2] 43 Stat. 253; 8 U.S.C. § 3.

[3] Selective Training and Service Act of 1940, U.S.C. Title 50, Appendix, § 301 et seq.

[4] 67 Ariz. at 343, 196 P.2d at 459.

[5] *Id.*

[6] *Id.*

[7] Patty Ferguson-Bohnee, *The History of Indian Voting Rights in Arizona: Overcoming Decades of Voter Suppression*, 47 Ariz. St. L.J. 1099, 1112 (2015).

[8] Kellene Ricks Adams, *David King Udall, Arizona Pioneer*, Ensign, August 1993, https://www.lds.org/ensign/1993/08/david-king-udall-arizona-pioneer?lang=eng# [https://perma.cc/T3WU-X3N5].

[9] Patrick O'Driscoll, *Udall Family is Latest Political Dynasty*, USA Today, Dec. 12, 2007, 5A, 2007 WLNR 24159045.

[10] Levi Stewart Udall, 1891–1960, Biographical Sketch, University of Arizona Library,

http://www.library.arizona.edu/exhibits/lsudall/index.html [https://perma.cc/J6GK-QWMK].

[11] Herbert M. Kritzer, *From Litigators of Ordinary Cases to Litigators of Extraordinary Cases: Stratification of the Plaintiffs' Bar in the Twenty-First Century*, 51 DePaul L. Rev. 219, 222 (2001).

[12] From Donald W. Carson, *Mo: The Life and Times of Morris K. Udall* by Donald W. Carson. ©2000 The Arizona Board of Regents, Reprinted by permission of the University of Arizona Press, 10.

[13] *Navajo Cty. v. Apache Cty.*, 26 Ariz. 74, 79, 221 P. 837, 839 (1924).

[14] Arizona Revised Statutes of 1913, Penal Code, section 602.

[15] 33 Ariz. at 439, 265 P. at 602.

[16] Ariz. Const. art. VI, §§ 3, 5, 9 (amended 1960); Hon. Ruth V. McGregor, *Arizona's Merit Selection System: Improving Public Participation and Increasing Transparency*, 59 Syracuse L. Rev. 383 (2009).

[17] Carson (2000), 10.

[18] *Id.*

[19] *Id.* at 14.

[20] *Id.* at 10.

[21] *S. Pac. Co. v. Arizona*, 325 U.S. 761 (1945).

[22] U.S. Const. Art. I, § 8, cl. 3.

[23] 15A Am. Jur. 2d Commerce § 35

[24] Sam Kalen, *Dormant Commerce Clause's Aging Burden*, 49 Val. U. L. Rev. 723, 792 (2015).

[25] 325 U.S. at 779–780.

[26] *State v. Jobin*, 58 Ariz. 144, 118 P.2d 97 (1941), aff'd by *Jones v. City of Opelika*, 316 U.S. 584 (1942), vacated, 319 U.S. 105 (1943).

[27] *Jones*, 319 U.S. at 126.

[28] See *Employment Sec. Comm'n v. Arizona Citrus Growers*, 61 Ariz. 96, 111, 144 P.2d 682, 688 (1944) (illness); *In re Hesse's Estate*, 62 Ariz. 273, 283, 157 P.2d 347, 351 (1945) (disqualification).

[29] Hon. Ruth V. McGregor, *Arizona's Merit Selection System: Improving Public Participation and Increasing Transparency*, 59 Syracuse L. Rev. 383 (2009).

[30] Carson (2004), 10.

[31] Timeline of Levi Stewart Udall and Louise Lee Udall, Whiting Depot, Papers of Levi Stewart Udall, http://whitingdepot.com/resources/Levi_and_Louise_Udall_timeline.pdf [https://perma.cc/D6MC-9BR3] (hereinafter "Papers of Levi Stewart Udall").

[32] McGregor, 59 Syracuse L. Rev. at 383.

[33] Search on Westlaw in Arizona Supreme Court cases for "ju(justice /s udall) & da(bef 1961)" (search conducted Oct. 26, 2017).

[34] *Hart v. Bayless Inv. & Trading Co.*, 86 Ariz. 379, 346 P.2d 1101 (1959).

[35] *Id.*

[36] *McIntyre v. Mohave Cty.*, 127 Ariz. 317, 318, 620 P.2d 696, 697 (1980).

[37] *Morrison v. Acton*, 68 Ariz. 27, 35, 198 P.2d 590, 595 (1948).

[38] 73 Ariz. at 228, 240 P.2d at 184.

[39] *Father and Son Preside Over Stake for 58 Years*, Church News, The Church of Jesus Christ of Latter-day Saints, Sept. 15, 1945, Papers of Levi Stewart Udall.

[40] *Id.*

[41] Letter from the Office of the First Presidency, The Church of Jesus Christ of Latter-day Saints, to President Levi S. Udall, St. Johns Stake (June 5, 1945), Papers of Levi Stewart Udall.

[42] Letter from Ezra Taft Benson to President and Mrs. Levi S. Udall (Sept. 12, 1945), Papers of Levi Stewart Udall.

[43] Levi Stewart Udall, 1891-1960, Biographical Sketch, *supra*, note 10.

[44] Justice Levi S. Udall, *What the Sunday School Has Done for Me*, *The Juvenile Instructor*, p. 326 (date unknown), Papers of Levi Stewart Udall.

[45] Honorary Degree for the Doctor of Laws, Levi S. Udall, University of Arizona, Mar. 1, 1960, Papers of Levi Stewart Udall.

[46] *Levi S. Udall Dies Following Attack at Family Picnic*, Apache County Independent News, Jun. 3, 1960, Papers of Levi Stewart Udall.

[47] Carson (2000), 13.

[48] O'Driscoll (2007).

[49] The Book of Mormon, Ether 1:16.

[50] *Harrison v. Laveen*, 67 Ariz. 337, 342, 196 P.2d 456, 459 (1948).

Chapter 18

J. Clifford Wallace: Promoter of the Rule of Law Worldwide

Narrowly Missing Out on the Supreme Court

Judge J. Clifford Wallace was a runner-up not once but twice for a U.S. Supreme Court nomination.[1] Despite being passed over to serve on the nation's highest court, Wallace left an enduring legacy in the law, not just in the United States, but around the globe. Through his international efforts in promoting the rule of law, Wallace arguably made a bigger impact on the law worldwide than if he ever received an appointment to the U.S. Supreme Court.

U.S. Supreme Court Chief Justice Warren E. Burger submitted the name of J. Clifford Wallace, a well-known conservative judge from California, as his choice to fill the void after Justice William O. Douglas announced his retirement in 1975. But Ford, the only unelected President in history, decided to appease Senate Democrats and nominated John Paul Stevens instead of the conservative West Coast judge.[2] Stevens was later known as the "Chief Justice of the Liberal Supreme Court" and the "liberal lion."[3]

Well-regarded by the Californians who were among President Ronald Reagan's closest advisers, Wallace was also leading contender for the vacancy created by Justice Potter Stewart's retirement in 1981. Reagan ultimately appointed a little-known Arizona state court judge at the time, Sandra Day O'Connor, who became the first female justice in the history of the Supreme Court.[4]

When another vacancy arose after Justice Lewis Powell announced his retirement in 1987, Wallace missed out again. President Ronald Reagan first selected Robert Bork, but the

Senate rejected the nomination. Reagan then nominated Anthony Kennedy to the vacant seat rather than Wallace. Justice Kennedy provided the key swing vote on some of the Court's most important decisions for the next three decades.[5]

The name of J. Clifford Wallace appeared on the short list of potential Supreme Court nominees four times between 1975 and 1987 for both President Ford and Reagan.[6] Legal analysts can only speculate on how decisions by the U.S. Supreme Court would have changed if Ford or Reagan had selected Wallace to fill those vacancies. Even though he never rose to the U.S. Supreme Court, Wallace said it was gratifying simply to have been considered. A fellow judge told him, "Well, Cliff, it's good to be trotted out with the prize cattle." Wallace later said, "So I don't feel any despondency or dejectment."[7] Ed Whelan, a former law clerk to Judge Wallace and later a law clerk to U.S. Supreme Court Justice Antonin Scalia, wrote in the conservative magazine *National Review*, "How much more faithful Supreme Court decisionmaking would be to the Constitution if Judge Wallace had been appointed either time."[8]

Developing Judicial Systems Overseas

Even though he never reached the pinnacle of the legal profession in serving on the U.S. Supreme Court, Wallace's footprint on the law cannot be ignored. As one of the longest serving federal appeals court judges, including 23 years of active service and over 45 years in total service, combined with his previous experience as a federal district judge, Wallace decided thousands of cases impacting countless people.

Besides his service on the bench, Judge Wallace also helped develop judicial systems around the world. He used his vacation time by sharing his decades of legal experience abroad. He traced his support for the "rule of law" movement, to impart the concepts and ideals of an independent judiciary and impartial judicial system, to 1972, when he began devoting personal vacation time to visiting judiciaries overseas.[9] Wallace visited more than 60 countries to help developing nations improve the rule of law. Wallace helped other countries develop an independent judiciary, streamline judicial administration, and strengthen the separation of powers. He traveled the globe extensively to promote these principles in fledging judiciaries ranging from the South Pacific to the Middle East, Russia, Australia, Peru, and China.[10] He visited every populated continent promoting American values in the rule of law. For example, Judge Wallace met with Shri P.R. Narasimha Rao, prime minister of India, in January 1994 on one visit promoting the rule of law.[11] Wallace embarked on a 10-day visit to Algeria in 2002. Wallace shared the values of the American legal experience with the northern African country. Wallace promoted with Algerian leaders the values of constitutional rights, including individual and collective rights and freedoms. Wallace also shared ideas on election disputes with Algerian officials.[12]

On his work with other countries, Wallace said, "I don't try to sell the American model. . . Very often it is not relevant to those individual countries. . . The idea is to try to work with these court systems to make them more effective based on their culture and . . . what fits best for them. . . The best thing we can do for a dictator is to give them a good independent judiciary."[13] Justice Scalia recognized the efforts of Judge Wallace in helping judiciaries overseas, "He has been a major force in spreading the principles and the practices of American courts around the world; I daresay no figure in American Law has done so much."[14]

An Early Career in the Law Following Military Service

A portrait of J. Clifford Wallace reflects a lifetime of devoted service. Raised in San Diego, California, which has a large military population, Wallace served as a petty officer, second class in United States Navy from 1946 to 1949.[15] After his service in the Navy, Wallace graduated from San Diego State University in 1952 and from Boalt Hall School of Law at University of California, Berkeley in 1956 where he served as editor of the California Law Review. Wallace is one of the most distinguished graduates of the law school that has produced other famous alumni, including U.S. Supreme Court Chief Justice Earl Warren, California Supreme Court Chief Justice Roger Traynor, U.S. Attorney General Ed Meese, William Prosser, author of the legal treatise Prosser and Keeton on Torts, and Judge Lance Ito, who presided over the infamous O.J. Simpson murder trial.[16]

After graduating from law school, Wallace worked as a successful trial lawyer in private practice for the law firm Gray, Cary, Ames & Frye, one of San Diego's leading law firms, focusing on civil litigation. In *Martinovic v. Ferry*, 222 Cal. App. 2d 30, 34, 34 Cal. Rptr. 692, 694 (Ct. App. 1963), he represented the owner of a cement truck in a personal injury negligence case involving a five-year-old child. The boy sustained injuries when he was run over by a cement truck operated by the defendant. The jury returned a verdict in favor the defendant cement truck owner and the boy's family appealed the decision. The California Court of Appeals agreed with the trial court and ruled that the Superior Court judge gave the proper jury instructions. The appellate court also agreed that the question whether the child contributed to his own injuries in walking in front of the cement truck which struck him was a question for the jury. In *Milick v. Baker*, 201 Cal. App. 2d 723, 20 Cal. Rptr. 270 (Ct. App. 1962), Wallace represented a landowner in an action between two adjoining landowners involving property located in San Diego. Like the *Martinovic* case, Wallace successfully represented his client's interests when the plaintiff appealed the decision to the California Court of Appeals. Wallace said, "It was an exciting part of my life. I wanted to be a trial lawyer and they gave me that opportunity. . . It brought out the better things in me. Going in to trial and representing people, you are doing something they can't do for themselves and you want to do it well."[17]

With 15 years of experience in private practice, Wallace accepted a position in 1970 to serve as U.S. District Judge for the Southern District of California. With the growing population and an increased federal court docket, Congress provided for the appointment of additional judges in 1970, including the establishment of three new vacancies for the federal court in San Diego.[18] The Southern District of California, located in downtown San Diego, comprises San

Diego County and Imperial County.[19] President Richard M. Nixon nominated Wallace on October 7, 1970, to the newly-created seat and Wallace received his commission after confirmation by the Senate. Wallace earlier turned down opportunities to serve as a state court judge.[20] On his decision to leave a successful private practice where he had just recently made partner and serve as a federal judge, Wallace said, "We prayed about it and concluded that there would be a greater opportunity for service. It was a hard decision for me to make, but it's one that was good for me, and, in the long run, it was good for my family."[21]

If Wallace had remained in private practice with Gray, Cary, Ames & Frye, he would have made significantly more money than serving on the bench. For years, Gray Cary Ames & Frye dominated the legal scene in San Diego as the top law firm. In 1993, Wallace's old firm merged with Silicon Valley top law firm Ware & Freidenrich becoming Gray Cary Ware & Freidenrich LLP.[22] Gray Cary then merged with Piper Rudnick and the United Kingdom-based firm DLA in 2004 in the largest merger in the history of the legal profession. The resulting mega-firm from the three-way merger, DLA Piper, became the third largest law firm in the world.[23] While federal judges receive generous compensation and benefits compared to ordinary Americans, partners at top law firms in private practice earn significantly more income than their judicial counterparts.[24] Wallace welcomed the opportunity to provide service and influence the law from the bench rather than working for a big law firm.

During his stint as a federal district judge, Judge Wallace decided cases involving a variety of issues. Wallace denied a challenge brought by fishermen who appealed a decision by the Food and Drug Administration (FDA) for detaining clams imported from Mexico because of unsafe sanitary conditions.[25] He also decided an action brought by the Internal Revenue Service (IRS) to compel testimony and financial documents from a certified public accountant, a case filed by a Marine who appealed a court martial decision for selling marijuana, and an action brought by a serviceman in the Navy who requested a discharge because of his claimed status as a conscientious objector during the Vietnam War.[26]

Wallace also decided an important case involving questions of fairness and the Supremacy Clause under the U.S. Constitution as a district judge. In *Burns v. Rohr Corp.,* 346 F. Supp. 994 (S.D. Cal. 1972), Judge Wallace decided a case brought by male employees who challenged a California state regulation that provided only rest breaks for female employees but not for male employees. Judge Wallace invalidated the California regulation and held that "the state regulation requiring rest breaks for women is contrary to the objectives of Title VII of the Civil Rights Act of 1964, and it is, therefore, preempted by Title VII by virtue of the Supremacy Clause."[27]

Leading the Influential Ninth Circuit

Less than two years of service as a district judge, President Nixon appointed Wallace again—this time to a seat on the U.S. Court of Appeals for the Ninth Circuit vacated by James Marshall Carter who took senior status. Wallace became one of longest serving judges on the federal bench with active service as a federal appeals court judge from 1972 until 1996 during which he also served as chief judge from 1991 until 1996. He assumed senior status, a form of semi-retirement, in 1996 but still continued to actively decide cases but at a reduced caseload for over two decades.[28]

As a federal appeals court judge, Wallace decided many high-profile and key cases establishing legal precedent interpreting the U.S. Constitution and legislation enacted by Congress. Because the U.S. Supreme Court hears only a limited number of cases, the influential Ninth Circuit is the court of last resort for over 99 percent of the cases it hears as the largest circuit court.[29]

Wallace interpreted the Sixth Amendment right to counsel in criminal prosecutions and established an important test for the ineffective assistance of counsel in several high profile and important cases. In *Bonin v. Calderon,* 59 F.3d 815 (9th Cir. 1995), Wallace considered the habeas corpus petition filed by notorious serial killer William George Bonin. Bonin, a truck driver, was charged in Los Angeles County with 14 counts of murder. Bonin was called the "Freeway Killer" because he placed the bodies of his victims along the sides of freeways in Southern California. After being convicted of four murders in California state court, Bonin sought relief in federal court arguing that he received ineffective legal assistance during his trial. Wallace wrote the opinion for the three-judge panel. The court first recognized that the Sixth Amendment right to counsel includes the right to counsel of undivided loyalty. The court then held that a person convicted of a crime is only entitled to habeas relief for a violation of his Sixth Amendment from conflicts of interest if he can "show: (1) that counsel actively represented conflicting interests, and (2) that an actual conflict of interest adversely affected his lawyer's performance."[30] The truck driver confessed to raping, torturing, and killing 21 boys and young men. The court denied Bonin's petition and he was later executed at San Quentin Prison in 2007, becoming the first person in California to die by lethal injection, after exhausting all legal appeals.[31] Previously, California used the gas chamber for executions.

While conservatives praised the decisionmaking of Wallace, others disagreed with his hard-line opinions, particularly criminal defense attorneys. "He's very bright," said San Diego criminal defense lawyer John Cleary. "But heartless."[32]

Wallace decided another criminal case interpreting the Sixth Amendment in *United States v. Manning*, 56 F.3d 1188 (9th Cir. 1995). The Ninth Circuit considered an appeal by a former Jewish Defense League activist extradited from Israel convicted of murder by mail bomb of a secretary who worked at a computer company. The court held that the government's seven-year delay in bringing the case did not violate the Sixth Amendment right to a speedy trial. The defendant, Robert Manning, refused to return to the United States after the indictment and contributed to the delay. The court ruled that Manning "cannot avoid a speedy trial by forcing the government to run the gauntlet of obtaining formal extradition and then complain about the delay that he has caused by refusing to return voluntarily to the United States." The court observed that Manning could have avoided any post-indictment delay by returning to the United States on his own accord.[33]

Along with criminal cases, Wallace also decided important civil cases. In *Data Disc, Inc. v. Systems Tech. Ass'ns*, 557 F.2d 1280 (9th Cir. 1977), the Ninth Circuit established the test where a court can exercise personal jurisdiction under the Due Process Clause. In *Data Disc*, Wallace wrote the opinion for the much-cited Ninth Circuit case requiring "substantial" or "continuous and systematic" activities in the state for exercising jurisdiction over a party.[34]

In an interview with Harry Kreisler at the University of California discussing the role of judges in democracies, Wallace reflected on the role that his religion plays in deciding specific cases as a judge. Wallace said, "I am sure that it [religion] has some indirect values. One of the things that you learn to do is you must be guided by the law and it is the Constitution, the statutes of the Congress that you must apply—not shaping them to our view of what society or whatever should be. So in that regard one has to be careful." Someone once asked Wallace if had to decide a case and it was against the tenets of his church but consistent with the Constitution, what would he do? Wallace responded, "That was an easy answer. You would follow the Constitution. That is why I have taken my oath [raising his arm]. If I can't do that, I should step down." Wallace elaborated that religion has an indirect influence in that it teaches that we should be looking outside ourselves for help. Wallace said that the main goal of judges is to "apply the Constitution and the statutes and we can't allow anything outside of that—even no matter how virtuous they are—to be an influence. That is what people expect of us."[35]

Promoting Judicial Efficiency

Throughout his career, Wallace gained respect in his efforts and expertise on court administration promoting judicial efficiency. Wallace said, "My interest in the larger picture of judicial systems started in 1976 when, as a scholar at the Woodrow Wilson International Center for Scholars at the Smithsonian Institute, I began my study of judicial administration."[36] As chief judge from 1991 until 1996, he oversaw administrative responsibilities for the nation's largest circuit, which decided 7,955 matters in 1995 and 7,813 matters in 1996.[37] Based on his years of court administration, Wallace advocated for fewer larger circuits in the federal court system and opposed repeated efforts to split the Ninth Circuit. Wallace wrote, "In the Ninth Circuit, we have observed that a single court of appeals serving a large geographic region promotes uniformity and consistency in the law and facilitates trade and commerce by contributing to stability and orderly progress."[38]

Judge Wallace received much deserved acclaim from the legal community for his service to the legal profession. In an ironic twist, Justice Kennedy, who assumed the vacant seat on the U.S. Supreme Court instead of Wallace in 1987, presented Wallace with the Edward J. Devitt Distinguished Service to Justice Award nearly two decades later in 2006. Named for the longtime federal judge in Minnesota, the Devitt Award is intended to serve as "the Nobel Prize for the American judiciary." The award, first established in 1982, honors a respected member of the federal bench. Wallace received recognition at the opulent Spreckels Theatre in San Diego for his contributions to the administration of justice and advancement of the rule of law at home and abroad during his judicial career.[39] Wallace also received the A. Sherman Christensen Award in 2016 for his work on the American Inns of Court movement. Wallace played an influential role in developing the idea of the American Inns of Court and advocated enthusiastically for its establishment. He accompanied Chief Justice Warren Burger on the 1977 Anglo-American Legal Exchange and served as keynote speaker at the organizational dinner of the first Inn of Court. Judge Wallace served as a regular adviser to Judge A. Sherman Christensen, for whom the award is named.[40]

Faithful Living

Besides his service as a federal judge for over four decades, Wallace actively served in the Church. As a teenager growing up in San Diego, California, he typically spent his Sundays at the beach or going to movies. In high school, a group of kids befriended him and invited him to attend an activity at their stake house. In the Church, a *stake* is a regional church organization comprised of several local congregations or wards. Wallace said, "I came from a very poor family, and the idea of going to a *steak* house was very appealing." He remembered being very hungry that evening, but "they only had green punch and store-bought cookies to eat." Still, Wallace enjoyed his association with the new group of friends and eventually accepted their invitation to go to church, read the Book of Mormon, and then be baptized. In the Church, Wallace served as a bishop, stake president, regional representative, and temple sealer.[41] The beloved father, grandfather, and even great-grandfather also served as President of the San Diego Temple from 1998 to 1999.[42]

In a speech given to Brigham Young University-Hawaii students, the former temple president emphasized the importance of learning in the temple. He taught, "Think of the Temple as an educational institution and you will begin to see the vision of the mandatory requirement of your education within the Temple." Wallace added, "The higher education taught in the Temple is of a different nature. In the Temple, new truth is revealed to you personally and individually by the Holy Ghost, the third member of the Godhead."[43]

Yet for all his distinguished service and many accomplishments, Wallace never believed in settling down. In an interview at age 88, Wallace said, "I'm still a work in progress. . . I think the great reward in this life will be when we've fulfilled the mission we were sent here to do."[44]

"Those who champion division seem to express a preference for a small court culture. This is indeed a romantic and appealing notion: a 'small town' where everyone knows everyone intimately. . . Large courts are not wrong—just different. In the long run, fewer larger circuits may be the better structure for litigants. I can remember the nostalgic days of the corner store with the pickle barrel. I might prefer to be a grocer in such an environment. But with the growth of society's demands, the supermarket has taken its place. We, too, need to keep an open mind in determining what model will best serve the long term interests of the people we serve." J. Clifford Wallace in testifying before Congress on court administration.[45]

[1] Ed Whelan, *Inaugural Judge J. Clifford Wallace Lecture*, National Review, Jan. 20, 2016, http://www.nationalreview.com/bench-memos/430054/clifford-wallace-lecture [https://perma.cc/KYJ6-NQXW] (hereinafter "Whelan (2016)").

[2] Bob Woodward, Scott Armstrong, *The Brethren: Inside the Supreme Court* (New York, NY: Simon & Schuster, 2005), 485.

[3] Jeffrey Toobin, *After Stevens: What Will the Supreme Court Be Like Without Its Liberal Leader?*, New Yorker, Mar. 22, 2010, 38 (quoting Clinton Administration Acting Solicitor General Walter Dellinger); Christopher L. Eisgruber, *How the Maverick Became A Lion: Affirmative Action in the Jurisprudence of John Paul Stevens*, 99 Geo. L.J. 1279, 1281–82 (2011).

[4] Ruth Marcus, *2 U.S. Judges, Senator Eyed for Powell Seat; Leading Candidates Bork, Wallace, Hatch Share Philosophy of Judicial Restraint*, Washington Post, Jun. 27, 1987, 1987 WLNR 2260871.

[5] Mitchell Gordon, *Getting to the Bottom of the Ninth: Continuity, Discontinuity, and the Rights Retained by the People*, 50 Ind. L. Rev. 421, 445 (2017); Liam Skilling, *Justice Anthony M. Kennedy*, 11 Haw. B.J. 30 (2007)

[6] Christine L. Nemacheck, *Strategic Selection: Presidential Nomination of Supreme Court Justices from Herbert Hoover through George W. Bush* (Charlottesville, VA: University of Virginia Press, 2008), 151–154.

[7] Alan Abrahmason, *"Law and Order" Judge Takes Over Key Appeals Court Post: Judiciary: J. Clifford Wallace Becomes Chief Judge of the Nation's Largest Circuit Court of Appeals*, Los Angeles Times, Feb. 4, 1991, 1991 WLNR 3939769.

[8] Whelan (2016).

[9] Judge J. Clifford Wallace to Speak at 2010 Commencement, University of Utah S.J. Quinney College of Law, Apr. 8, 2010, https://law.utah.edu/news/judge-j-clifford-wallace-to-speak-at-2010-commencement/ [https://perma.cc/6QR7-LLCD].

[10] University of California, Berkley School of Law, Judge John Clifford Wallace Lecture Series, https://www.law.berkeley.edu/events-calendar/judge-john-clifford-wallace-lecture-series/ [https://perma.cc/R62M-4TWX]; Rachel Sterver, *Federal Appeals Court Judge J. Clifford Wallace Seeks Inspiration, Chances to Serve*, Church News, The Church of Jesus Christ of Latter-day Saints, Jan. 10, 2017, https://www.lds.org/church/news/federal-appeals-court-judge-j-clifford-wallace-seeks-inspiration-chances-to-serve?lang=eng [https://perma.cc/37XC-KHXN]; Rachel Sterver, *A Life Defined By Service*, Deseret News, Jan. 7, 2017, 2017 WLNR 581782.

[11] *Id.*

[12] *US Court of Appeals Judge Begins 10-day Visit to Algeria*, BBC International Reports, Apr. 9, 2002, Westlaw Newsroom.

[13] University of California, Berkeley, Conversations with History, Judges and the Rule of Law, J. Clifford Wallace, Senior Judge, United States Court of Appeals for the Ninth Circuit, Interview with Harry Kreisler, Mar. 10, 2009, at 44:00, https://conversations.berkeley.edu/wallace_2009 [https://perma.cc/N93U-SVKX] (hereinafter "University of California, Berkeley (2009)").

[14] Tyler Ward, *Justice Kennedy, Elder Oaks Honor J. Clifford Wallace*, J. Reuben Clark Law Society, The Thread, Vol. 1, Issue 1, December 2006.

[15] Federal Judicial Center, Wallace, John Clifford, https://www.fjc.gov/history/judges/wallace-john-clifford [https://perma.cc/RPJ8-B45X].

[16] Jesse H. Choper, *Dave: Student, Friend, and Hero*, 94 Or. L. Rev. 629, 632 (2016); Tung Yin, *Really, Who Is Uncle Zeb?*, 3 Green Bag 2d 115 (1999).

[17] University of California, Berkeley (2009), at 11:00.

[18] Public Law 91-292, 84 Stat. 294.

[19] 28 U.S.C. § 84.

[20] University of California, Berkeley (2009), at 11:00.

[21] Sterver (2017).

[22] Chris Kraul, *Gray Cary to Merge with Law Firm Ware & Freidenrich,* Los Angeles Times, Oct. 21, 1993, at 2, 1993 WLNR 4189830.

[23] Michael Kinsman, *San Diego Law Firm Set to Become World Player*, San Diego Union-Tribune, Dec, 7, 2004, 2004 WLNR 13347853; DLA Piper, History, https://www.dlapiper.com/history/ [https://perma.cc/EC7H-JQ2D].

[24] See Christopher E. Smith, *Federal Judicial Salaries: A Critical Appraisal*, 62 Temp. L. Rev. 849, 863 (1989).

[25] *Goodwin v. United States*, 371 F.Supp. 433 (S.D. Cal. 1972).

[26] *United States v. Barnes*, No. 71-342-CW, 1971 WL 455 (S.D. Cal. Nov. 22, 1971) (IRS action); *Small v. Commanding Gen., Marine Corps Base, Camp Pendleton, Cal.*, 320 F.Supp. 1044, 1045 (S.D. Cal. 1970), aff'd, 448 F. 2d 1397 (9th Cir. 1971) (Marine court martial appeal); *Rastin v. Laird*, 320 F.Supp. 1047, 1048 (S.D. Cal. 1970), rev'd, 445 F.2d 645 (9th Cir. 1971) (application for discharge as conscientious objector).

[27] 346 F.Supp. at 998.

[28] Federal Judicial Center.

[29] Jerome Farris, *The Ninth Circuit--Most Maligned Circuit in the Country--Fact or Fiction?*, 58 Ohio St. L. J. 1465 (1997).

[30] 59 F.3d at 825.

[31] Rebecca Trounson, *"Freeway Killer" Bonin Executed*, Los Angeles Times, Feb. 23, 1996, 1996 WLNR 5244933.

[32] Abrahmason (1991).

[33] 56 F.3d at 1195.

[34] 557 F.2d at 1285.

[35] University of California, Berkeley (2009), at 6:00.

[36] Testimony of The Honorable Clifford Wallace, Senior Judge and former Chief Judge, U.S. Court of Appeals for the Ninth Circuit, before The Subcommittee on Administrative Oversight and the Court of the Senate Judiciary Committee, April 7, 2004, https://www.judiciary.senate.gov/imo/media/doc/Wallace%20Testimony%20040704.pdf [https://perma.cc/7BC2-ELDH] (hereinafter "Wallace (2004)").

[37] Jerome Farris, *The Ninth Circuit--Most Maligned Circuit in the Country--Fact or Fiction?*, 58 Ohio St. L. J. 1465 (1997).

[38] Hon. J. Clifford Wallace, *The Ninth Circuit Should Not Be Split*, 56 Ohio St. L.J. 941, 944 (1995).

[39] Greg Moran, *Judge to be Honored in Hometown*, San Diego Union-Tribune, Oct. 16, 2017, B1, 2006 WLNR 18067671; David Lat, *Who's The Nation's Foremost Federal Judge?*, Above the Law, November 20, 2015, 2015 WLNR 34534176.

[40] United States Courts for the Ninth Circuit, Public Information Office, Judge J. Clifford Wallace to Receive the 2016 American Inns of Court A. Sherman Christensen Award, News Release, Sept. 19, 2016, http://cdn.ca9.uscourts.gov/datastore/ce9/2016/09/19/Wallace_Sherman_Award.pdf [https://perma.cc/DNN6-KR66].

[41] Sterver (2017).

[42] LDS Church Temples, San Diego California Temple Presidents, http://ldschurchtemples.org/sandiego/presidents/ [https://perma.cc/22UQ-EM8V].

[43] J. Clifford Wallace, The Higher Education Offered in the Temple, speech given at Brigham Young University-Hawaii, Oct. 26, 2016, https://devotional.byuh.edu/media161025 [https://perma.cc/DTA2-TQ8B].

[44] Sterver (2017).

[45] Wallace (2004).

Afterword

Because of space and time limitations, many prominent lawyers and judges are regrettably excluded. A number of church leaders have also been lawyers, starting with Oliver Cowdery. Selected Church leaders with legal backgrounds include Stephen L. Richards, James Henry Moyle, Henry D. Moyle, Marion G. Romney, Stephen L. Richards, Albert E. Bowen, Ernest L. Wilkinson, Howard W. Hunter, D. Todd Christofferson, and Quentin L. Cook. Many General Authorities have also been lawyers, including L. Whitney Clayton, Bruce Hafen, Marion D. Hanks, Marlin J. Jensen, and Lance B. Wickman.

Certain political leaders are also omitted, including Orrin Hatch, largely because much has already been written about these individuals. Many prominent law professors and university leaders are also not included. There are many worthy law professors at the University of Utah and Brigham Young University that could have been featured. Other notable lawyers in higher education include Robert Daines, Cole Durham, Noah Feldman, E. Gordon Gee John Morley, Nathan Oman, Kevin Worthen, and Michael K. Young. Many judges, including N. Randy Smith, Dee Benson, Thomas Lee, David Sam, Ted Stewart, Robert Clive Jones, Dale Kimball, Lloyd D. George, David L. Evans, Matthew Durrant, David Ebel, David G. Campbell, Lawrence J. Block, Randall Radar, and others are also omitted. Eric Baxter, Sean Reyes, Hugh W. Colton, John K. Edmunds, Randall Guynn, James W. Parkinson, David P. Petermann, Hannah Clayson Smith, Keith N. Hamilton, Katrina Lantos Swett, Troy Dow, Brent Hatch, and LeGrande Young (father of NFL quarterback Steve Young) were also considered for this book. Future researchers may consider exploring in greater depth the contributions of these persons and others not included in the text.

Because of space considerations and the aim of the text, each chapter focuses on professional accomplishments with little emphasis on personal and family connections. Family relationships and upbringing, however, play important parts in the life of each person, especially for members of the Church who consider the family central to the Creator's plan for the eternal destiny of His children. Future researchers may consider full length biographies for each of the individuals profiled in this book to explore their lives in greater detail.

Finally, the book does not profile George Alexander Sutherland, one of the "four horsemen" who served on the U.S. Supreme Court. While Sutherland lived in Utah and attended Brigham Young Academy (now Brigham Young University), he was not a member of The Church of Jesus Christ of Latter-day Saints. Although Sutherland himself never joined the Church, he maintained strong relationships with members of the Church and Brigham Young University throughout his life. Much has already been written about Sutherland, including two biographies.

While no member of the Church has yet reached the U.S. Supreme Court, perhaps a member of The Church of Jesus Christ of Latter-day Saints will someday occupy one of the seats on the nation's highest court.

Index

Corporation Service Company (CSC), 117
Covington & Burling, 209
Cox, Archibald, 150
criminal law, 57, 66, 117, 223
Crow Tribe, 90
Crowder, Enoch, 34
Cruz, Ted, 135
Cuba, 29
Cutler, Judy Goffman, 107
cy pres doctrine, 216
dairy farm, 99
Daubert, 102
Dawson, Kent, 103
Days, Drew, 145
Dean, John, 72
death penalty, 43, 44, 172, 173, 238
Death Valley National Park, 201
Declaration of Independence, 22, 215
Delaware, 115, 116, 117, 118
Delta, Utah, 57
Denver Nuggets, 71
Deukmejian, George, 212
Devitt Award, 240
Distinguished Service Medal, 34
DLA Piper, 236
Donahue v. Warner Bros. Pictures, 201
Donahue, Jack, 202
door law, 58
Double Jeopardy Clause, 165
Douglas, William, 232
Due Process Clause, 19, 55, 56, 145, 175, 190, 239
Dunes Hotel, 101
Eastern States Mission, 204
Echo Hawk, Larry
    advocate for tribal people, 44–46
    Idaho Attorney General, 42–44
    Idaho governor's race, 46–47
    law professor, 47–49
    Obama Administration, 49–52
Edmunds, John, 158, 185
Edward I, 14
Edward, Harry, 78
Edwards, Hunt, Hale & Hansen, Ltd., 100
Einstein, Albert, 92
Eisenhower, Dwight D., 16, 227
El Paso, Texas, 198
empirical analysis, 6, 150, 186

Encyclopedia of Mormonism, 95
Endangered Species Act, 214
Ensign, John, 1
entrapment, 183
environmental law
    Jordan, 117
    Milan Smith, 214
Equal Protection Clause, 142
Establishment Clause, 133, 148, 149, 163, 164, *See also* freedom of religion
Estrada, Estrada, 72
Evers, Medgar, 62
exclusionary rule, 147, 186
exoneration, 106
experimental medications., 75
expert witness testimony, 102
faculty athletics representative, 49
faith-based initiatives, 133
Family Proclamation, 64
Family Search, 95
Faust, James E.
    church leadership, 64–66
    civil rights leader, 62–63
    early legal career, 56–59
    Utah Bar Foundation, 61
    Utah Legislature, 59–61
    Utah Supreme Court, 55–59
Faust, Marcus, 63
FDA, 76, 236
Federal Bar Association, 24
Federal Deposit Insurance Corporation, 131
Federal Tort Claims Act, 117, 163, 167
Federalist Society, 144
feeder-court, 73
Field, Fred, 72
filibuster, 73, 74
Fleming, J. Clifton, 93
football, 49, 166
Ford v. Wainwright, 172
Ford, Gerald, 144, 186
Foreign Intelligence Surveillance Court, 176–78
Foreign Intelligence Surveillance Court of Review, 177
Fort Bridger Treaty, 44
Fort Hall Indian Reservation, 44
Fort McDowell Indian Reservation, 219
Fortas, Abe, 63

New York Bar, 31
New York City, 33
New York Times, 135
New York Times v. Sullivan, 142, 215
Nicholas II, 32
Nixon, Richard, 142, 236, 237
North Carolina, 130
Northwestern University, 87, 158
Notre Dame University, 144
O'Connor, Sandra Day, 17, 149, 150, 215, 232
O'Melveny & Myers, 212
O'Neill, Tip, 157
Oaks, Dallin H.
    BYU President, 189
    church service, 191–93
    Illinois Supreme Court, 182–83
    influence in Milan Smith, 212
    influence on Bybee, 3
    private practice, 184–85
    recruitment of Hawkins, 85, 86
    relationship with Faust, 63
    relationship with Rex Lee, 141, 143, 151
    Supreme Court clerkship, 183–84
    University of Chicago, 158, 185–88
    Utah Supreme Court, 189–91
Obama, Barack, 49, 164, 215
obscenity, 158
Office of Legal Counsel, 3, 144
Office of Professional Responsibility, 4
Office of the Legal Counsel, 4–5
Oklahoma, 164
Old Mormon Fort, 99
Order of the Coif, 87
Oregon. *See* Mosman, Michael
originalism, 135
Otis, James, 135
painting, 107
parental rights, 193
Parker v. District of Columbia, 77
Parkinson, James, 166, 167
Patient Protection and Affordable Care Act, 75
Paul (Apostle), 111
Pawnee people, 42
Peace Corps, 159
Pearl Harbor Day, 139

Pedrick, Willard, 86
Pennsylvania, 120
Philadelphia Intellectual Property Law Association, 123
Phoenix, 226
Pickwickians, 22
Pike v. Bruce Church, Inc., 143
pioneers, 144
Plato, 2
plural marriage, 19
polygamy, 19, 89, 221
port of Arica, 31
Portland Seven, 173
Potter v. Murray City, 18
Poulos v. New Hampshire, 88
Pouren, Jan, 32
Powell, Collin, 2
Powell, Lewis, 37, 172, 174, 232
prayer, 49, 60, 86, 149, 187
Presentment Clause, 127, 140
Presley, Elvis, 203
privacy, 77, 174, 180, 201, 203
prosecutor, 117, 131, 173–74
Prosser, William, 235
Proverbs, 127
Provo, Utah, 91
publicity rights, 203
Quinn, D. Michael, 36
racial segregation, 88
radioactive fallout, 163
railroad, 224
Reagan, Ronald, 72, 127, 131, 145, 232
Rehnquist, William, 4, 186
Reid, Harry, 1, 103
Reinhardt, Stephen, 6, 9
religious discrimination, 149
Rexburg, Idaho, 171
Reynolds v. United States, 89
Richards, Preston
    claims in Mexico, 198–99
    early interest in law, 197
    right of publicity, 201–3
    Senate campaign, 203–5
    Seventeenth Amendment, 134
    U.S. Department of State, 197–98
    work in California, 200–201
Richards, Preston D.
    relationship with Clark, 33, 34
Richards, Stephen L., 196
Richards, Willard, 196, 204

About the Author

Brian Craig is an educator, lawyer, and writer. He is a faculty member at Purdue University Global and an adjunct instructor at Brigham Young University-Idaho. He is also a legal writer for Wolters Kluwer providing expert legal analysis on new developments in the law. He previously taught at the University of Minnesota Law School and worked as an attorney for Thomson-Reuters. He received his undergraduate degree in political science from Brigham Young University and his law degree from the University of Idaho College of Law. He lives in Providence, Utah with his wife and children.

Made in the USA
Columbia, SC
17 March 2019